STREETS

OF

CORPUS CHRISTI

Murphy Givens

STREETS

OF

CORPUS CHRISTI

Murphy Givens

www.nuecespress.com

Corpus Christi, Texas

Library of Congress Control Number: 2019905496

Givens, Murphy STREETS OF CORPUS CHRISTI

Includes index.

1. South Texas — History.
2. Nueces County — History.
3. Corpus Christi — History.

ISBN   978-1-7339524-0-8

Published by Nueces Press, Corpus Christi, Texas.

Cover design by Jeff Chilcoat

Front cover photos: View of Chaparral Street, page 52 (inset) and page

Rear cover photos: View of Chaparral Street, page 52 (inset) and page

www.nuecespress.com

Publisher's Notes

For 20 years Murphy Givens wrote a weekly column on a subject of South Texas history. Some of his columns recounted the histories of various streets in the city, telling who lived on them worked on them and what were the businesses and residences that gave life to the streets. Because of the format of the columns in the Caller-Times, it was difficult to include more than one photograph of the street. Readers were unable to picture how streets, businesses and homes appeared from an article with only one photograph. This volume solves that shortcoming by providing many photographs from different eras and locations on each street.

Givens has chosen photographs that most people have never seen to illustrate each street. Many were taken by Doc Frederick McGregor in the 1930s and 1940s. However, others come from many sources including Karl Swafford postcards and business and family records. They provide a visual history of Corpus Christi showing bygone scenes.

Corpus Christi grew rapidly in the twentieth century, from a town of less than 5,000 people in 1900 to 325,000 today. Such growth caused the destruction of old buildings from the nineteenth century so that new larger buildings could replace them. The downtown and bluff areas saw most of the original buildings replaced. In addition, the need for improved automotive highways caused more destruction. The Harbor Bridge access roads, Interstate 37 and Crosstown Expressway all caused many old homes and businesses to be moved or torn down. Hurricane destruction caused more to be demolished or replaced. Changing demographics and movement of populations to suburban areas led to still more changes. Today only a few buildings date to 1900 and only a handful go back to the1850s.

A map of Corpus Christi in 1875 is provided on page 157. This map shows the original configuration of downtown and uptown streets before name changes and the Crosstown, I-37, Harbor Bridge and Shoreline improvements were made. The map will allow you to picture the locations about which you are reading.

One of the interesting things that I realized while reading the manuscript was the mix of businesses and residences on the streets. Before the proliferation of the automobile as a mode of transportation, citizens walked most places in town. Groceries, butchers, eateries and hardware stores needed to be close to customers. There were far more of them and they were much smaller into the 1930s and were interspersed in the neighborhoods.

Unfortunately, street names are subject to change at the will of city government. Often a street is named to honor a person. Years later, the person has been forgotten and the name might be changed to commemorate another person or event. Sometimes street names are changed to simplify the finding of one's way. Corpus Christi has seen its share of the changing of street names. As a student of local history, I find this practice deplorable as it diminishes our ability to envision our history. In the last chapter of Streets, Murphy has detailed the origin of street names. In that section you will see many name changes and be able to understand the changing dynamics of our city.

I hope you enjoy this trip back in our history.

Jim Moloney
Nueces Press

Preface

Having written many columns on the history of Corpus Christi's original streets, which appeared over the years in the Caller-Times, I thought it might be worthwhile to put them together, augment the written material (to make a short story long) into a more complete whole. The project began in late 2017.

From the outset, it was never intended to be about *all* the city streets, which would be an endless task and encyclopedic in length. It was limited to the streets in the historic downtown, uptown, Ocean Drive and North Beach. In addition to the geographic limitations, the work was always envisioned as being limited in time to the 19th Century and the first five decades of the 20th Century. But in the writing, the narrative wouldn't always behave and sometimes strayed beyond the imposed constraints. Every writer discovers sooner or later that he doesn't always control the material; sometimes it controls him.

The story is concentrated on the city's early history through the 1930s and 1940s. Corpus Christi was founded in 1839 so the narrative covers roughly one hundred years. It is also concentrated on the 1930s and 1940s because we have a wealth of photos for those years in the "Doc" McGregor Collection. Another reason to concentrate on the 1930s and 1940s is that this period served as a bridge, as I see it, between old and new Corpus Christi. In addition to the McGregor photos, we have detailed city directories available for those years, which provide a useful record of what was where. When the directories failed, newspapers on microfilm were helpful.

The easiest way to tell a story, as writers learn early, is to tell it chronologically, to begin with the beginning and end with the ending; simple advice that is always right in the abstract. But that's not possible within this framework since each street, and each building on that street, has its own chronology. The narrative by necessity shifts back and forth in time as we progress along each street. That may make it difficult to curl up around for an evening of sustained reading, but I would hope people will find this work of some value or as interesting to read as it was for me to write.

I would like to express my sincere gratitude to the people at the Corpus Christi Museum of Science and History and the Corpus Christi Central Library who helped track down photos that were used in this book.

Murphy Givens
June 2019

Table of Contents

Chapter 1. Water Street

From the arroyo to the port entrance, crossing downtown east-west streets from Laguna to Resaca, and includes Shoreline Boulevard and the seawall.

Water Street is awash in history. For a century before the seawall was built Water Street was the first street along the shore. It was from Water Street that early residents lived in close communion with the bay and Gulf beyond.

The story of Water Street begins with Henry Kinney. In 1839, he landed at the mouth of an arroyo, what the Spanish also call "rambla" or watercourse, a salty estuary that was later named Blucher's Creek. Kinney moved to Texas from Illinois, where his venture to build a canal from the Mississippi River to Lake Michigan collapsed, leaving him bankrupt. He came to Texas and opened a store at Aransas City, near where Rockport is today. He bought wool and hides and dealt with what was then known as the Mexican trade.

When Kinney landed at Blucher's Creek in late 1839 he was preparing to move his store from Aransas City to a site on Corpus Christi Bay. The attractions of the site included a high bluff and plateau overlooking a large bay. The beach was a place where goods had been unloaded for shipment to Mexico, called the Old Indian Trading Grounds.

The Old Indian Trading Grounds was a place where smugglers landed goods on the beach to avoid paying customs duties and then loaded them on pack trains destined for Mexico. Trader John J. Linn in 1829 landed a load of tobacco at the site with plans to smuggle it into Mexico. Henry Gilpin also landed in 1829 with goods for sale in Mexico.

The arroyo where Kinney landed emptied into the bay about where Cooper's Alley intersects with Water Street today. The bay at this point had the deepest water along the shore and for that reason the first piers were built nearby. Another natural watercourse was to the north, later called Hall's Bayou, where the port entrance is today.

The city grew between the two inlets and the bluff and the bay, with the lower section called "The Beach" and higher ground called "The Bluff." Water Street stretched between the two inlets along the shore.

Piers and wharves off Water Street reflected the city's maritime ambitions, despite being hampered by a shallow bay clogged with mudflats. The first pier was built by Hiram Riggs in 1844, located past the end of Lawrence Street. The base consisted of brush and mesquite mattresses filled in with shell to weight it down and topped with planks. The pier washed away in the early 1850s. To the south was William Mann's wharf, built in 1848 near where Cooper's Alley joins Water Street. Mann's wharf had a track for handcars leading to a warehouse and complex of buildings. Mann, like Kinney, dealt in the Mexican trade.

Ohler's Wharf was built in 1849 from the end of Peoples Street. The Government Wharf built by John Willet in the 1853 later became the Central Wharf, which stretched into the bay from between Laguna and William streets. The Staples and Sidbury wharves were built in the 1870s to unload shipments of lumber. The Staples Wharf was located off Lawrence Street where the old Riggs' wharf had been. It was destroyed by a storm in 1875.

South of the arroyo where Kinney landed became the 100 block of South Water. The arroyo was the dividing line between street's north and south addresses. Here, on the water side, was Mann's red house, which got the name from the reddish color of the shellcrete bricks. Anna Moore Schwien's mother, a slave named Malvina, said there were deep pits in the south bluff where the builders dug out the red clay to make the bricks for Mann's place.

During an Indian raid people forted up behind Mann's walls. The buildings were built around a central courtyard in the Spanish style. The main structure was three stories high, the largest building in town at the time, which included a store, rooms, and the Mann family residence. Traders arriving from Mexico to do business with Mann would stay in rooms at the Mann house. Mann's pier was in front of the buildings.

Anna Moore Schwien said after the Civil War the Mann place was used as a hotel, called the Virginia House. It was on the site of the later Guth Park, which is now an empty lot.

In the 1920s and 1930s, before the seawall was built, beginning in 1939, Water Street south of the arroyo was dominated by the city's Municipal Wharf. On the east side of the street at 99 South Water, was Gulf Hardware followed by the 40 & 8 Arena. The 40 & 8 was an old converted cotton warehouse where sporting events and rodeos were held. Behind the 40 & 8 was Frank Gomez's Yellow Cabin Bait Stand and across the wharf, to the south, was the San Antonio Machine Supply Company warehouse.

On the west side of South Water was the Purple Cow Drive-In followed by the home of Mrs. Eddie Segrest. The Purple Cow location, at 309 South Water, must have been coveted. After the Purple Cow there was Zackie's Play House and still later there was Pick's Drive-In downtown. The U&I Restaurant occupies that site today.

North of the arroyo, said Annie (Schallert) Bagnall, her parents lived in a house where she was born in 1862. "Mr. and Mrs. Prokop Hoffman lived across the street from us." In the next block, the 200 block, was the old Mullen home, at 203 North Water, which was said to have been one of the first homes built in Corpus Christi.

Conrad Meuly's bakery was in the 200 block past the Laguna intersection. Meuly, from Switzerland, came to Corpus Christi at the time of Zachary Taylor's encampment in 1845.

2. *Corpus Christi's Municipal Wharf was built on a landfill off Cooper's Alley in 1913, replacing the old Central Wharf as the town's main shipping pier. Near the entrance on the north side was the 40 & 8 Arena. On the south side was the SAMSCO warehouse complex. Most of the wharf was demolished when the seawall was constructed.*

Meuly was involved in the trade expedition to Santa Fe that was in reality a scheme to bring New Mexico under Texas control. Volunteers and merchants called the Santa Fe Pioneers left Austin in June 1841 with wagons and ox-carts carrying merchandise valued at $200,000.

Meuly invested $16,000 in trade goods for the venture, an enormous sum in those days. After much hardship on the trip, Meuly and the other members of the expedition were captured by Mexican soldiers. The Texans were forced to walk 1,400 miles to Mexico City. Those who fell behind were executed and their ears cut off to prove to higher authorities that they hadn't escaped. Meuly and the others who survived were imprisoned until they were released in 1842.

Once back in Texas, Meuly opened a "bread-and-biscuit" bakery in Corpus Christi in 1845. He married Margaret Rahm and built a large two-story home on Chaparral, with fancy ironwork, and bought a 17,000-acre ranch near Banquete.

During the Civil War, Meuly championed the Union cause. After a mob threatened to hang him, Meuly moved the family to the ranch 30 miles west of Corpus Christi. This was in 1862. In late 1863, Confederate Gen. Hamilton Bee and staff stopped at Meuly's Bee

3. Water Street, looking north, from south of the Municipal Wharf before the seawall.

4. The Purple Cow Drive-In on Water Street (where the U&I is today) shown in 1939

called Meuly a traitor and vowed to hang him. Meuly, a brave if obstinate man, said, "General, issue your orders. I am here." Bee did not carry out his threat. At war's end Meuly agreed to supply beef to Union troops in Brownsville. He was in Brownsville when

5. Conrad Meuly, a baker who originally came from Switzerland, survived the disastrous Santa Fe Expedition of 1841. He opened a bakery in Corpus Christi when Zachary Taylor's troops were concentrated in the settlement. During the Civil War he dared a Confederate general to carry out his threat to hang him.

he caught yellow fever and died on July 9, 1865. He left a widow and 12 children.

Down the block from Meuly's bakery was Cornelius Cahill's store and home, which stood facing the Central Wharf. Cahill came to Corpus Christi from Peru, Ill., where he knew Henry Kinney, the founder of Corpus Christi, before Kinney came to Texas. Cahill's two-story building was built in 1848 of shellcrete bricks that faced the long wharf that stretched far out into the bay. It housed a store and family dwelling on the second floor. City aldermen held their meetings at Cahill's in the 1850s, dances were held there, and mass was conducted at Cahill's before the first St. Patrick's Church was built in 1857.

Cahill built a three-story building on Chaparral in 1858, north of Conrad Meuly's home. Cahill's place on Water Street housed a store on the first floor and City Hotel on the second. A grand ball was held on March 14, 1860 to celebrate the opening of the City Hotel.

In the yellow fever epidemic of 1867, which claimed 135 people in Corpus Christi that summer, parents lost children, children lost parents, and in some cases entire families died.

Many orphans were adopted by families that lost their own children. Cornelius and Catherine Cahill, who lost two children to the fever, adopted two nieces and a nephew who were left orphaned.

Cahill's on Water Street stood a long time. The weather-beaten building was torn down with great difficulty after it was damaged in the 1919 storm. Dynamite blasts left only small breaks in the thick shellcrete walls, hardly larger than the space made for the dynamite sticks, so workers were forced to undermine the foundations. They used tractors to pull down the walls before they could bring the old building down.

Three mail boats made a tri-weekly run from Indianola to Corpus Christi. They docked at the Central Wharf, across from Cahill's on Water Street. The mail boats were the Emily, the Agnes and the Henrietta. This was after the Civil War. Before the war, the mail boats docked at Ohler's Wharf.

"The coming of the mail boat was announced by the captain blowing a cow-horn within a mile of the town," longtime newsman Eli Merriman said. The mail boat arrived on Sunday, Wednesday, and Friday. "The mail was brought up from the wharf on a dray by a man named Webber who delivered it to postmaster Horace Taylor." The mail boat runs ended with the coming of the railroads in the 1880s.

A cattle chute on Central Wharf was used to load cattle on the steamships. "We could hear the cattle bellowing way up at our house (blocks away)," said Lillie Anderson Rankin. One resident recalled cattle jumping into the bay, with men rushing in on horseback to herd them to shore.

Central Wharf was a busy place. The Corpus Christi Gazette, on May 1, 1875, reported that the steamer Mary left Central Wharf on April 27, 1875 with 178 bags of wool, 31 bales of hides and skins, five casks of tallow, 266 beeves, 74 calves, 115 mutton and other freight." Next day the schooner Anna M. Dickenson left with 398 bags of wool, 4,128 dry hides, 294 wet salted hides, 30 bales of skins, and 5,000 horns.

North of Cahill's, John Graham ran a café that featured, said the Nueces Valley on Oct. 3, 1857, "fresh fish, oysters, and hot coffee."

Graham commanded a militia company during the Civil War called the Mounted Coast Guards. The company was mustered into service on April 1, 1862, with Graham as captain and members including John Riggs, Frost Allen, William Cody, Matthew Cody, William Chism, John Carr, John P. Dunlap, William P. Dunlap, August Holthaus, James Hobbs, Maurice Levy, William Mussett, Elias T. Mussett, Thomas Mussett, Edwin McLaughlin, Felix Noessel, William Ohler, Luther Owings, George Pfeuffer, Emanuel Scheuer, Naman Staples, Charles Weidenmueller, John Woessner, Green Williams.

John Mircovich, who came from Yugoslavia with his brother Mateo, opened the Bay Saloon and Restaurant at 224 N. Water in 1889, between Laguna and William on the bay side of the street. The Bay Saloon was converted to the Bay Grocery when Nueces County voted "to go dry" in 1916. After the buildings were destroyed in the 1919 storm Mircovich built a new home and grocery on Waco Street.

In this block, in the 1930s, there was a service station, a welding shop and, on the north corner of Laguna (now Sartain), there was the Ocean View Café, which later became Lorena's Beer Garden, run by Mrs. Lorena King. By the early 1940s a new building was constructed on this site for Shoop's Grill, which moved south from its former location near the Princess Louise Hotel.

6. *The new Shoop's Grill was at 200 North Water. The first Shoop's opened near the Princess Louise. Bob Shoop moved to the new location, at Water and Laguna about 1939.*

Bob Shoop moved to the new location about 1940. At that time, you could order a roast prime rib dinner for 75 cents at Shoop's Grill. Or you could get a "Shoop Steak dinner Ben Bennie" for $1. Shoop's old site is a parking lot today across from the Education Service Center.

In the 300 block of Water, between William and Lawrence, was an ice plant built in 1878 and owned by Richard King and John Greer. Before it was built, huge blocks of lake ice packed in sawdust were shipped on schooners from Maine. After King's death in 1885 and Greer's soon afterwards, the ice plant was sold to George Blucher. Kate Smith Anderson (Mrs. Adolph Anderson) lived next to Blucher's ice factory for 40 years. "I would gather the bark that fell from the wood at the factory for my own use. I have seen many a cord of wood unloaded at his place for boilers at the factory."

Near the ice plant, on the water side, was John Superach's fish and oyster business. When the Caller printed its first edition, on Jan. 21, 1883, they sent down to Superach's for a bucket of oysters for the pressmen. It was so cold the oysters froze into a block of ice in the bucket. Andrew Anderson said Superach built a pen in the water where he kept turtles for the commercial market.

The Magnolia Saloon, in 1860, was located in the 300 block of Water. The Ranchero, on May 18, 1861 reported that the Magnolia "has been fitted up and opened. A marble-topped billiard table, the finest in western Texas, is at the services of the knights of the cue."

7. *Goodyear tire store in the 1940s at 322 N. Water Street, between William and Lawrence. The south end of Water was dominated by car dealerships and automobile service firms.*

Down the street was James Hunter's Livery. Hunter, a Confederate cavalry officer in Terry's Texas Rangers, opened his livery in 1871. When bandits took hostages and burned Thomas Noakes' store in the Easter raid of 1875, Hunter was almost captured but escaped on a fast horse and rode to Corpus Christi to sound the alarm. He was the Paul Revere of the Nuecestown Raid. His livery was where the Water Street Seafood restaurant is today.

In the 300 block in the 1930s were body shops, a Goodyear tire store, a sheet metal shop, and Phil Scott's Auto Laundry. This building was turned into a bar in the late 1930s, Forest Casey's Barge Inn, then Cecil Hagewood's auto paint and body shop in the 1940s.

In the 400 block, past the Lawrence intersection, were two wool warehouses owned by Perry Doddridge and Uriah Lott. Elizabeth Hart's store, built in 1848, was in this block. Mrs. Hart, from Ireland, opened a store in the Zachary Taylor's old commissary building at Taylor and Chaparral in 1848 then built her own shellcrete structure on Water Street.

The Hart family left Wexford, Ireland in 1833 and landed at Copano in 1834. The father died of cholera and was buried on the beach. Mrs. Hart and two daughters traveled by oxcart to Refugio and camped next to the mission walls. Mrs. Hart nursed the colonists sick with cholera. Many died and were buried in their blankets. Elizabeth Hart remarried but her second husband died in the Goliad massacre. Mrs. Hart and daughters evacuated to Mobile, Ala., where Rosalie married Jean Marie Priour. Mrs. Hart moved to Corpus Christi and opened a store in 1848. Rosalie and husband joined her. In the Civil War, Mrs. Hart moved to her ranch on the Aransas River. She died in 1863. Rosalie returned to Corpus Christi and taught school in her mother's store. Her family lived in a house at the Salt Lake. Jean Marie Priour died in 1880 and Rosalie in 1903.

In an upstairs room in a building on the corner of Lawrence, Henry and William Maltby ran their pro-Confederate newspaper, the Ranchero. Henry Maltby came to Corpus Christi as the owner of a circus that performed at Kinney's Lone Star Fair in 1852. The circus moved on but Maltby returned and three years later was elected mayor. He started the Ranchero newspaper with his brother William in 1859. As the country moved toward war,

8. *The 400 block of Water, looking south, presented a busy scene in the 1930s. On the right was Allen Furniture and on the left Kinsel Motors. The parking lot was for the Elite Café.*

the Maltby brothers argued for Southern secession. William joined a Confederate artillery company and was captured by Union forces on Mustang Island in 1863. With the help of his older brother, Union Gen. Jasper Maltby, he was allowed to return to Texas in 1864.

Years later, William Maltby and Eli Merriman published the Corpus Christi Free Press. William Maltby died in Corpus Christi in 1880. Henry Maltby died in Brownsville in 1906.

In the 1930s and early 1940s, in the 400 block of Water, from Lawrence to Schatzel, were several auto dealerships, including Kinsel Motors, at 414 Water.

The Elite Café was on the west side of the street north of the Water Street entrance of Allen's Furniture. Elise Black bought the Elite from Clifford F. Kenney, about 1935, and renamed it the Blackstone Café.

In the 500 block of Water was the old Byington house, used by Zachary Taylor as his headquarters in 1845. Myrtle Calloway, a visitor, was staying in this house in March 1902 when she came down with smallpox. The house was quarantined, with a yellow flag flying from the roof, until she recovered and the quarantine was lifted. In 1910 part of the old house was demolished and the rest of it used as a warehouse.

Eli Merriman built a home at 505 N. Water Street in 1900. It was on the lot where the old J. T. Swift home, built in 1847, once stood. Merriman's daughter Marion (Clemmer) recalled that in the front yard of the home was a plant which produced blossoms that gave a narcotic effect. One of their chickens behaved as if it were intoxicated, caused, they believed, by the plant. The chicken followed a guest as he was going downtown. The drunken chicken walking behind the unsuspecting visitor was a source of great amusement for the Merriman children. The Merriman home was wrecked in the 1919 storm.

9. *The Pleasure Pier and the Pier Cafe in 1932.Nueces Hotel's Three Palms on the left.*

10. *The Pleasure Pier was a favorite place for a stroll before the seawall took its place.*

In the 1930s, the 500 block of Water was best known for the popular restaurant sitting next to the Pleasure Pier. This was the Pier Café, at 524 North Water, across from, and a little south of, the famed three palms of the Nueces Hotel garden.

The Pier Café was owned and operated by John Govatos, who came from the small Greek seacoast village of Metamorfosi with his brother Clem and his cousin John Nicols. John Govatos opened the Pier Café in 1926. It was moved to the south side of the pier and remodeled several times. It afforded a good view of the bay, the Pleasure Pier and the Nueces Hotel's Tres Palmas. At the Pier Café in 1939, a seafood dinner, with shrimp, crabmeat or oyster cocktail and broiled redfish, trout, or fried shrimp in butter sauce, cost 85 cents. When the Pleasure Pier was dismantled during the construction of the seawall,

11. John Govatos' Pier Café was two blocks from the water after the seawall was built. No longer on the bayfront, the restaurant lost its waterfront appeal and soon closed.

the Pier Café, away from the water's edge, lost its allure and John Govatos moved up to the Nixon Café on the bluff with John Nicols.

The rest of that block, in the 1930s, was home to Lyon's Auto Service, Cooley's Auto Repairs, and Emmett's Garage. By the 1940s, where Lyon's had been, there was a new Firestore store and Cooley's had become Buck's Garage run by Jud Smith.

The Ladies Pavilion was built in 1902 and 1903 over the water off Peoples Street. It was built by public subscription under the auspices of the Woman's Monday Club as a social center to replace Market Hall. The club sold stock to raise funds to build the facility. It was opened on Aug. 7, 1903. A tableau presented at the Ladies Pavilion was called "A Dream of Beautiful Women." The town's most fashionable women — Mrs. Leo Kaffie, Mrs. Moise Weil, Mrs. Roy Miller, Mrs. Walter Timon, among others — struck fixed poses of famous women. Clara Driscoll reclined on a couch as Cleopatra. The Ladies Pavilion was also where the city's first conventions were held. The Texas Bankers, the Texas Medical Association, and the Texas Press Association held conventions at the new Ladies Pavilion. The Ladies Pavilion didn't last long. It was destroyed in the hurricane of 1916.

In the 19th Century, at the Peoples Street intersection with Water were two identical buildings, the Hunsaker on the south side of Peoples and the Ohler building on the north side. Much of the activity at the 1852 Lone Star Fair occurred in front of Hunsaker's and Ohler's. Both buildings were constructed for Edward Ohler by Henry W. Berry from shellcrete bricks made in his kiln at the foot of south bluff.

Judge Edmund J. Davis had a law office in the Hunsaker building after the Civil War, before he was elected governor. The building was sold to Will "Dad" Grant and became known as the Grant Building (another Grant Building was at Chaparral and Starr). It was torn down after the 1919 storm. The Sherman Building (later the Jones then the Nueces Building) was constructed on the site.

12 and 13. Above, the 500 block of Water Street across from the Texas Star Service Station with the Nueces Hotel down the street. Below, women at the Texas Star fill a gas tank, air up the tires and wash the windshield in what had been male jobs before the manpower shortage in World War II.

14. *The Ladies Pavilion was built off Water Street between the end of Peoples and Schatzel streets. It opened on Aug. 7, 1903 and quickly supplanted Market Hall as the town's social center. The Ladies Pavilion was destroyed by the 1916 hurricane.*

Across Peoples Street from the Hunsaker building was the Ohler building. A photograph of the Ohler structure, taken in the early 1850s, is perhaps the oldest known photo of Corpus Christi. The back of the photo identifies it as a landmark structure built on the waterfront in 1849. Based on a comparison of Hollub's 1874 sketch of the waterfront, it was almost certainly the Ohler building.

Edward Ohler was in Veracruz during the Mexican War. He was an army sutler who made a fortune selling goods to the U.S. Army. After the war ended he moved to Corpus Christi. The Corpus Christi Star on Oct. 17, 1848 noted the arrival of the Ohlers on the schooner Uncle Bill, which docked at the Mann wharf. Ohler brought his wife, two sons, and a supply of merchandise "with the view to settling permanently in Corpus Christi."

Maria von Blucher in a letter to her parents mentioned the arrival of the Ohlers. Her husband Felix knew them from Veracruz. She described Ohler's wife Matilda as pretty, vain, and lazy, who was attended by several slaves. "At the table," Maria wrote, "stands a black woman with a mighty fan of peacock feathers, shooing off the flies." Ohler opened a grocery and dry goods store on Water Street in a building constructed by Henry W. Berry.

Corpus Christi was a small town. Soon everybody was talking about a scandalous affair between Henry Kinney, who was fond of other men's wives, and Matilda Ohler. Maria Blucher wrote that "Mrs. Ohlers (sic) is the paramour of Col. Kinney. Felix (Blucher) is not shocked at Mrs. Ohlers' affair and often goes there in the evening. The most ignominious aspect of this is that Mr. Ohlers, because of his pecuniary relation with Kinney, tolerates the affair and even favors it." This had all the elements of a good comic opera: the vain and pretty wife, the avaricious husband, the licentious rich man.

Andrew Anderson, who lived next door, said Mrs. Ohler would sit on the porch upstairs and ring a silver bell to summon a slave. One of her slaves called Old Rachel was accused

15. *Edward Ohler, an army sutler from Veracruz, came to Corpus Christi in 1848 at the end of the Mexican War and built a two-story building at Peoples and Water in 1849. In the early years, the Ohlers lived on the second floor and operated a store below. They later built a home on North Broadway. The photo is believed to date from the early 1850s.*

of stealing some silver and was sentenced to receive 25 lashes at the whipping post. Anderson watched as the constable whipped her with a leather strap.

Anderson recalled that Mr. and Mrs. Ohler would dress up and take a drive to North Beach; Ohler bought much of the property there. They rode in a carriage pulled by four black horses in splendid harness and attended by a coachman and footman in top hats. They must have presented quite a spectacle in the dusty frontier town of Corpus Christi.

Lt. John Kittredge landed at Ohler's wharf under a flag of truce in August 1862. Kittredge commanded the federal blockading fleet in the Gulf and was the scourge of the coast. People called him "that pirate Kittredge" and used his name to frighten children. After he demanded the surrender of Corpus Christi, and after that demand was rejected, his warships bombarded the town. This came to be called the battle of Corpus Christi.

Ohler was put in jail as a suspected Northern spy. With the city under blockade and food scarce, Mrs. Ohler was accused of jacking up prices on foodstuffs. The town's low opinion of her dropped even lower.

After the war, Mrs. Ohler, with the rest of the family, moved to Indianola, to the satisfaction of those who remembered her wartime profiteering.

Ohler's building was torn down in the 1870s. George F. Evans built a wool warehouse on the site. Evans owned a store on Chaparral and a ranch near Banquete. The Evans warehouse was later sold to Randolph Robertson to become the American Bottling Works, which bottled and sold Coca-Cola.

Next to the Ohler building was Capt. John Anderson's place and next to Ohler's wharf was Anderson's wharf. Anderson's schooners "Flour Bluff" and "Two Brothers" docked there. Anderson came to Corpus Christi in 1845 on a ship carrying supplies for the army

16. John Anderson's wind-powered grist mill, next to his home on Water Street, ground up salt collected from the Laguna Madre for use in curing meat and hides at beef packing houses along the coast. Capt. Anderson died in 1898. His grist mill and cottage were torn down two years later. The Nueces Hotel was built on the site of Anderson's home and grist mill.

of Gen. Zachary Taylor. He returned after the war with Mexico and built a home in the 600 block of Water Street in 1852.

When Kittredge's warships threatened Corpus Christi, Anderson took his family to the country. They could hear shells exploding and afterwards returned home to find a hole in their roof and their old gray cat missing an ear. The Andersons moved into a salt warehouse at Anderson Point at Flour Bluff to sit out the war. Capt. Andrew Anderson, in later years, recalled Civil War events involving his father, though he was only a young boy at the time. "While the Yankees were threatening to occupy Corpus Christi, a Frenchman and his wife were anxious to get out of the line of battle. They promised Captain Anderson $150 to take them in his sloop, the White Pelican, to Peñascal.

"There was an ox-cart road from Peñascal to Brownsville and after reaching Peñascal they could go by land to Brownsville and from there by water to New Orleans. Captain Anderson agreed to take them but before they reached Flour Bluff they were overtaken and captured by the Yankees (stationed on Mustang Island after November 1863). The Yankees came out of the cove while Anderson's boat was sailing around the outside of the cove. At Aransas Pass (the channel), the Union major in command made arrangements to send the French couple on to New Orleans to their great relief.

"Captain Anderson asked to be allowed to return to Corpus Christi and after holding him a day and a night they agreed to let him go. The major inquired of him as to the supply of provisions, sugar and coffee, in Corpus Christi and being told that provisions were short, the major commanded that his sloop be well stocked with supplies for the people in Corpus Christi. Upon Captain John Anderson's arrival, neither the supplies were well-received nor his intentions in bringing them well-considered. Many of the citizens refused to accept any of the provisions.

"Of course, news from the outside was very rare during the blockade days, and Captain Anderson succeeded in bringing back from Aransas Pass some Northern newspapers. These were passed from hand to hand until they were worn out and the print rubbed off.

"Some of the Confederate soldiers, while in a state of drunkenness, fell to discussing the Yankee major's kindness to Captain Anderson and came to the conclusion that Captain Anderson must be a spy and should be hanged as such. They were overheard by a friend of Anderson's, Bill Tinney, who ran to Anderson's house to warn him.

"Captain Anderson got away by boat and went back to Aransas Pass. Here he explained the situation to the very surprised Yankee major. The major then said since such was the case Anderson should stay at Aransas Pass and pilot the Yankee ships in and out of the bay. He worked in this capacity at Aransas Pass for two years, until the end of the war.

"During the time Captain Anderson piloted the Yankee boats around these coastal waters he sometimes made secret trips, at his own risk, across the bay to visit his family. He was often accompanied by some of the Yankee soldiers." One night, Captain Andy said, he awoke and saw guns stacked up in the yard and the blue coats of Yankee soldiers moving around. "It was not unusual for these visitors to move around in town a little, and although there was a small encampment of Confederate troops up on the bluff, no encounter was known to have taken place. The Confederate soldiers were mostly just cowboys."

At war's end, Andrew Anderson recalled, his father went to New Orleans where he was ordered to take charge of the steamer "Planter" full of Negro troops — three regiments, consisting of 700 or 800 men — and land them at Corpus Christi.

A year later, Andrew's father-in-law, Will "Dad" Grant, was hired to transport the Negro soldiers to Port Isabel on his sloop "May."

"On the voyage a storm blew up not far from Port Isabel," Andrew Anderson said, "and the boat was in such danger that she was beached, but the troops were saved and marched by land to their destination. This was the last of the Civil War as far as Corpus Christi was concerned."

After the war, Capt. John Anderson built a windmill to grind salt and to power a saw to cut firewood. The salt came from the Laguna Madre and the wood from the Nueces River bottoms. Anderson acquired four old cannonball relics of Kittredge's bombardment and used them as ball bearings on his windmill. They allowed him to shift the blades into the wind.

Capt. John Anderson died in 1898. His grist mill and cottage were torn down two years later. In 1912, the Nueces Hotel was built on the site of the Ohler building and Anderson's windmill. When the Nueces opened in 1913, it quickly became the pride of the city. In reality, it was too much hotel for a small town of 10,000, but the local investors behind building it believed the city was being held back because it lacked a first-class tourist hotel.

The Nueces Hotel was certainly first class. The six-story building, the tallest south of San Antonio, was built between Chaparral and Water Streets, fronting on Peoples, for $413,000. The hotel had more than 200 rooms, an elegant ballroom, Sun Parlor and Tropical Gardens.

17. *The Nueces Hotel, between Chaparral and Water streets, off Peoples, held its formal opening on Jan. 18, 1913. The six-story building was the tallest structure south of San Antonio. The hotel in 1961 was converted into a retirement home. After the building was damaged by Hurricane Celia, it was razed in 1971.*

In 1926, a new hotel was built on the bluff, the Plaza (later named the White Plaza). To compete, a 103-room wing was added to the Nueces Hotel. When the site where the Plaza was built was cleared, three palm trees in the yard of the Henry Redmond house were dug up and transplanted in the Nueces Hotel garden. The stately palms, called Tres Palmas, became the emblem on the Nueces Hotel's menu cards and stationary.

On Nov. 17, 1932, Henry Rudd, the hotel barber, was shaving the hotel's owner, W. W. Jones, when they heard gunshots. Jones ran through the lobby up to the mezzanine where the hotel manager, Arthur Dowd, had been shot to death in his office.

The killer, Isaac Davis, was the husband of a maid who had been fired. He shot Dowd eight times. Less than two weeks after the shooting, on Nov. 26, Davis was found guilty after a two-day trial and assessed the death penalty.

The hotel fell on hard times in the 1960s and was converted into a retirement home. The final blow came on Aug. 3, 1970 when the hotel was damaged by Hurricane Celia. The Nueces was razed in 1971 and its contents auctioned.

Dick Swantner paid $2,600 for the marble-faced clock from the lobby and donated it to the Corpus Christi Museum of Science and History, as time caught up with the grand old Nueces, once the pride of Corpus Christi.

18 and 19. The dining room of the Nueces (above) and the lobby below.

20. *The Dragon Grill opened on March 26, 1946 in the old Elks Club Building at Starr and Water streets. The Dragon Grill was famous for its entertainments, fine cuisine, and illegal gambling. In August 1953 Doc Mason, the owner, was charged with keeping a gambling house. He closed the Dragon Grill and moved to Las Vegas.*

Scogin Brothers Garage was built next to the Nueces Hotel just past the site of the Anderson cottage. It later became the Nueces Storage Garage. At the north end of the 600 block, at Water and Starr, was the old Arlington home used as a boarding house.

On the corner of the 700 block a storage building was owned by Edward Grant. His home was next door. In later years the Elks Club was on this site and then the Dragon Grill.

The Dragon Grill, a dinner club that featured illegal gambling, was established on North Beach by Linn K. "Doc" Mason. He came to Corpus Christi in 1926 and opened a private club above the Manhattan Cafe on Peoples Street.

In 1930 he opened the Dragon Grill on North Beach. The club burned on Jan. 15, 1944 and Mason leased the Elks Lodge building in Corpus Christi, at the corner of Water and Starr streets, a block north of the Nueces Hotel. Mason hired nationally known architects and interior designs to transform the building into a nightclub *par excellence* at a cost of $260,000. It opened on March 26, 1946 and never experienced a slack time thereafter. Guests entered through hand-hammered copper doors. The main dining room, the Zodiac Room, featured floor-to-ceiling murals between panels in coral and silver. It was a place of elegant evening gowns and tuxedos, of reflecting mirrors, the soft light of candles, of steak and lobster and cognac. Someone at the time said the Dragon Grill looked like, and even smelled like, money. The second floor included living quarters for Chinese cooks and private rooms for high-stakes gamblers. On the third floor was the Jalna Room, an elegant supper club, and beyond that were gambling rooms with roulette wheels and blackjack tables. Access to this illegal domain was controlled with a system of warning lights and buzzers. The building was honey-combed with secret rooms and hidden passageways.

In August 1953 an enterprising policeman gained entry to the Jalna Room and. Doc Mason was charged with keeping a gambling house. Not long afterwards, Mason sold out to the Town Club. He died in Las Vegas when he was 85 and was buried in Corpus Christi.

21 and 22. In the late 19th and early part of the 20th century, Water Street was interrupted by bay tides and there was no street as such for three blocks, from Taylor to Belden. The city built a retaining wall of rocks and boulders along that stretch of Water Street to stabilize the shoreline before the seawall was built. In the above photos, taken on May 8, 1935, workers add a smooth concrete facing over the rock revetment.

23. A rooftop view of the 700 block of Water Street shows a line of cars parked along the shoreline before the seawall was built. On the left was Doc Mason's Dragon Grill and down the street was the Princess Louise Hotel.

24. Kyle Dowdy's hamburger and A&W root beer stand at 725 Water on the corner of Taylor.

In the 19th Century, near the north end of the 700 block, was architect Charles Carroll's office. Carroll designed St. Patrick's Church in 1881. Mary Carroll, one of his four daughters, became school superintendent; Carroll High School was named for her.

25. Mary Sutherland wrote about the city's history in "The Story of Corpus Christi."

On the corner of Taylor and Water Street, east of the Vaky Apartments, was the home of H. R. Sutherland Sr. and wife Mary, who wrote the book "The Story of Corpus Christi," printed in 1916. Mary Sutherland was a fierce Southern nationalist, a diehard Confederate who never quite became reconciled to losing the war. She was born Mary McCrae in 1850 in Selma, Ala. She married Hugh Sutherland, a Confederate captain in the Ninth Regiment of Alabama Volunteers, and they moved to Corpus Christi in 1876.

In her book she tells of the discovery of Corpus Christi and writes that a Mexican village on the site was wiped out in an Indian attack. Only a small boy survived, she said, and returned to live out his days on King Ranch. She writes of the legend of a rich silver mine two days' ride from Corpus Christi. She tells of the landing and encampment of Zachary Taylor's army before the Mexican War and the bombardment of the city during the Civil War. She writes about early settlers and pioneers and tells stories of times long past.

Besides writing the "Story of Corpus Christi," she was instrumental in building the Confederate memorial fountain on the bluff and erecting a monument in Old Bayview Cemetery dedicated to the Confederate dead buried there. Her husband Hugh died on July 4, 1906. She died in 1930. Both were buried in old Bayview. Her son, Hugh Sutherland Jr., became one of the town's leading attorneys and county judge of Nueces County.

26. *The Seaside Hotel, shown on a 1907 postcard, was the former home of Capt. John Dix. The Seaside Hotel was a popular tourist resort. In 1908, William Jennings Bryan stayed there after he lost the presidential election to William Howard Taft.*

In the 1930s and 1940s, the 700 block of North Water hosted a fish market, the 15 Cent Taxi Service, an A&W root beer and hamburger stand. By the 1940s there were several used car lots in that block.

In the 19th Century, at the end of Taylor Street, was the home of John Dix, a retired ship captain. He served on a privateer in the War of 1812 and journeyed to the South Pacific. He moved to Corpus Christi in 1849 and built a home and planted salt cedars by the bay.

During the Civil War Dix was an ardent Unionist. Confederates believed that he was communicating with Union blockade officers by flashing a lantern light to send pre-arranged signals. Local Confederates threatened to hang him. (Dix and several other Union sympathizers, like Conrad Meuly, Edward Ohler and John Anderson, made themselves objectionable to Confederate neighbors at a time when it was dangerous to do so.)

After the war, Dix was appointed chief justice of the newly reorganized Nueces County government. The town's former Confederates, including those who had threatened to hang him, were disqualified for the post. Dix was chief justice of Nueces County when he died in 1870.

Anna Moore Schwien said Dix's wife, Mary Eliza Hayes Dix, taught school at her home after the war. She taught colored girls in the morning and white girls in the afternoon. The home became a boarding house, known as the Dix House, run by Eliza Ann Sullivan, who previously ran a boarding house in San Patricio. The Dix home was sold and converted into the Seaside Hotel. The conversion took place just after the turn of the 20th Century. An ad in the Caller in June 1904 said the Seaside "is the only hotel on the beach." Jack Ennis, a pioneer oilman from East Texas, bought the hotel after 1906.

27. The Seaside Pavilion, adjunct of the Seaside Hotel, was built on a pier in the bay in 1908. The Seaside Hotel and the Seaside Pavilion were destroyed by the storm on Sept. 14, 1919.

Ennis added the Seaside Pavilion on a pier in the bay. Among the more famous guests of the Seaside Hotel were William Jennings Bryan and wife, who stayed there two weeks after Bryan lost the 1908 presidential election to William Howard Taft. Bryan delivered a stirring speech at the Waterways Convention on Nov. 17 before leaving for Mexico. Bryan, known as an electrifying orator, had visited Corpus Christi 10 years before, in 1898. A man wrote later that he did not go to the meeting where Bryan spoke but he opened the window of his hotel room and could hear his every word, crystal clear, though he was three blocks away.

When Ennis died in 1910, he left the Seaside to Nancy Ferguson, daughter of a friend. The Seaside Pavilion lost its pier in the 1916 hurricane and three years later the Seaside Hotel and the Pavilion were destroyed in the 1919 storm.

In the 1930s, in the 900 block of North Water, there was the Princess Louise Storage Garage. On the beach side of Water in the 1000 block the Confederate sloop Hannah was burned in 1862 to prevent her capture by Union warships. Wool dealer Ed Buckley, of Byrne & Buckley, built a home nearby, at Mann and Water, where the Princess Louise Hotel was later built. Mr. and Mrs. J. B. Murphy lived on the north end of this block.

After the 1919 hurricane destroyed the Seaside Hotel and Pavilion, the Chamber of Commerce offered a $10,000 bonus to anyone who would build a resort hotel on the waterfront. The offer was taken up by Walter Foster, a former railroad conductor. He bought property at Mann and Water, where the Ed Buckley home once stood.

Foster's 110-room hotel was built in 1927. He named it the Princess Louise after his wife, Louise Devereaux. The hotel's pink stucco walls offered a stylish contrast with the red-tile roof. The hotel opened on Saturday night, Jan. 7, 1928. The first guests were Mr. and Mrs. J. C. Robertson from St. Petersburg, Fla. After Louise Foster died in 1936, Walter turned over the management of the hotel to a longtime employee, Leslie Greer.

28. *The 900 block of Water in the 1930s. A Sinclair service station is on the left and the Princess Louise Hotel at the corner of Mann and Water.*

29. *The Princess Louise on March 25, 1936. The hotel opened in January 1928 and became a downtown landmark. It was converted into La Posada Apartments in 1965.*

When the seawall moved back the shoreline, the Princess Louise was stranded two blocks inland and never the same afterwards. Walter Foster died in 1948 and left the hotel to his secretary, Mary Ethel Noble, who converted it into the La Posada Apartments in 1965, which are still there today.

30. *Robert Ritter's Hotel and Bath House was built on a pier over the water between Resaca and Fitzgerald streets in 1891. It was a popular place for dances and entertainments.*

In 1891 Robert Ritter built the Ritter Hotel and Bath House on a pier over the water between Fitzgerald and Resaca.

The Caller on Jan. 8, 1893 reported that a ball held at Ritter's Pavilion was in honor of Adelaide Lovenskiold and Belle Skinner who were leaving for a tour of the North. The paper said the Ritter pavilion was decorated with evergreens, flowers and bunting. When the grand march was struck by the Favella quartet, 50 couples fell in line, and the program of dances was taken up. The ball broke up as the sun rose. Ritter's Pavilion was destroyed by a storm in the 1890s.

At the intersection of Water and Fitzgerald, in the 1500 block, was the home of Col. John M. Moore. Before he moved to Corpus Christi, Moore owned the Alabama Coal & Mining Company and a large plantation. He sold his Alabama holdings and moved to Corpus Christi in 1858. He brought some of his slaves with him.

Moore contracted to dredge a channel across the bay. He used slaves to work the dredge boat. Work was stopped before the start of the Civil War when funds ran short. J. C. Riddle, dredge boat captain, complained about "not having a cent" to pay his workers.

During the Civil War, Moore was involved in blockade-running and served as a purchasing agent in Mexico for Confederate authorities. During the occupation after the war, two Union regiments camped at that end of town and the Moore home was taken over by Gen. Charles Russell for his headquarters. Thomas Noakes visited Russell at the Moore home to lend him his painting of the battle of Corpus Christi.

Moore was one of the first members of the school board, with William Rogers and Nelson Plato, in 1873 and he was elected to a three-year term as mayor in 1877. He dabbled in oil exploration and drilled for oil around Spindletop long before the great discovery. He died in 1892. Moore's home at 1505 Water Street was a two-story structure surrounded by an iron fence. It was sold to J. H. C. White in the 1880s. At the rear of the Moore home was an adobe house where Moore's daughter (Hannah Conklin) taught school.

31. *An unusual building in the 1400 block of Water was the Lighthouse Restaurant, which was there for a short time. It was built on the site of the Bayside Inn and was operated by William E. Sorrell and wife who lived on the premises. There was another lighthouse restaurant on Ocean Drive past Airline (page 275). It was also short-lived.*

32. The Water Street Tourist Park, in the 1700 block, was between Hughes and Brewster streets. Tourist camps gave this stretch of Water Street the appearance of North Beach.

33. The Humble Service Station, at 2021 Water Street, sat in the junction between Water and Chaparral, just across from the bascule bridge.

Near John M. Moore's home on Water were the remains of the old earth walls of Fort Marcy built by Zachary Taylor's soldiers in 1845. These were dirt embankments, or redoubts, but there really was no "fort" except on paper. The embankments were used to protect a Confederate battery during the battle of Corpus Christi in 1862. The walls could be seen after the turn of the century; Alex Weil Sr. recalled playing on the old redoubts as a youngster. Over time they were leveled and built over.

34. *David Hirsch Elementary, built in 1912, was located on North Water Street at the rear of where the Museum of Science and History is today. The school was closed in 1962 and the building torn down in 1966.*

David Hirsch Elementary was one of three new ward schools built in 1912, at a cost of $11,000 each, and opened in 1913. Besides David Hirsch the other two were George Evans and Edward Furman, all based on the same design to save money.

David Hirsch was a brick structure built at 1907 North Water, within rock-throwing distance of Hall's Bayou. It was around the site now occupied by the Museum of Science and History. It was named for wool merchant and banker David Hirsch who served as the first president of the school board.

David Hirsch students came from the Irishtown area north of the courthouse, and from North Beach.

Mrs. Ameta McGloin, a teacher at David Hirsch, recalled that streetcars passed the school on their North Beach run. One who attended the school was Theodore Fuller, who recalled his school days in his memoirs "When the Century and I Were Young"

"Three grade schools in Corpus were the last word in the era's modern school architecture. Our school, David Hirsch, was one of these."

Fuller wrote that his teacher, Miss Pearl Bauerfein, thought they needed a pencil sharpener in their room and asked the students to contribute a nickel each. "I think the hand-turned sharpener was a dollar but it may have been as much as a dollar and a half.

35. The David Hirsch Elementary baseball team is shown in perhaps the late 1920s, though the date and identities are unknown.

With 30 to 35 students in the class, a nickel each should do the job." After three days Miss Bauerfein wrote on the blackboard "collected" and "needed." Since some kids didn't bring a nickel they were still short by 25 cents. A boy named Jack Giles (his father, Dr. H. R. Giles, would later be elected mayor) contributed a whole quarter. Fuller was impressed. "Had I possessed a quarter, it would never have entered my mind to have done as Jack did. My envy was boundless."

Atlee McCampbell, another student, recalled that during recess the boys would shoot marbles on the playground or play baseball on a nearby field. David Hirsch was damaged in the 1919 storm and stood empty for six years before it was re-opened in 1925.

Rodolfo Pena Garcia told me his family, immigrants from Mexico, lived in a cabin at the Big Chief Camp when his father took him to be enrolled at David Hirsch in 1954. "The teachers and principal showed us great kindness and patience. The teachers would stay after school to teach us English and the principal took me to the school library so I could choose two books which I could take home and keep, to advance my ability to learn English. My second-grade teacher assigned a Spanish-speaking boy, David Garcia, to explain things as well as teach me English."

The school was closed in 1962. One year later the school building was used as a backdrop to film an episode of the TV series "Route 66." Students from Casa Linda Elementary School were brought in to help film the scene. It was 19 degrees when the scene was shot on the Hirsch playground, with girls jumping rope and boys playing basketball.

The David Hirsch school building was torn down in August 1966.

36. *Cars wait in the 1900 block of Water Street for the bascule bridge to be lowered. On the right was the Leo Gunderland Grocery Store. The photo dates from about 1955.*

In the 19th Century, the Stanley Welch home was at the north end of Water Street. It was followed by a small bridge over the slough where the ship channel is today. Hall's Bayou was a natural watercourse that drained into the bay. In the 1870s when North Beach was called Brooklyn there was a small wooden bridge across the bayou. Naturally it was called Brooklyn bridge

In the 1930s, between Resaca and Hughes, there were several fish markets and grocery stores, including the Midway Grocery, Midway Café and Midway Gardens, all operated by Charles M. Lassiter and his relatives. This section of Water Street began to take on the appearance of North Beach with tourist-oriented business attractions, including the Water Street Tourist Park and the Big Chief Camp near the David Hirsch School. On Water and Chaparral, in the approach to the bascule bridge, there were a number of service stations, bars, and cafes, ready to cater to a captive audience.

Great changes came with the destruction of the 1919 storm, when the seawall pushed back the bay, and when the I-37 terminus cut across the 1000 and 1100 blocks. Water Street was left high and dry and two blocks inland after the seawall was built.

Though it was no longer on the water the street never lost its historic importance. From Blucher's Creek, where Kinney first landed, to the Central Wharf, from Cahill's building to Anderson's windmill, from Ritter's pavilion to the old earth fortifications left by Zachary Taylor, much of the city's history is connected to Water Street.

37. Gutzon Borglum's bayfront plan in 1928 featured a vertical seawall, not a stepped design, with a statue of Christ beyond the breakwater. Voters turned down a bond issue, funds from state and federal sources were unavailable, and Borglum left for his monumental work in the Black Hills of South Dakota.

SEAWALL AND SHORELINE: Work began in 1939 on a project that would change the city's appearance, adding the seawall, two T-heads and an L-head. But it was a mess at the time, with dredges pumping mud from the bay bottom. The idea for a seawall goes back at least to 1874, after a hurricane flooded the downtown, and again in 1890 when the Caller ran an article on how the city might look at the beginning of the 20th century and the article forecast building a seawall "500 feet from the shoreline, filling up back of this wall and utilizing the ground."

It was a bold plan, far ahead of its time, and predictably went nowhere. But the idea stayed around. In 1909, County Judge Walter Timon tried to convince Corpus Christi Mayor Dan Reid of the need for a seawall. The idea went no further, but after two severe storms in 1916 and 1919, people remembered Timon's proposal.

Timon was asked to look at seawalls along the Atlantic coast and make recommendations on what would best serve the city's needs. When he returned he drafted what was called the Timon Plan to build a seawall and a breakwater. The federal government required the breakwater to be in place before it provided funding for building the port. The breakwater was started in 1924, two years before the port opened for business, but there was no money for a seawall.

In 1928 the city hired sculptor Gutzon Borglum to design a seawall. The man who would eventually sculpt Mount Rushmore had family ties here. The plan Borglum drafted called for a grand boulevard behind the seawall with parks along the bayfront and an imposing 32-foot statue of Jesus standing inside rock jetties in the bay with his arms uplifted as if to

38. *Work began on the bayfront improvement project on Jan. 1, 1939. The project completely altered the city's waterfront appearance. Dredged fill from the bay bottom extended the city at some points to more than 1,000 feet into the bay. A 12,000-foot seawall was built from the port to Craig Street to the south. The seawall and levee behind it raised the city's waterfront elevation to 14 feet, 3.7 feet above the high-water mark in the 1919 storm. Two T-heads and one L-head, the seawall, and new Shoreline Boulevard atop the levee, were completed in two years at a cost of $2.2 million.*

calm the raging waters. Borglum's seawall design did not include the stepped design that was eventually adopted. Borglum's was a straight wall with castellations, or castle-like effects, though he did describe the seawall as serving as a great amphitheater facing the bay, so perhaps it was his artistic vision which eventually inspired the final design.

There was a fierce fight over the statue of Christ, the city was unable to get state or federal help to pay for the undertaking, and local voters turned down a bond issue to build the seawall. Borglum left for the Black Hills, with a parting shot for Corpus Christi — "I don't think I have ever seen a town where the crooks and respectable people are so like scrambled eggs."

The seawall plan laid dormant for another decade. In 1938, Corpus Christi voters were asked to approve a $650,000 bond issue. There was already $200,000 in the kitty. There

39. *An aerial shot shows the white strip of dredged fill from the bay bottom between Water Street and the location of the new seawall.*

was some opposition. Walter Foster, who owned the Princess Louise Hotel, opposed the project. Foster's hotel was a few steps from the water, but the seawall plan would push the waterfront east by almost two blocks, leaving the Princess Louise high and dry.

But the opposition was very weak and that first bond issue passed by a vote of 1,431 for to 108 against. The following year voters easily approved another $1.1 million bond issue, 1,078 to 83.

One of Timon's ideas was revived that called for the state to give Corpus Christi the state's share of ad valorem taxes from seven South Texas counties — Nueces, Jim Wells, Jim Hogg, Brooks, Kleberg, Willacy and Duval — to help pay for the seawall. That was done with little opposition in the Legislature.

The project began on Jan. 1, 1939, the 100th anniversary of the city's founding. Mayor A. C. McCaughan chose a Dallas engineering firm, Myers & Noyes, to design and oversee the project and he hired J. DePuy of San Antonio who built the breakwater in 1926 as the

40. *Contractor J. DePuy designed a special device to use to furnish the forms, pour the concrete, and after that section of concrete was set to lift up and move to a new section. The stepped seawall was completed, section by section, with DePuy's contraption.*

prime contractor of the project. The city almost repeated the same mistake it made with the bascule bridge. When the port was built, federal engineers argued that the proposed bascule bridge would be too small for the larger ships being built. The city ignored that advice and built the cheapest bridge it could build. That blunder plagued the city for the next three decades.

Similarly, on the seawall, city officials opted for the cheapest possible seawall. They wanted a straight wall of steel-sheet piling and concrete to separate land and water. They wanted a narrow 24-foot parkway on Shoreline. They opted for the cheapest of all the alternatives. But a civil engineer, Edward Noyes of Myers and Noyes, resisted and argued that a stair-step design for the seawall, as he proposed, would cost more but would give Corpus Christi a bayfront "second to none" in point of function and beauty. He argued for a 200-foot-wide parkway atop the levee and finally compromised on an 80-foot-wide parkway. Noyes won the argument.

The contractor, DePuy, started work at three points, at the bascule bridge, Pleasure Pier, and Municipal Wharf. The Pleasure Pier was dismantled and tenants on the Municipal Wharf were forced to move. DePuy designed a 40-foot-long metal shed on railroad wheels under which the 40-foot lengths of the stepped seawall were poured of reinforced concrete.

On the north near the ship channel, creosoted pilings were driven to provide a footing for the embankment, which was built of dredge spoil from the bay bottom. Behind a temporary seawall, the bottom of the bay next to the shore was laid bare.

The bottom clay called fill was scooped out by dredges and pumped into the outlines of

41. Aerial view of the two new T-heads and L-head during the last phases of construction before the project was completed in March 1941.

the T-heads and L-head and used to raise the elevation between Water Street and the seawall. On top of this reclaimed land would run the parkway, in effect a levee. The parkway was first called Bayshore Boulevard then Shoreline.

Warehouses at the port had been built to a higher grade but tourist cabins and other waterfront structures had to be raised two to three feet with fill pumped in under them. The Pier Cafe had to be raised as well as the Nueces Hotel garden.

Work on the seawall was completed in March 1941. From scratch to finish it took two years and cost $2.2 million. The city had been extended almost two blocks into the bay and the bayfront itself had been elevated to 14 feet above sea level — 3.7 feet above the high-water mark of the 1919 storm.

The seawall, from the ship channel on the north end to the foot of Craig Avenue on the south, stretched two miles and every foot, it was said, of the 12,000-foot wall was built to withstand a load pressure of 260 tons. There would be no reprise of the kind of storm surge

42. *Corpus Christi's $2 million seawall nears completion at the end of 1940. The new stepped seawall would prove to be a scenic amphitheater facing the bay.*

that wrecked the downtown in 1919. The yacht basins, the L-head and two T-heads were part of the project. Another L-head, off the end of Twigg, was planned but the state closed its purse, saying it had spent enough on storm protection for Corpus Christi.

The original plan also called for a tube tunnel under the ship channel to be built later but, because of the war, that was dropped.

The seawall was a storm-protective measure. It's why the state agreed to pay for it. But when it was finished, it was clear that it was the greatest beautification program in the city's history. Edward Noyes was responsible for the seawall design; it was his stepped seawall design that provided seating for that great amphitheater on the bay.

The seawall's clean lines along two miles of the bayfront, facing the rising sun, dramatically improved the city's appearance and it did give Corpus Christi a bayfront "second to none in point of beauty."

43 and 44. First cars drive on Shoreline Boulevard (above) when the roadway was opened on March 29, 1941. The new T-heads and L-head (below) were also opened to traffic.

+

Chapter 2. Chaparral Street

From the arroyo going north to the port entrance, crossing Laguna (later Sartain), William, Lawrence, Schatzel, Peoples, Starr, Taylor, Twigg, Mann, Aubrey, Belden, Power, Palo Alto, Fitzgerald, Resaca streets.

Corpus Christi from its earliest times had three main streets which ran north-south — Water, Chaparral and Mesquite. Of the three, Chaparral was the main commercial street. It was sometimes called Front Street and Mesquite Back Street.

At the south end of Chaparral, beyond Cooper's Alley, was a brush thicket that may have given it its name. Guth Park was here later. The arroyo between Cooper's Alley and Laguna Street was the dividing line between North and South Chaparral. This division was later shifted to Cooper's Alley.

South of Cooper's Alley, on the east side, was W. N. Staples' lumberyard. He sold it to E. D. Sidbury. North of Cooper's Alley, in the 100 block, was William "Billy" Rogers' home, on the corner on the west side of the street. Rogers survived a massacre on the Arroyo Colorado near the Rio Grande at the start of the Mexican War. He returned to Corpus Christi, became a prominent rancher, was elected sheriff, bought the St. James Hotel, and built Market Hall. Rogers' home at 101 Chaparral burned on Oct. 1, 1871. After the fire, he organized the city's first fire volunteer department. His replacement home, built on the same site, was torn down in 1941. A parking lot is on that site today.

Across from Rogers' home, in the 20th Century, was the San Antonio Machine Shop building. For the rest of the block, in the 1930s, there was the CPL district office at 110, followed by the main CPL office building in a modern brick structure constructed in 1931 on the corner (where the City Police Headquarters is today). On the west side of the 100 block was the Caldwell Cypress Cisterns, at 117, followed by the Nueces Battery.

Past Laguna on the east side, in the 200 block, was Conrad Meuly's home, which was built in 1854. Meuly's two-story house had 14-foot ceilings and walls as thick as an ancient fortress. It was built of local materials — clay, oyster shell and lime — and the front of the house was decorated with iron grillwork.

The Meuly home was the scene of an attempted lynching on May 15, 1866. A drunken loafer named Jim Garner shot and killed a storekeeper named Emanuel Scheuer. A mob grabbed Garner and hustled him down Chaparral looking for a place to hang him. It was with an increasing sense of panic that he pleaded, "Give me a trial, boys! Give me a trial!" The mob stopped at Meuly's and they tried to attach the rope to the wrought-iron balcony when Margaret Meuly ran them off. She would not allow her house to be used to lynch a man.

Garner was taken to the end of the street and hanged from a stunted mesquite tree. It was said that old man Garner, the hanged man's father, came to take the body away and said he had gotten a good long rope by the proceeding. Dr. Arthur Spohn, when he first arrived in town, had his office in the Meuly house and boarded with the family.

1. The Conrad Meuly home at 210 N. Chaparral in 1936. The house, built in 1854, had a distinctive wrought-iron front shipped from New Orleans. The old house survived the bombardment of Corpus Christi during the Civil War and hurricanes of 1874 and 1919. It was torn down in the 1950s.

The Meuly home was torn down in the 1950s to clear the site for a Fedway department store, which was later remodeled and enlarged to house the Education Service Center.

Past Meuly's was Cornelius Cahill's three-story building. He had an older building on Water Street, facing the Central Wharf. Cahill held a party in 1859 to celebrate the opening of his new store. The building was in ruins by the 1880s.

At the north end of the block was the Gravis boarding house shaded by a screen of oleanders. The Gravis place was built in 1846 by John A.F. Gravis, a former Texas Ranger. It was called the California House in 1849 to attract prospective miners as they passed through on their way to the goldfields. Gravis, with Henry W. Berry, built many of the early shellcrete structures in town. But the building trade was not very lucrative then. When Gravis died of yellow fever in 1854, his estate consisted of a Spanish pony, a two-wheeled gig, and a six-shooter, which sold for $27.

His widow Irenah married Berry, her husband's business partner. Irenah Gravis Berry continued to run the boarding house, which for a time was called the Sierra Madre Hotel. She would send one of her boys out with a bell fixed to a long wooden pole to summon the boarders at meal times. A two-story brick building on this site was later occupied by the auto dealership of J. C. Blacknall, with the Colonial Hotel on the second floor. On the west side of the 200 block, past Laguna, was Frederick Belden's warehouse, an adobe-like building that was used to store supplies for Zachary Taylor's army in 1845.

2. *In this street scene, lining the east side of the 200 block of N. Chaparral, Conrad Meuly's "home with the iron front" is followed by J. C. Blacknall's Dodge and Plymouth dealership. Above Blacknall's is the Colonial Hotel and past the William Street intersection is the Savoy Hotel in the next block. Down the street can be seen the Medical-Professional Building and Jones Building, with the Nueces Hotel blocked from view.*

Near the north end of the 200 block was the La Retama Saloon in a shellcrete building. The Ranchero in its March 31, 1860 edition reported that the La Retama "is the name of the new saloon, opened opposite the Sierra Madre Hotel, Chaparral street." A fracas at the La Retama on Aug. 4, 1860 led to the fatal shooting of Deputy Sheriff Thomas (Tom) Nolan, brother of Sheriff Matthew (Mat) Nolan. This building was later used as a store.

The west side of the 200 block was burned in a big fire on July 14, 1892. The fire consumed the E. Molander and M. Ley cottages on the south end of the block, the J. B. Mitchell warehouse, the William Biggio residence, the William Daimwood home, and Royall Givens' grocery in the old La Retama building. The most destructive fire in city history led to building a pipeline to the Nueces River and establishing the city's first water system. A 1900 Sanborn insurance map shows the south end of the block empty except for water cisterns behind the burned homes. Mifflin Kenedy's office in a small frame building on the corner of Chaparral and William, next to Royall Givens' store, survived the fire.

In the 1930s, on the east side of the 200 block, was Winerich Motor Company, which sold Studabaker and Rockne motorcars, followed by the Meuly residence, a used car lot, and the Blacknall auto dealership on the corner. On the west side of the block was a Humble service station, where the Nueces County Appraisal Office is now, Clarence McVay's Waffe House, a boarding house called the Chaparral, followed by J. A. Stovall's Corpus Christi Radiator Works and Guaranty Finance on the corner.

3. *Central Power & Light's main office building at Chaparral and Laguna shown on Sept. 4, 1940. The CPL building was constructed on the site of an old grocery store owned by A. Longoria. The CPL building was purchased by the city in 1988 to house the police department and municipal courts.*

In the 300 block, across William Street, was one of the oldest buildings in town. This was the old Kinney House, a hotel built in 1845 on the northwest corner of Chaparral. It was diagonally across the intersection from the Berry boarding house.

The Kinney House was sold in 1848 to George Noessel, who had owned hotels in Matagorda and Bastrop before he came to Corpus Christi. He renamed the Kinney House the Corpus Christi Hotel. Army officers, including the later Civil War general Phil Sheridan, stayed at Noessel's. After the army moved the Eighth District headquarters from Corpus Christi to San Antonio in 1855, Noessel converted the hotel into a grocery and dry goods store.

Noessel's featured a sign of an Indian chief and displayed a Comanche buffalo hide shield. The Ranchero, on Feb. 23, 1861, said the shield was made of "bull hide ornamented with red flannel, feathers, little bells, a brass plate, doubtless taken from the lock of some unlucky traveler's carpetbag. It is a curiosity worth seeing." In 1882 the Noessel building (the old Kinney House) was rented to become the first home of the Corpus Christi Caller.

4. *In the 300 block was the Kinney House, left, built in 1845. It was sold to George Noessel and for years housed Noessel's grocery store. To the right was Noakes Brothers Machine. Shop, which advertised that its machinists could repair anything from a clock to a steam engine.*

Past the Caller's office, after 1883, came the Noakes Brothers' Machine Shop. An ad just after the turn of the 20th Century said Noakes Brothers' machine and blacksmith shop contained the latest machines and could fix anything from a clock to a steam engine. An ad in 1906 said Noakes was selling Cadillacs, that there were already four in town, and the shop would keep the machine in repair for six months, barring accidents or punctured tires.

Beyond Noakes was F. Lachman's tailor shop then Joseph Groome, a bootmaker, followed by Prokop (also spelled Prokoff) Hoffman's dry goods and grocery store near the end of the block. On the corner was a restaurant and saloon run by Jacob Ziegler, who also ran a hotel-cum-boarding house on Mesquite. The Nueces Hardware store was later on the old Ziegler site.

On the east side of the 300 block on the northeast corner was the wool commission firm of Byrne & Buckley. Next door was a grocery and dry goods store owned by Waymon N. Staples. In the October 1859 Ranchero, Staples advertised hoopskirts, family groceries, whisky, and said he would accept wool, hides, stock, lead, gold or silver in exchange. He also owned a lumberyard which he later sold to Edward Sidbury.

Mary Sutherland told a story about one of Staples' customers who had his own notched-stick system of accounting, as related by Joseph Fitzsimmons, a bookkeeper for Staples. A rancher came in twice yearly to settle up, Fitzsimmons said. "One day he came in for his

5. *DeWitt Reed's auto dealership where Noessel's once stood, at Chaparral and William. Past Reed was the Stag Buffet, Cage Hardware, Nueces Furniture and Nueces Hardware.*

account. I called the amount, he hesitated before taking the bill. 'No, sir, that's not right,' he said, laying it on the desk and reaching in his pocket he brought out a stick covered with notches.

" 'You have charged me twenty cents too much.' Running his finger down the stick he said, 'This is ten dollars; this is five; one-seventy; two forty-five; tobacco, twenty-five; ax for John, seventy-five; one wash pot for the old woman, two-thirty; one dollar, what the devil? Oh, yes, two gallons of whisky for Old Jerry's wake,' and so on to the end of the stick. The clerks added wildly, the overcharge of twenty cents was actually found, and the old man settled up and cut a new stick."

When Staples moved out to Last Street the Staples building housed David Hirsch's store, beginning in 1869. The family lived upstairs while on the ground floor Hirsch operated a general merchandise and men's clothing store. He became a major wool dealer, bought Martha Rabb's Magnolia Mansion on the bluff, founded the Corpus Christi National Bank and served as the first president of the school board. Hirsch moved his wool store to the 400 block of Chaparral.

The Crescent Hotel was next door to the Hirsch place. An ad in the Caller in 1883 said the hotel was under the new management of Nick Constantine and had reduced its prices to $1.50 and $2 a day. It was bought by Capt. Fred Steen, who had lost a leg in a ship collision at Brazos Santiago. Steen and wife Nevada renamed the Crescent as the Steen Hotel.

George Roberts' Favorite Saloon was north of the Crescent/Steen Hotel. The Favorite Saloon advertised "choice liquors, fine cigars, and polite bartenders." The Favorite had a ten-pin alley and rooms above. On the corner, past the Favorite, was the Frank & Weil

44

6. Reed Auto at the corner of Chaparral and William later became Gillespie Buick, owned by Henry C. Gillespie Jr. The dealership was later moved to South Water.

Store where E. Frank and Charles Weil sold dry goods and ranch supplies.

In the 1930s and early 1940s, the 300 block of Chaparral, on the west side of the street there was Reed Auto where Noessel's once stood. Reed was later sold to Henry Gillespie and became Gillespie Buick. Past Reed was the Stag Buffet, Cage Hardware, Nueces Furniture and Nueces Hardware on the corner. On the east side was Mervin Douglass' café, Douglass Eat-a-Bite, with the Savoy Hotel Rooms above. It was followed by a paint store, hobby shop, barber shop and, on the corner, McNabb-Collins Motors, owned by Otis McNabb and Ned Collins. Mrs. Alma Bonner's Model Rooms were above.

When Zachary Taylor's army was encamped at Corpus Christi in 1845, Charles Bryant, an architect from Maine, built the Union Theater at the corner of Lawrence and Chaparral. It hosted plays and entertainments for the troops. In 1850, Bryant was killed and scalped by Indians on Chocolate Bayou near the Wood Ranch.

A new hotel was built on the site of Bryant's Union Theater. It was named after the St. James Hotel in Kansas City, but it was also the last name of the man who had it built, J. T. James, a cattle rancher on Mustang Island. Before the hotel was finished James sold it to William Rogers, who paid $13,000 for the hotel and spent $5,000 to get it ready to open. When Rogers died in 1877 William Biggio became the manager of the St. James. Biggio

7. In the 400 block of Chaparral was the St. James Hotel, built in 1869. It stood on the corner of the old Union Theater, built in 1845 to stage entertainments for Zachary Taylor's troops.

was the pilot of the Confederate ram Webb, a sidewheel steamer, which was burned by its crew at the mouth of the Mississippi and Biggio was among those taken prisoner.

Under Biggio's management the St. James became known as the headquarters of cattle ranchers, cowboys, politicians, gamblers and gunmen. The hotel saloon, the Gem, run by P. H. McManigle, was one of the places in town where men gathered in the evenings to discuss the events and adventures of the day.

William Daimwood opened a men's store in the building and Dr. D. H. Lawrence kept an office in the St. James.

It was said that Biggio would never turn a man away hungry, whether he could pay for a meal or not. Biggio retired in 1905 and died soon afterwards. The St. James in the 1930s was operated as a rooming house. When it was torn down in 1937, one of the most famous landmarks in South Texas was gone. Three years later, Lichtenstein's fourth and last department store was built on the site.

On past the St. James Hotel, in 1896, a man named Foster and his wife opened a snake-collecting business next to the St. James. They bought rattlesnakes and shipped them away. After one of their rattlesnakes escaped, complaints forced the snake couple to move on.

North of the St. James was a variety store, similar to a five-and-dime, owned by J. Levy, who moved to Corpus Christi from Banquete. The Bluntzer building was later constructed on the site of Levy's store. Cage Hardware was later in this building.

On past Levy's was a wool warehouse where, in the 1870s, David Hirsch was located, after he moved from the 300 block. Near the north end of the block was Herman Meuly's News Depot, which sold newspapers, stationery, and McGuffey's readers.

Past Meuly's was a vacant lot used to park wagons. Gugenheim-Cohn Department Store was built on this site in the 20th Century.

8. *After the St. James Hotel was dismantled in 1937, the corner of Chaparral and Lawrence was used as a parking lot before the new Lichtenstein's was built on the site in 1941.*

Across from the St. James, on the east side of Chaparral, was the wool firm of Edey & Kirsten. Uriah Lott, Perry Doddridge and Allen M. Davis bought out Edey & Kirsten. Doddridge opened the first bank in town in 1871 in the old Edey & Kirsten building. He built the Doddridge Bank building on the site in 1883.

The second floor of the building was used for the Myrtle Club, a private men's club, with a saloon, billiards, reading room, and tables for card games. Most of the prominent men in town belonged to the Myrtle Club.

The Doddridge Bank collapsed during a national depression in 1893. In February 1919, the Corpus Christi Caller moved from the Noessel building into the Doddridge Building. During the 1919 hurricane, the newspaper office was submerged in the storm surge. The press on the first floor was swamped, though the editorial offices and composing room on the upper floor escaped damage. The Caller was printed in Kingsville until the big duplex press was repaired, but the city light plant that provided the power had been destroyed. The Caller got a Fordson tractor and used a long belt to connect the drive shaft to the press. With some careful "driving" the Caller's press was back in operation.

In the mid-1920s the Caller moved to Mesquite Street and the Doddridge Building was remodeled to house J. E. Garrett's Texas State Bank & Trust and, in the 1930s, the Faust Café, run by Meydon Lymberry. Before 1941, the Doddridge Building was torn down or renovated to house Buttrey's Ladies Wear.

9. *Girls ride their bicycles in front of Perry Doddridge's bank, built in 1883, at the corner of Lawrence and Chaparral. The Doddridge Bank was on the east side of Chaparral across from the St. James Hotel.*

North of the Doddridge Building was Wheeler's store. Lt. E. H. (Elijah Harvey) Wheeler arrived with Union occupation forces after the war, married Sarah McCampbell, and opened a shoe store. Wheeler's promised to refasten buttons on ladies' shoes for free.

Next door to Wheeler's was Julius Henry's store with living quarters on the second floor. Henry arrived in Corpus Christi in 1858, penniless, and chopped cotton for John Dunn for $4 a month and board. When Henry Kinney, the town's founder, came to a melodramatic end in Matamoros in 1862, Julius Henry and Martin Hinojosa were with him.

There are conflicting accounts of Kinney's death. In the official version, Kinney was shot to death in June 1861 during a street disturbance between rival gangs in Matamoros. Judge M. P. Norton, Kinney's friend and confidante, wrote that Kinney was "shot down in the street during a difficulty."

The author Coleman McCampbell related that Kinney "became involved in a petty skirmish between two factions of Mexicans, the Crinolinos and Rohos. While attempting to pass through a breach in a wall, a bullet pierced his heart. He toppled, dying instantly."

10. *Corpus Christi founder Henry Kinney was killed in Matamoros in February 1862.*

The other account said Kinney was killed in February 1862 when he was shot outside the front door of his former lover, Genoveva Perez. He was shot in the early morning hours by Genoveva's new husband, Cesario Falcon. We don't know where Kinney was buried, which reminds me of a prophetic poem by the Spanish poet Federico Garcia Lorca, who was murdered during the Spanish Civil War and himself buried in an unknown grave:

> *"Then I realized I had been murdered.*
> *They looked for me in cafes, cemeteries and churches . . .*
> *   but they did not find me*
> *They did not find me?*
> *No. They never found me."*

After Kinney's death, Julius Henry returned to Corpus Christi and, after the war, opened a general store on Water Street then built a new building on Chaparral. Past Henry's was Gradwhol's dry goods, which later became Friend & Cahn's Bank, and finally, after the bank failed, the Bank Saloon run by Jap Clark. Charles Parker's barber shop was next door.

11. *The Doddridge Building, shown on Nov. 12, 1931, was known as the Garrett building after it was sold to J. E. Garrett. It was torn down or renovated for Buttrey's Ladies Wear.*

Near the end of the block was Blumenthal & Jordt furniture store in a wooden building with three gables. The firm later became Jordt-Allen and then Allen Furniture. It moved into a new building in 1912. At Jordt-Allen Furniture after the 1919 storm, the water inside had risen to five feet or more and all the furnishings for sale were covered with thick, black oil. Frank Campbell Allen, co-owner of the store, said the building between Water and Chaparral served as a canal for the floodwaters.

On the corner was an old barn-like structure that had been shipped in component parts from New York by William R. Grace, mayor of New York City, who was a business partner of Matthew and William Headen, wool merchants.

Longtime newsman Eli Merriman said that the Grace building was shipped to Corpus Christi in 1859. It arrived in sections and was put together with wooden pegs. The Grace-Headen building was occupied by J. W. Westervelt, a ship chandler, in the 1890s. After the turn of the 20th Century it was sold to William (Bill) Rankin, who owned and operated several grocery stores in the downtown area. Rankin said that when he was growing up in the 1860s his ambition was to own that structure. "I thought I would be a millionaire if I could own that building."

Rankin later sold the building to Hugh Sutherland Sr. A grocery store was operated on the first floor with law offices on the second. The Oil City Café took over what had been

12. The Grace-Headen building, which was shipped in pieces from New York to Corpus Christi about 1859, was later remodeled to house Rankin's Grocery. In the 1930s it also housed the Oil City Café. The Sun Pharmacy building was constructed on this site.

the Liberty Café in a corner of the building in about 1930. The old Grace-Headen building was torn down in the mid-1930s and a new structure was built on the site just north of the Medical-Professional Building and Allen's Furniture. The new building eventually housed the Sun Pharmacy.

In the 400 block of Chaparral, after 1942, on the west side of the street was the new Lichtenstein's Department Store where the old St. James Hotel once stood. There were four Lichtenstein locations. The first Lichtenstein's was in a frame building on Chaparral that later became a grocery store, in the 600 block. The second location was in the Uehlinger Building, which was torn down in 1934 to build a new Montgomery Ward store. The third location was on the corner of the 500 block of Chaparral. And the fourth location was at Chaparral and Lawrence, where the old St. James Hotel once stood. The building was finished and opened in December 1941. The Cosmopolitan Apartments building was constructed on this site.

Lichtenstein's was followed by Randall's Women's Wear, Max Engle's Smart Shop, Corpus Christi Book & Stationary, Betty Maid women's clothes, Baker's Shoes, and the Lerner Shop, which was the site of the home of Dr. George Robertson, who died in the yellow fever epidemic in 1867. Zale's Jewelry was later on this location.

On the east side of the street was Buttrey's Ladies Wear where the Doddridge Bank once stood, followed by Clayton Richardson's shoe store, Stever Jewelry, the Centre Theater, Hackley's Men's Store, the Medical-Professional Building, Allen Furniture, Hall's Clothier, and the Sun Pharmacy on the corner, where the old Grace building had been.

When it was built in 1929 the 10-story Medical-Professional Building was known as the

13. *Lichtenstein's fourth location, at Chaparral and Lawrence, was occupied in December 1941, the week before Pearl Harbor was attacked. At the ribbon-cutting ceremony, Morris Lichtenstein Sr., grandson of the founder, said, "We like to feel that this store is more than a store, that it is a part of the lives and hopes of Corpus Christi." The Lichtenstein building was demolished to make way for the Cosmopolitan Apartments complex.*

Pope Building, from the owner, W. E. "Uncle Elmer" Pope. Elmer Pope, a state legislator, ran for governor but lost to Miriam "Ma" Ferguson. On the tenth floor was the Medical-Professional Hospital where "Uncle Elmer" died of a stroke in 1944. The building was later converted into the Sea Gulf Villa Apartments.

The next building south of the Centre Theater was a jewelry store owned by Ben, who moved to Chaparral Street from a store in the 600 block of Mesquite. Stever's son, Jim Stever, geologist and author, said his father did not do well at the Mesquite location because of stiff competition from Taylor Brothers in the same block. But Stever prospered at the store next to the Centre Theater where many of his customers were from the Naval Air Station. "Whenever Tyrone Power came into the store," Jim Stever said, "the sales girls scrambled to see who would get to wait on the famous movie star." Power, a fighter pilot in the Marine Corps, was stationed at the Naval Air Station before he was shipped to the Pacific.

14. *Two months after the attack on Pearl Harbor, the new Centre Theater on Chaparral joined the war effort with its marquee message pushing war bonds. Theater-goes could buy war bonds at the Victory Booth in the lobby.*

15. *A large turnout honored Admiral Chester W. Nimitz of Texas, fleet admiral and theater commander in the Pacific, with a parade down Chaparral Street on June 18, 1946. In his speech afterwards, Nimitz said Corpus Christi would always be a Navy town.*

16. *The Corpus Christi National Bank (left), at the corner of Schatzel and Chaparral, was opened in 1890. Among the bank's organizers were Robert J. Kleberg of King Ranch and merchant David Hirsch, who became the bank's first president.*

One feature of the 500 block of Chaparral was a large mulberry tree behind a paling fence in the front yard of Bob Berry.

Next door to the south was Max and Otto Dreyer's candy store, where youngsters could find firecrackers, toys, and soft drinks. On the corner was D. Schwartz's dry goods store. Schwartz lived in New York and hired a local manager. The Nueces Valley said Schwartz "has a large stock of dry goods, boots and shoes. This house is connected with New York. They do a heavy business."

Corpus Christi National Bank was built in 1890 on the Schwartz-Dreyer-Berry site. The bank was founded by David Hirsch. It was first located in a small building on Chaparral and was said to be the smallest national bank in the country, with only $50,000 in capital. Within a year the bank moved into a new building on the corner of Schatzel and Chaparral.

In the money panic of 1893 a man tried to withdraw $5,000 in savings from Hirsch's bank. People were allowed to withdraw small sums but not large amounts. The customer, however, was adamant, demanding all his money. Thomas Hickey, the cashier, offered to give him the entire $5,000 if he would take it in silver. That would have been a heavy load to carry so the man left his money in the bank.

Next to Bob Berry's to the north was George Mew's ship chandlery, followed by Frederick Brose, cobbler. On the corner was the Uehlinger Building which housed Lichtenstein's store and then Gugenheim-Cohn after it moved from the 400 block. Montgomery Ward's was built on the old Uehlinger site in 1934.

On the northeast corner was Keller's Saddlery. The building was decorated with the painting of a white horse. Fred Gold, another saddle-maker, later moved into Keller's old

17. *Keller's Saddlery, with a white horse advertising the business, was at the corner of Schatzel and Chaparral. That business was followed by E. Morris' dry goods store, and Norwick Gussett's hide warehouse, with a rooster weathervane. Mexican wool-sellers called Gussett's place "la tienda del gallo." The photo dates from the late 1880s or early 1890s.*

building. Past Keller's was E. Morris's dry goods. Morris was shocked one day in 1874 when a cow and a calf trotted through his store. The cow was being driven home, the newspaper reported, and took a shortcut. Past E. Morris was the Pat McDonough building, with a stationery business on the ground floor and club rooms upstairs.

The Shaw building at Chaparral and Peoples was remodeled to become Norwick Gussett's store and bank. Gussett, the founder of Gussettville on the Nueces River, became one of Corpus Christi's richest wool merchants in the 19th Century.

Gussett came to Corpus Christi from Ohio with Zachary Taylor's army, family accounts say. He was a muleskinner whose job was to haul water from the Nueces River. In the war in Mexico, Gussett was wounded at Cerro Gordo and for the rest of his life kept in his pocket a piece of polished bone taken from his hip. After the war, Gussett married Harriet Elizabeth Jamison and they had a daughter, Clara Matilda. They moved to Oakville and from there to Fox Nation, a stagecoach stop on the Nueces River across from Fort Merrill, named for the Fox family. The name was changed to Gussettville.

Gussett's wife died in 1863. After the Civil War, Gussett moved to Corpus Christi and married Margaret Evans. He became a buyer of wool and hides and opened a store on Chaparral. Traders from Mexico called his store, identified by a rooster weathervane, "la tienda del gallo." He established his own bank and operated a fleet of schooners (named for his daughters) to take wool and hides to New York. In one year, 1873, he purchased more than three million pounds of wool. Though he never achieved a rank higher than sergeant, he was known as Colonel Gussett out of respect. He died on Sept. 28, 1908.

18. After 22 years in the Uehlinger Building, Lichtenstein's moved into a new three-story brick building on the east side of Chaparral at Schatzel. The new store (shown in the 1930s) featured the city's first elevators and fire sprinkler system.

19. Flags hang over the 500 block of Chaparral for an unknown celebration in 1941. It may have been the dedication of the Naval Air Station on March 12 of that year. Just visible on the right was Lichtenstein's Department store, which was about to move to its new location. On the left, also just visible, was Corpus Christi National Bank. Montgomery Ward was at the end of the block, west side, while the Jones Building was on the east side next to Peoples.

20. *The corner of Schatzel and the 500 block of Chaparral in the 1930s. On the right with the striped awning is Lichtenstein's at its third location. Down the block on the east side is the Jones Building and the Nueces Hotel beyond. On the left is Corpus Christi National Bank, followed by Thomas' Model Pharmacy, Montgomery Ward, and the City National Bank.*

In the 1930s and 1940s, the 500 block of Chaparral, on the west side of the street, featured Corpus Christi National Bank on the corner followed by Thomas' Model Pharmacy and Montgomery Ward on the north corner. Across the street, past Schatzel, was Lichtenstein's third store before it moved a block south. Past Lichtenstein's was the Federal Clothing Store, the Vogue Women's Shop, Dempsey's Men's Store, Barry-Hendrix Drugs (later Walgreen's) in the Jones Building.

Dempsey's Men's Store had been a women's clothing store, the Elite, owned by Mrs. Hester McLean. Her home on Lower Broadway was where the Caller-Times constructed a new building in 1935. The Jones-Sherman Building was on the corner where Gussett's bank and wool warehouse long stood.

21 and 22. *The 500 block of Chaparral, looking south, shows the Barry-Hendrix Drug Store in the Jones-Sherman Building on the east corner. Thomas' Model Pharmacy was across the street south of Montgomery Ward. Corpus Christi National Bank on the Schatzel Street corner was undergoing renovation. Below, an interior view of Thomas' Model Pharmacy. Thomas moved to Corpus Christi from Missouri and opened a pharmacy across from Market Hall in 1901. He was one of the first pharmacists in Corpus Christi to install a soda fountain in his drugstore. He moved to several locations before he settled at 517 North Chaparral.*

23. *A shot of Chaparral in 1910 shows streetcar rails being laid in the 500 block. Barely visible on the right was the Bismarck Café, which was located at 510 Chaparral. Daniel Hewitt, street railway promoter, arrived in Corpus Christi from Tyler to start the Corpus Christi Street and Interurban Railway. It made its first run on March 28, 1910. Within a year, Hewitt sold it to V. S. and Earl Heinly of Denver. The Heinly brothers expanded the line and operated it for three years before they sold it to a Philadelphia syndicate in 1914.*

24. *The 700 block of Chaparral, looking south, about 1925. In the distance on the right was the Kress store and beyond that, on the corner of Peoples was the City Bank Building.*

25 and 26. DeRyee & Westervelt's pharmacy at the corner of Chaparral and Peoples was followed by William Funk's soft drink stand, John Hall's tin shop, and Mrs. Merriman's boarding house. DeRyee's drug store building was knocked down in 1908 to build the City Bank Building (below). That building, with modern cladding, is still on that location.

27. *In 1902, wagons hauling well casing pipe leave Chaparral Street for King Ranch. The large building in the center was E. H. Caldwell's Hardware Store and the small building with a slanting porch roof was Lichtenstein's first store, before it moved to the Uehlinger building. The Nueces Hotel was built on the site where Lichtenstein's and Caldwell's stood.*

In the 600 block, at Peoples and Chaparral, on the northwest corner, was the DeRyee Drug Store in a shellcrete building. Dr. William DeRyee collected driftwood on the island to frame the doors and windows.

DeRyee's front window always displayed some curiosity, like a duck with its bill clamped in an oyster shell. DeRyee, a chemist, came to Corpus Christi in 1857. DeRyee's drug store was torn down in 1908 to build the City Bank Building, which still stands.

North of DeRyee's was William Funk's soft-drink stand followed by Johnny Hall's tin shop, decorated with a stove sitting on a pole. One story told was that Hall was hired by the rancher Mifflin Kenedy to install the gutterwork on his mansion on the bluff. Kenedy was such a demanding taskmaster, it was said, that he forced the tinner Johnny Hall to redo the work three times before he would pay him.

After Hall's was by Eli Merriman's mother's boarding house. Mrs. E. T. Merriman combined two adjacent houses to establish what she called the Oriental Hotel Merriman.

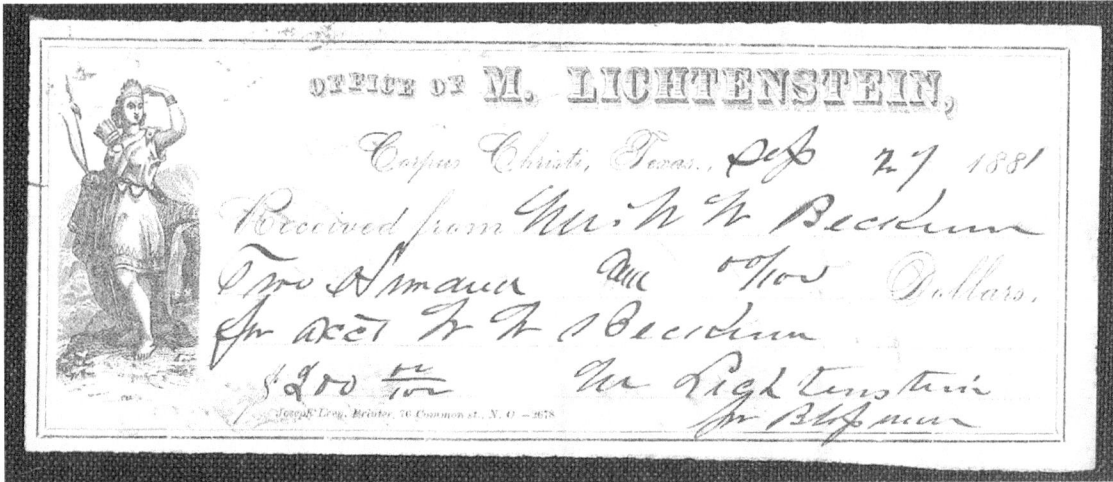

28 and 29. Above, a receipt from Morris Lichtenstein from 1881. Below, a line drawing of Lichtenstein's second location in the Uehlinger Building, which stood diagonally across Chaparral and Peoples intersection from the original store. After Lichtenstein moved into a large new brick building at Chaparral and Schatzel, the Uehlinger Building was torn down to make way for a new Montgomery Ward store built on that site.

30. *John Woessner's wool warehouse was on the east side of Chaparral at the north end of the 600 block, shown in the 1880s. North of Woessner's, on the other side of Starr Street, was George French's wholesale and retail grocery store located in the old Holthaus Bakery building. South of Woessner's was Mitchell's Hardware.*

Across from DeRyee's, on the east side of Chaparral, at the corner of Peoples, was a long wooden building with a slanting front porch roof. This building housed Morris Lichtenstein's first store, after he moved his operation from Indianola in 1874. Lichtenstein sold ladies' and men's apparel and made regular trips to New York to buy the latest fashions. In 1889 Lichtenstein moved into the Uehlinger Building, which later was torn down to make way for the new Montgomery Ward building.

Next door to the Lichtenstein store was James McKenzie's paint shop. McKenzie's was followed by J. B. Mitchell's hardware and furniture store, which had been Mitchell & Evans for many years. Mitchell's two-story building was later occupied by E. H. Caldwell's hardware store.

The Kearney cottage followed Evans & Hickey. Dr. Thomas Kearney was brought to Corpus Christi from Cuba during the yellow fever epidemic of 1867. The old Kearney cottage later housed the Customs Office.

At the end of the block was John Woessner's store and a wool warehouse. His residence was behind the store, on Starr. Dances were held in the second-floor hall of the wool warehouse. Walter Timon once recalled that Woessner's warehouse had the best dance floor in town, which was "springy and fine."

31. The Nueces Hotel, on the corner of Peoples and Chaparral, held its grand opening on Jan. 18, 1913. The six-story building, the tallest structure south of San Antonio, cost $413,000. The hotel boasted more than 200 rooms, an elegant ballroom, Sun Parlor and Tropical Gardens. After it was damaged by Hurricane Celia, the building was razed in 1971.

32. The 600 block of Chaparral presented a busy scene on Saturday, April 2, 1932 with long lines of people waiting to see the second day's showing of the hit movie, "Tarzan, the Ape Man" at the Palace. This was the heyday of the downtown, its golden age, before the city spread out south and west and left the downtown behind. J. C. Penney's moved to a new building at Chaparral and William in 1949 and finally closed its downtown store in 1978.

33. In 1925, the Simon-Cohn department store anchored the corner of Chaparral and Starr, which was later the site of the W. T. Grant store, beginning in 1933.

In the 1930s and 1940s, on the west side of the 600 block of Chaparral, was the Texas State Bank & Trust in the old City Bank Building. A corner location in that building was renovated for Vo-Craft Shoes. Down the block, going north, was McCrory's Five-and-Dime, Muttera's Federal Bakery, Mangel's of Texas, Franklin's, Kress's five-and-dime department store and W. T. Grant's.

Muttera's Federal Bakery was established in 1919 when Fred and Mae Muttera moved to Corpus Christi from Springfield, Ill. Their first bakery was swept away in the 1919 storm. Fred Muttera bought near the original site and re-opened Muttera's Federal Bakery. When he died in 1935 his widow Mae and his son William (Bill) ran the bakery. The bakery was closed in 1958.

North of Muttera's, in the late 1920s and 1930s, was the Metropolitan Café run by Hispanic civil rights leader Ben Garza. After Garza's death, the Metropolitan Café became Bill Maddis' Restaurant and later the building was occupied by Franklin's Women's Wear.

On the opposite of the street was the Nueces Hotel, with K. P. Hrissikopoulos' Olympia Confectionery, E. J. Hitt's Cigars, and Lester's Jewelry. It was followed by the Palace Theater, L. R. Loving's Clothing Store, Liberal Loans and Betty Maid dress shop. On the corner was J. C. Penney's on the old site of Woessner's warehouse.

34 and 35. Sales events at Penney's in July and August 1932. The original J. C. Penney's store in Corpus Christi was on the corner of Chaparral and Starr on the site where John Woessner, a buyer of wool and hides, had a store, warehouse and home. A two-story brick building was erected on the site by H. R. Sutherland and leased to Penney's, which opened in 1925. The store later moved into a new building at Chaparral and William.

36. *Rooftop view (from the Nueces Hotel) of the 700 block of Chaparral shows Cooper's Clean Bakery on the corner with Starr (right). This was the old Holthaus Bakery, a shellcrete building constructed in 1866. Across the street was the Grant building which housed Davis Drug Store.*

37. *Mayflower Café, in the old Holthaus building, in 1935. The Mayflower was torn down for a K Wolens Department store. In this scene, cars passing on Chaparral advertised the movie "Red Dragon" showing at the Palace starring Barbara Stanwyck and Robert Young.*

38. *The 700 block of Chaparral in the 1930s, looking north from the Starr Street intersection, shows the Davis Drug Store with Draughon's Practical Business College upstairs, followed by Richardson's Shoes, the White Kitchen Café, the Nueces Shoe Repairing shop, the Roosevelt Grill, and the Ritz Theater. The old Ranahan home was next door to the Ritz.*

In the 700 block of North Chaparral, James Ranahan died while he building a structure on the northeast corner of the block, past Starr Street.

Ranahan was a brickmaker and builder from Belfast who came to Corpus Christi in 1849. His brick kiln was on the slope of the bluff near the top of Taylor Street. In late 1866 he was building a two-story shellcrete structure at Chaparral and Starr when he collapsed and died.

The building was later finished and housed the Holthaus grocery and bakery, run by a German man, August Holthaus, and his French wife. Robert Adams worked for the Holthaus couple as a 15-year-old in 1862. August Holthaus died during the yellow fever year of 1867 and, six years later, Mrs. Holthaus sold the building to George French. He operated a retail and wholesale grocery business at the site.

The Corpus Christi Gazette, on Jan. 6, 1873, ran this item: "Mr. George French announces to the public that he has opened business in Corpus Christi. His store is on the corner of Chaparral and Starr streets in the old Holthaus building."

39. The Ritz Theater on Nov. 23, 1934. Next to the theater was Jack Brown's cabinet shop in the Ranahan home, built in 1854 by James Ranahan. The Ranahan home was hit by a shell or cannon ball during the bombardment of 1862. It was later known as the Fitzsimmons home.

After the turn of the 20th Century, the Holthaus building was occupied by E. P. Cooper's Clean Bakery and by the 1930s it housed Charles Payne's Mayflower Café. The Mayflower was closed and the building pulled down to make way for a new K Wolens store, which opened on June 19, 1941. In the middle of the 700 block on the east side of the street was the Horne Apartments, constructed in 1899, across the street from where the Ritz was built in 1929. The Horne Apartments, owned by Helen Horne, were badly damaged in the 1919 storm but survived. By the 1930s she was advertising "three-room modern furnished apartments."

On the northwest corner, past Starr, was the John Grant building, constructed in 1908 on the site of an old Chinese laundry. The Grant building housed the City Drug Store, which was later G. E. Davis's drug store. Draughon's Business College occupied the second floor. The streetcar line after 1912 ran from the City Drug Store corner to the Breakers Hotel on North Beach.

40. *On the west side of the 700 block of Chaparral Street in 1935 was the Rio Theater next to the Mayflower Cafe. Past the Starr Street intersection, in the 600 block, were Penney's, Grant's, Kress and the Palace Theater.*

At the north end of the block was James Ranahan's home, a shellcrete structure built in 1852. During the bombardment of Corpus Christi in 1862 the Ranahan home was hit by a shell or cannonball which left a gaping hole in its lime-white wall. The Ranahan home was also known as the Fitzsimmons home. It later housed Jack Brown's carpentry shop next door to the Ritz Theater. When the building was torn down in 1938, house-mover Ed Brennan, known for his feats of strength, was killed when one of the walls crushed him.

In the 1930s, on the east side of the 700 block, at the Starr Street corner was the Mayflower Café where the Holthaus bakery once stood. By 1941, K Wolens was on this site. For the rest of the block there was the Rio Theater, the Horne Apartments, and Vaky Court Apartments at the north end of the block. In earlier years, where Vaky was built, there was a movie theater called the Airdome. On the west side at Starr was the Davis Drug Store and Draughon's Business School upstairs, the White Kitchen Café, Nueces Shoe Repairing Company, the Roosevelt Grill, Ritz Theater, and Brown's Carpentry Shop in the old Ranahan building.

The Nueces Shoe Repairing Company, in the middle of the 700 block, was more than its name suggested. It was said that a man arriving in town after a long, hot trip could get himself spruced up here. The business, operated by Jim Dimotsis and George Strates, not only provided shoe repairs and polishing, but also cleaned and pressed suits, blocked hats, and furnished hot and cold baths.

41. The 700 and 800 blocks of Chaparral, in the 1930s, (east side, facing north) included the Vaky Court Apartments, at 722, Mrs. Royall Givens' home, at 802, and the Railway Express office at 810. Mrs. Givens' home was past the intersection with Taylor Street.

On the east side of the 800 block was Mrs. Royall Givens home, across Taylor Street from the Vaky Court Apartments. Royall Givens bought what had been known as the old Russell home. It was built between 1853 and 1855 by Charles Russell (not related to Union Gen. Charles Russell) after he married Mary Eliza Dix, the daughter of Capt. John Dix.

When the war ended and Corpus Christi was occupied by Union soldiers, U.S. officers used this house for their quarters and as the provost marshal's office. Citizens who wanted to affirm or reaffirm loyalty to the Union went to this house to take what was known the Ironclad Oath, which ended with, "I will faithfully support the Constitution and obey the laws of the United States and will, to the best of my ability, encourage others to do so. So help me God."

Royall Givens, a prominent fish and oyster dealer, bought the house in 1888. Mrs. Royall Givens (Leona Gussett) in an interview said, "Our house is said to be very old. It was used for officers' quarters during the Civil War and they say the oath of allegiance was signed in this house at the close of the Civil War." Royall Givens' seafood cannery and packing sheds on North Beach were destroyed in the 1919 hurricane. He died in 1928 and Leona Givens died in 1948. The house was razed soon after her death.

In the 1930s and 1940s, the Givens home was followed by a Railway Express office with the Givens Apartments upstairs, a barber and beauty supply shop, a beauty salon, and car lot on the corner.

Across the street from the Givens house, at 801 Chaparral, was the Church of the Good Shepherd, before it was moved to South Broadway in 1926. After the church was the parsonage followed by the Otto Dreyer home, built in 1881. Dreyer and his brother Max

42. *The south end of the 800 block of Chaparral, at the Taylor Street intersection, with R. G. Guy's Foods on the corner, where the Church of the Good Shepherd was located before it moved to South Broadway and Park in 1926. On south side of Taylor was Brown's cabinet shop and the Ritz Theater. Across Chaparral from Guy's, not visible, was Royall Givens'*

43. *In the 900 block of North Chaparral was the shellcrete home of William Baker Wrather, built in 1860. Wrather organized the first local troop of Confederate volunteers. A silk flag sewn by the town's young ladies was presented to Wrather by Mary Woessner on the courthouse steps. He married her and they lived in the Wrather house. It was a refuge during the war, when federal troops made raiding forays, and it was a haven during the 1919 hurricane. It was demolished after it was wrecked by Hurricane Celia. Next door was the Dan Reid home, built in 1850. It was used as an apartment building in the 1950s.*

44. The T. P. Rivera house (left), at 1001 North Chaparral, was sold to Walter Timon in 1902. Judge Timon sold it to the First Methodist Church in 1945. It was torn down in 1962. The Rivera/Timon home was followed by "Doc" McGregor's studio and residence.

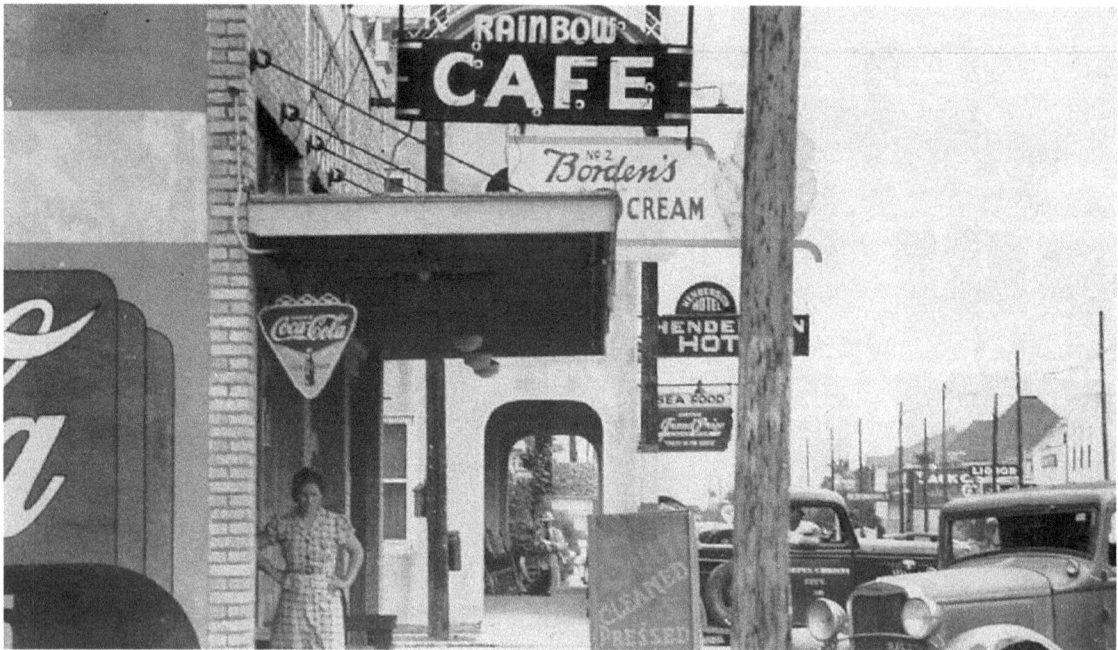

45. The Rainbow Café was followed by the Henderson and Giles hotels.

owned a candy store in the 500 block of Chaparral. The Dreyer home was moved and the site cleared in 1957. Artesian Park was north of the Dreyer home. In the 1930s, after the Church of the Good Shepherd was moved, Guy's Food store was located on the site, across

46. *The Giles Hotel, owned by Dr. H. R. Giles, in the 1100 block of Chaparral, north of Henderson Hotel. After Giles' death, it was sold and became the Whitehouse Hotel.*

from the Givens' home (this Guy's store was later Peterson's). Where the parsonage had been was Corpus Christi Beauty Shop followed by the old Dreyer home and Artesian Park.

Down the street on the east side was the shellcrete store and home of William Baker Wrather. At the beginning of the Civil War, Wrather commanded a militia company of Confederate soldiers. In a ceremony on the courthouse steps, he accepted a Confederate flag from Mary Woessner. After the ceremony, the captain and Miss Woessner were married. The old Wrather house was demolished after it was wrecked by Hurricane Celia.

Next to the Wrather place was Dan Reid's home, on the corner. This two-story house was built about 1850. Reid, an architect and builder, designed and built many of the downtown structures, including the First State Bank on Mesquite. He was elected mayor in 1908. The Reid place was sold in 1950 and torn down soon afterwards.

In the 1930s and early 1940s, the east side of Chaparral in the 900 block featured the Park Café on the corner, followed by the Masonic Temple, G. E. Covey's gunsmith shop in the old Wrather building, and the Reid place.

On the west side of the block were three homes followed by the Guaranty Title Company building, which was constructed in 1926. The building was restored in the 1980s.

On the west side of the 1000 block, at 1001, was the Tito Rivera house. Rivera was captured by Comanches as a boy but he was purchased, for $125, by Robert Neighbors, superintendent of Indian Affairs. In the 1870s Rivera moved to Corpus Christi and worked as cashier in the Doddridge Bank. He owned a stationery and book store and was elected to the City Council in the 1880s. The Rivera house, built in 1885, was sold to Walter Timon in 1902. It was torn down in 1962.

47. The former Giles Hotel owned by Dr. H. R. Giles was sold after his death in 1948. It was owned and operated by J. L. Whitehouse. It was later managed by Roy Griffin and wife Hetty before it was torn down in 1956. Buildings in the 1100 block of Chaparral were razed to build an access route to Harbor Bridge. The terminus of I-37 cuts across that block today.

Past the Rivera house, later, was Doc McGregor's photo studio. McGregor bought a home on that site, built in 1928, which he enlarged over the years. He had been trained as carpenter by his father. In the 1100 block in the 20th century was the Giles Hotel, owned by Dr. H. R. Giles, later which became the Whitehouse Hotel in the early 1950s before it was razed in 1956. The Henderson Hotel was also in this block. I-37 construction leveled stores and homes in the 1100 block of Chaparral, between Aubrey and Belden streets.

Aerial photographs of the construction show how much of the city was cleared for the interstate pathway, which claimed roughly two blocks of Mesquite, Chaparral and Water.

The Herman Cohn home was in the 1300 block. Cohn was the co-founder of Gugenheim-Cohn department store. In 1914, he built a mansion on South Broadway, considered the city's finest home. Near the old Cohn home on Chaparral was the Hoover Hotel which opened in 1926. In the 1400 block was the August Ricklefsen home.

Chaparral, or Front Street, stretched from the arroyo to Hall's Bayou, covering 17 city blocks. The street was home to Conrad Meuly's house with the iron front, the old Kinney House hotel in the 300 block, the St. James Hotel, Mrs. Merriman's Oriental Hotel, from the Holthaus Bakery to the Pig Stand No. 1 by the bascule bridge.

48. *The 700 block of Chaparral in the 1930s, with Vaky Court Apartments on the left and the Ritz Theater on the right. Old streetcar rails in the middle of the street were later removed.*

49. *The Elite Café on Chaparral at the Mann intersection in the late 1930s.*

50. *Herman Cohn, co-founder of the Gugenheim-Cohn department store, stands on the front porch of his home at 1911 N. Chaparral, about 1900. His young son, Joseph Adolph Cohn, is sitting in the buggy.*

51. *The Pig Stand No. 1, at 2016 N. Chaparral, was the last business listed before the street ended at the bascule bridge. The Pig Stand was always at its busiest when the bridge was raised for a passing ship. In the 1930s, a man named Roy Whitehurst ran Pig Stand No. 1. There were two other Pig Stands, one on Port and one on Leopard.*

52. *The bascule bridge was raised for a ship in February 1939.*

Chapter 3. Mesquite Street

From the arroyo to the port entrance, crossing Laguna,
William, Lawrence, Schatzel, Peoples, Starr, Taylor, Twigg,
Mann, Aubrey, Belden, Power, Palo Alto, and Fitzgerald streets.

Mesquite Street was sometimes spelled Mezquit, since spelling in old times was not subject to strict rules. It was the city's second most important street after Chaparral, the main street in everything but the name. Mesquite was also called Back Street, a reflection on its second-class status compared to Chaparral, which was Front Street.

In the 100 block of Mesquite, on the east side of the street, was the Pellegrino home. It was on the corner. Matt Pellegrino, who would one day become a city detective, lived here, in the home of his father, Frank Pellegrino.

Before the 1919 storm struck, Matt Pellegrino was planning to go to Matamoros to see a bullfight. It was raining so hard he decided not to go. When the storm hit, Pellegrino led his family and others through the raging storm tide to safety on the bluff. On Monday morning he went down to see what was left of the Pellegrino home and found "bales of cotton and boats floating around the house. We were wiped out. Didn't have anything left. The house was there but everything was ruined."

Down from Pellegrino's home was the Corpus Christi Mattress Factory, which later moved out to Laredo Street. Past it was the Corpus Christi Steam Laundry, owned by John Selvidge, whose first location was at Chaparral and Starr, in the 700 block, before he moved to Mesquite, on the south edge of town.

Because of the encroachment of the bluff, there was almost nothing on the west side of Mesquite until William Street, except for one business. On the corner on the west side of the 100 block was the grocery store of Vicente Lozano.

Lozano, from Bagdad, Mexico, came to Corpus Christi in 1891. He worked in the fishing business then got a job as a clerk in Peter Baldeschwiler's grocery store selling charcoal for five cents a bucket and cleaning the oil lamps. When he was 20, in 1899, he married Elvira McCarthy and in 1902 opened his own store at Mesquite and Broadway. He built a new building on Staples and moved out there in 1913.

In the 1930s in the 100 block of Mesquite all the buildings were on the east side of the street. The Pellegrino house on the corner was followed by Perfecto Cleaners, Crystal Water and Stanley Tomlinson's Trading House, which sold used furniture. Stanley's was moved to the 300 block of Mesquite and then out to Agnes.

In the 200 block of Mesquite, on the east side of the street, was the store of Frederick Belden, an early merchant who was engaged in the Mexican trade. He settled in Corpus Christi in the 1840s. He had been in business in Matamoros where he married Mauricia Arocha. He was a friend of Zachary Taylor when the army was concentrated at Corpus Christi in 1845 and early 1846.

Capt. W. S. Henry, who dined with Belden and Mauricia, said they gave him a dish called "themales." He said, "I know of nothing more palatable."

1. Workers gather in front of the Corpus Christi Steam Laundry at 112 N. Mesquite in 1907. The laundry was established in 1904 at Chaparral and Starr by John Selvidge.

Before the army left Corpus Christi to march to the border, in early March 1846, Mauricia Belden held a dinner party for Gen. Taylor and some of his officers. At the dinner she asked the general about the prospects for war. Taylor said if war broke out he intended to capture Mexico City.

Mrs. Belden bet him he would never get there. While Taylor didn't capture Mexico City — Winfield Scott did — he sent Mrs. Belden a silk dress from Mexico. Frederick Belden died in 1867 and Mauricia died in 1896. The old Belden home was converted into a boarding house run by an Irish woman named Annie Dugan.

On the corner was the home of photographer Louis de Planque, whose photo studio was behind the home, fronting on William Street. De Planque was one of the most important photographers in Texas from the Civil War into the 1890s.

He came from Prussia and arrived in Matamoros in 1864, when it was the hub of the Cotton Road and wartime boom town. He opened a studio and photographed civilian and military leaders, Confederate and Union. He photographed Richard King, Mifflin Kenedy and many prominent Corpus Christi leaders who were on the border during the war.

After the war, in 1867, a hurricane ruined his studios and he moved to Indianola. His studio was again destroyed in the great hurricane of 1875.

He opened a studio in Corpus Christi and his business prospered. People would stroll past his window at Mesquite and William to see the latest display of street scenes.

De Planque died of a stroke on May 1, 1898. He was 56. An obituary in the Caller said he was one of the best photographers in the country, a real artist, and one of the more kind-hearted men who ever lived in the city. Only a few of his thousands of photos taken over the years have survived.

2. Louis de Planque dressed up for a Columbus Day parade. The photograph was probably taken by his wife, Eugenia. One of the tragedies of Corpus Christi history is that thousands of his glass-plate negatives of local scenes and people were lost or destroyed.

3. *The Roy Murray Ford dealership in 1938, at the corner of William and Mesquite. In the 19th Century, it was the location of photographer Louis de Planque's home and studio.*

4. *President Taft traveled to South Texas in October 1909 to visit the Taft Ranch. He came to Corpus Christi and spoke to a crowd on the side of the bluff, an area later called Spohn Park.*

In the 20th Century, past the Belden home, was the Russell-Knight auto dealership at 204 Mesquite. The building became a popular restaurant, the Rendezvous Grill, in the 1930s. Near the end of the block was a blacksmith and wagon wheel shop. Later, Roy Murray Motors was located on the de Planque corner and more recently La Bahia Restaurant.

On the west side of the block was the sloping ground of the bluff. In the middle of the block, in the 1850s, was an adobe building where Fr. Bernard O'Reilly taught school.

5. *The long narrow Spohn Park, with a World War I artillery gun display, is wedged between Broadway, Mesquite, Laguna and William. The photo was taken from Upper Broadway looking toward the Roy Murray Ford dealership at the corner of Mesquite and William.*

After the school closed, the Corpus Christi Female Academy occupied the building, about 1860, until the academy was moved north on Mesquite, in the 700 block. The O'Reilly building housed the Post Office for a time in the 1870s and after it was torn down the site was used as a parking lot for teams and wagons. This was directly across Mesquite from the old Belden home.

In 1909, a speaker's platform, or pergola, was built on the side of the bluff where Spohn Park is today for President William Howard Taft to make his speech. Taft was visiting his half-brother Charles at the Taft Ranch. The president spoke about the importance of harbor improvements, a subject dear to Corpus Christi.

After Taft's departure, Eli Merriman, editor of the Caller, ran into Annie Dugan, who ran the boarding house across from where the president spoke. She said, "Mr. Merriman, why didn't you put in the Caller that the President of the United States made a speech in front of my gate? I would have liked to have sent a copy to Ireland."

The 200 block of Mesquite was visited by two presidents, in 1909 by President Taft and by Zachary Taylor in 1846, two years before he became president.

There were several businesses located on the east side of the 200 block of Mesquite, across from Spohn Park, in the 1930s. Most notable was the Rendezvous Grill at 204. The Corpus Christi Press and printing office was at 206 and at the end of the block was Heyser-Edwards Motors, a Ford dealership, which later became Roy Murray Motors.

On the corner of the 300 block, on the east side of the street, was Thayer's Yankee Notions store, which sold guns, cigars, guitar strings, perfume, Montgolfier balloons, and eight-day clocks. North of Thayer's was Fogg's Livery, a busy place in town in the age of

6. *Pitts Livery stabled horses, rented buggies, conducted funerals, and serviced the town's first automobiles. It was owned by B. H. Pitts and was located on the site of John Fogg's livery, which dated back to the 1860s. Coleman Furniture was built on this site in the 1930s.*

the horse. Fogg's included the main livery building, wagon sheds, and hay storage building, all in the middle of the block.

An ad for Fogg's from the 1870s said, "The public are informed that John Fogg still holds forth at his old stand on Mezquit Street." Fogg also operated a saloon and a San Antonio-Brownsville stagecoach line. When a drunk shot a storekeeper in 1866, Fogg led the mob that hanged the culprit at the end of Chaparral.

Fogg so distrusted banks, it was said, that he kept his money hidden on his property. A man who had done some work for Fogg went to his home to get paid. Fogg went out back around his chicken house and returned with a handful of gold coins. After Fogg died on Oct. 30, 1896, his backyard became a favorite digging place for treasure hunters, who dug by lantern light at night and left big holes in the morning.

Fogg's Livery later became Pitts' Livery, which sold and serviced the town's first automobiles. Roy Terrell, whose family owned a ranch on the Oso, noted in his memoirs that his first automobile ride, when he was 12, was in a taxi from Pitts' Livery. "My father sent this taxi to our house to pick us up and take us to the railroad station, a distance of four blocks, but what an experience! We were catching a train to Calallen to visit our uncle, Cal Allen, my mother's brother."

Later, on the north corner of the 300 block, was the Russell boarding house run by Kate Fletcher and Myrtle Russell. It moved into the old Timon house in the 600 block.

In the 1930s, Coleman Furniture was built on the Pitts' Livery site. Past it, in the 1920s and 1930s, was Zip Battery owned by Cipriano "Zip" Gonzalez. Zip Battery was at 318

7. *Zip Battery Service, at 318 N. Mesquite, was owned by Cipriano "Zip" Gonzalez, standing at far left with his service vehicles. Zip's employees shown here, left to right, were Willie Jordan, C. Trevino, Bob Williams, and Walter Lawrence. The photo was taken in 1927.*

North Mesquite near the Lawrence Street intersection, where the old C. W. Johnson Produce stand was located. Gonzalez explained that he got his nickname because people couldn't pronounce "Cipriano" and just called him Zip. The business was later moved to South Staples Street. Past Zip's, on the corner, was the B. F. Goodrich store in the 1940s.

On the west side of the 300 block, on the corner with William, was the Baldeschwiler home. The Baldeschwilers were among the earliest to settle in Corpus Christi. Blaize Mathias Baldeschwiler and his wife, Swiss immigrants, came to Corpus Christi in 1844. She ran a boarding house and Blaize did carpentry work. Their son Andrew followed in the carpentry trade and married Margaret Murphy of San Patricio. After the turn of the century, Peter Baldeschwiler lived in the family home, rented rooms, and ran a grocery store.

In 1928, a new building was constructed on the Baldeschwiler corner that housed J. L. and Frank Tribble's Meat Market. Down the block was Stanley's Trading Post, a used furniture store owned by Stanley Tomlinson. He later moved to Agnes Street. On the west side of the 300 block, in the 1930s and 1940s, businesses included Tribble's Meat Market and Angela Chapa's Café; she ran another café on Waco. This was followed by Noble Gulley's Bike Shop, McCoy's Furniture (where's Stanley's had been), J. M. Ferrell's Little Bar, the Morgan family's Crescent Bakery, an auto glass firm and a parking lot.

In 1946, Theodore Weber, who moved to Corpus Christi from Boston and invested in real estate, built the three-story Weber Building, at 317 North Mesquite. In 1952, Abe Katz, a Valley produce grower known as the Onion King, built the Katz Building next door on the corner of Lawrence. Both buildings are still there.

8 and 9. Above, the editorial staff and delivery boys of the Daily Herald in 1907, standing in front of their offices in the Mireur Building at 409 Mesquite. Below, in 1897, people gather for a snowball fight in the 400 block of Mesquite in front of the Constantine Hotel during a rare snowstorm. On the right was Gray's Racket Store, a forerunner of the five-and-dime.

10. *The Bidwell Hotel, formerly the Constantine, stood at the corner of Mesquite and Lawrence. Just visible to the east was its more famous competitor, the St. James Hotel.*

In the 400 block of Mesquite was the Constantine Hotel on the corner with Lawrence. After the Ropes Boom collapsed in 1893, Nicholas Bluntzer bought property at fire-sale prices all over Corpus Christi. One of those was the Constantine Hotel. The name was changed to the Bidwell. One of its 25 bedrooms was turned into a bathroom, a novel idea at the time. The Caller ventured to say, "Surely there is such a thing as being too nice, this craze about washing all over."

The Constantine Hotel was leased by the government during the Spanish-American War to house the officers of the Longview Rifles, a militia unit moved to Corpus Christi for coastal defense. A local unit, the Kenedy Rifles, was being trained for duty in Cuba. The Longview Rifles erected tents on North Beach while their officers found more agreeable accommodations in the Constantine Hotel. The Bidwell Hotel was turned into a furniture showroom in 1940 and torn down in 1999.

Past the Constantine-Bidwell was saloon row. The Richelieu Bar was followed by a pool hall and the Magnolia Bar, which was later changed to the Alamo Bar. After that came the Buckhorn Saloon and across the street was the Palace Bar. After voters approved prohibition in 1916, the Richelieu Bar became George Allison's Domino Parlor and the Alamo Bar became the Alamo Café.

Near the end of the block was Farrell J. Smith's Grocery on the lower floor and the Miramar Lodge of the Knights of Pythias on the upper floor. The knights called it a "castle." On the corner was the home and store of Cheston C. Heath. Heath & Son's Emporium sold groceries, crockery, tin and iron ware. Capt. Heath first built a store and warehouse at Aransas Wharf on St. Joseph's Island. His operation was destroyed in the 1875 storm and he moved to Corpus Christi. Later, on the site of Heath's Emporium, the Citizens Industrial Bank was located.

On the west side of the 400 block, on the corner opposite the Bidwell, was Robert Ritter's Bazaar, which opened in the 1880s. It was called a racket store because it sold children's

11. *Heath & Son, which sold groceries, crockery, and iron stoves, was on the east side of the 400 block of Mesquite, between Lawrence and Schatzel. Cheston C. Heath, a ship captain, first built a store and wharf on St. Joseph's. He moved to Corpus Christi, was elected mayor in 1886 and his son, Cheston L., became president of the school board.*

12. *On the west side of the 400 block of Mesquite, past Lawrence across Mesquite from the Bidwell Hotel, was Robert Ritter's racket store. It was called a racket store because it sold whistles and tin drums and children's toys that made a loud racket.*

13. *The 400 block of Mesquite Street looking south about 1895. Uehlinger's Bakery on the right was followed by a blacksmith shop that was later Joe Mireur's store and on the corner was Ritter's Bazaar, or "Racket" store. Three stately homes on the bluff (from left to right) were the Centennial House, Mifflin Kenedy's home, and Martha Rabb's Magnolia Mansion.*

toys that made a noise. Robert Ritter's racket store building on the corner of Mesquite and Lawrence later housed Weil Brothers Grocery, which was opened in 1903 by Alex and Moise Weil. They ran the store until 1945.

Past Weil's was a blacksmith shop, which was later the site of Joe Mireur's shop, which was followed by the Uehlinger bakery. Mireur, born in Corpus Christi in 1879, learned the saddle and harness business as apprentice worker for Fred Gold, who had saddle shop on Chaparral. He bought the shop from Gold in 1903. In 1909, he bought the lot and building on the west side of the 400 block of Mesquite and moved to that location.

Mireur was elected to the City Council and served as finance commissioner in the A.C. McCaughan administration, from 1937 to 1945. He once told the story of politics in those times. When the McCaughan ticket was running under the banner of the Progressive Party, Mireur said, Joe Simon was a candidate on the opposing ticket and made a speech in Artesian Park, saying, "They call themselves the Progressive Party and one of the candidates for commissioner is in the harness business. There hasn't been a horse on the streets of Corpus Christi in 10 years."

Past Mireur's was Eidson's Department Store near the end of the block, before it was moved to Chaparral.

The Ziegler place may have been located on the corner of Mesquite and Schatzel. It's hard to be certain since no printed reference gives a specific location. It was variously referred to as Ziegler's Hall, Ziegler's House, and Ziegler's Hotel. More properly, it was probably a rooming house. There is also mention of Ziegler's Restaurant and Saloon.

14. The Weil Building on the corner of Mesquite and Schatzel, across from City Hall, in the 1930s. This corner may have been the site of Ziegler's Hotel in the 1860s and 1870.

The Ranchero on March 9, 1861 refers to Ziegler's restaurant on Chaparral. This was at the north end of the 300 block where Nueces Hardware was located later. Others refer to Ziegler's on Mesquite. For a time in the 1870s, Ziegler ran the St. James Hotel. He owned and operated several businesses at more than one location.

Ziegler, who came from Germany, arrived in Corpus Christi in the 1850s and opened a rooming house, or hotel, and a restaurant and bar. An ad in 1869 said the well-known house of Ziegler's "has been fitted up and renovated in a style unsurpassed in Western Texas. The table will be well supplied with the best meats the market affords." The Weekly Advertiser on April 8, 1870 said, "Louis de Planque, the photographer, has fitted up rooms at the Ziegler building, on Mezquit street, and will be ready to receive visitors."

Jacob Ziegler died on Nov. 4, 1883. Ziegler's original establishment, it is believed, was on the southwest corner of Mesquite at Schatzel.

In the 1930s, the 400 block of Mesquite on the east side of the street featured the Bidwell Hotel and the Bidwell Hotel Café, a domino hall that later became George Allison's Lunch and Bar, Ed Rouse's Furniture, the Smith Grocery with Knights of Pythias Hall above, and August McGregor's furniture store and the Citizens Industrial Bank on the corner.

On the west side of the street in the 1930s: Weil Brothers Grocery was followed by the Caller-Times, before it moved to Lower Broadway. Frank and Mae Brandon's Cadillac Hotel (also called Cadillac Rooms) was above the newspaper office. Next door was Joe Mireur's leather and saddle shop, followed by the City Garage and Western Auto in the Weil Building on the corner, where, it is quite probable, the old Ziegler's Hotel once stood.

15 and 16. *Market Hall was built in 1871 on Market Square bordered by Peoples, Schatzel and Mesquite. The building was financed by private builders who leased stalls to butchers and vendors on the lower level. City offices, the volunteer fire department, and a municipal auditorium were on the second floor. Market Hall is shown below in 1907.*

A triangle of blocks between Schatzel and Peoples is fan-shaped, with the small end under the bluff and the large end on the bayfront. The Schatzel-Peoples triangle contains the 500 blocks of Water, Chaparral, and Mesquite. At the top of the fan between Schatzel and Peoples, in the 500 block of Mesquite, was Market Hall in Market Square. This was the civic heart of old Corpus Christi.

In the 1880s, Robert Simpson's grocery stood on the corner of the east side of the 500 block. Simpson, from Delaware, was a single man who lived in a boarding house.

17 and 18. William S. Rankin's grocery took in the lower floor of the McCampbell Building, at Mesquite and Peoples, in the 1880s. The upper floor contained law offices for John McCampbell and John S. Givens. Rankin said his store sold "the finest smoke-cured bacon for 15 cents a pound; the best of Wisconsin cheese for 20 cents; and so much fresh country butter I had to tell farmers to take it back home and eat it themselves. Oh, my, those were the days." The two-story brick Seeligson Building (below) was constructed on the site of the old McCampbell building. Various businesses leased space in the Seeligson Building, including Carl Haltom, an optometrist.

19. *The First State Bank was established by Vincent Bluntzer in 1907. It occupied a rented room in the J. W. Leatherwood Building, across from Market Hall, until a new structure was built at the corner of Mesquite and Schatzel in 1908. The building, designed by Dan Reid, stood out because of its distinctive round tower. There were offices in the tower. First State became State National and later merged with Corpus Christi National Bank.*

On the site of Robert Simpson's store was built the First State Bank, a red-brick building with a round tower. The bank was founded in 1907 by Vincent Bluntzer. It first occupied a rented room until the new building was finished in 1908.

The First State Bank building was designed by Dan Reid in the firm of Reid & Sutherland. The building stood out from the structures around it because of its distinctive round tower on the Mesquite-Schatzel corner. There were offices in the tower, including one occupied by surveyor A. M. French.

First State's name was changed to State National Bank and in 1956 it merged with Corpus Christi National Bank. The First State Bank structure was stripped of its red-brick façade, its round tower was removed, and it gained a façade of black granite with gold anodized aluminum screens. It became the headquarters of the First Savings Association.

Next door was Conrad Uehlinger's saloon in a shellcrete building with an Alamo-shaped roofline. It had a hitching rail in front. It was said that late at night when Uehlinger's closed there was the loud clop-clop of horses' hooves as cowboys rode back to the ranch. The Alcove Chili Parlor later occupied the old Uehlinger saloon building. H. M. Kelley, who came to Corpus Christi in 1913, ran the Alcove Chili Parlor, which was across the street from the new City Hall. Kelley's wife Agnes recalled that the firemen would come over to get coffee and called her husband "Alcove" Kelley.

20. A view of the 500 block of Mesquite Street in 1926, looking north, from the Schatzel intersection, shows the First State Bank on the right and City Hall on the left. The First State Bank building, designed by Dan Reid, stood out because of its distinctive round front and tower with offices above it.

The McCampbell Building on the corner had law offices upstairs and William Rankin's grocery store below. Rankin's father James came from Scotland in 1854 and ran a livery stable on Mesquite.

During the bombardment of Corpus Christi in the Civil War, the Rankins camped out on a sheep ranch west of town. After the war, when William was 10, one of his chores was to go out in the country to fetch butter. "We got three pounds of butter for $1, nice country butter."

Rankin became a house painter when he was 16. In 1875, when bandits raided Nuecestown and Corpus Christi took fright, Rankin was at work painting the McCampbell Building. "I had never carried a gun in my life, but that night I was assigned to guard the outskirts of the city as part of the armed patrol."

Soon after the raid, Rankin went into the grocery business in a store on Chaparral and then moved into the ground floor of the McCampbell Building. In those years, Rankin said he could buy the finest smoke-cured hams for 15 cents a pound and the best Wisconsin cheese for 20 cents. You could go to the market with 25 cents and get enough meat for six

21. Corpus Christi's volunteer firemen in front of Market Hall. The date of the photo is unknown but was probably taken not long after 1871 when Pioneer Fire Company No. 1 was founded and Market Hall was built.

people, with a soup bone thrown in for the dog. Now you can't get even the soup bone." Bill Rankin died in 1948 when he was 92.

The west side of the 500 block was dominated by Market Hall. From the earliest times, this block was called Market Square, with a clutter of ramshackle sheds occupied by butchers and vegetable vendors. In 1871 William "Billy" Rogers and Richard Jordan built a two-story building on the site. They rented stalls on the first floor to butchers and vendors and provided free space on the second floor for the mayor and aldermen. A large hall was reserved for dances and social events.

One of the biggest events of the year was the Firemen's Parade and Ball, observed on the last Tuesday of November. There was a parade during the day, featuring fire engines and hose carts covered with flowers, and competitive events between fire units. A supper and dance followed at Market Hall.

The large auditorium on the second floor was used for traveling shows and entertainments. In 1873 the Nueces Valley reported that the Royal Japanese Troupe, a company of acrobats and jugglers, played before a full house in Market Hall.

Capt. Andrew Anderson recalled some of the entertainments held at Market Hall. "Two of the popular shows were 'Ten Nights in a Barroom,' and 'The Yankee in Texas.' Another play we liked was 'Rip Van Winkle.' The actors wore high stovepipe hats, beaver hats." He also recalled the medicine shows. "I remember especially how they would sell Hamlin's Wizard Oil from a wagon. Four fellows would sing beautifully and the whole street would be full of people listening to the singing. Finally, someone arranged for them to give an entertainment at Market Hall. You paid 25 cents to hear them sing and they had a full house every night for a week or more. They sold lots of Wizard Oil."

22. A new three-story brick City Hall was built on the site of old Market Hall in 1911. Lumber from Market Hall were salvaged and used to build a home on the bluff.

At a dance at Market Hall in 1876, some mischief-maker sprinkled cayenne pepper on the dance floor and when the dancing began the moving feet stirred up the pepper and started fits of sneezing and coughing. The paper was outraged and said the culprit "should be ferreted out and severely punished."

The town's bell-tower, housing the fire bell, was atop Market Hall. The fire bell was rung to signal the beginning of the work day, lunch hour, quitting time, and if course when fires broke out. The council in a budget-cutting exercise stopped paying a full-time ringer and the fire bell was later knocked to the ground during a storm. It was left at ground level and mounted on a concrete base at the west end of Market Hall.

North of Market Hall was a small building of the same design, intended to house city offices, but it was leased to bring in extra revenue. Market Hall and its auxiliary building were torn down in 1911. A new brick City Hall (with an irregular shape, like the other modern buildings on Schatzel) was built on the site. Lumber from Market Hall was salvaged to build a home on the bluff (the Edward Grant house at Tancahua and Lipan). The demise of Market Hall marked the end of one era and the beginning of another.

In the 1930s, on the east side of the 500 block, the State National Bank was on the corner, the dominant building on that block. It was followed by the Alcove Coffee Shop and the two-story brick Seeligson Building, on the site of the old McCampbell Building. Various businesses leased space in the Seeligson Building. City Hall took the opposite side of the street containing various city offices, the Chamber of Commerce, and the city library.

23. *R. G. Blossman's Grocery was on the corner of Mesquite at Peoples. Blossman was one of the town's leading grocers. The Furman building was constructed on the old Blossman site.*

In the 600 block, on the east corner, was the grocery store run by R. G. Blossman and his business partner, Capt. James Thompson. The store sold wine, liquor and groceries. An 1881 ledger from Blossman's showed that sugar was priced at one cent a pound, bacon 11 cents, ham and beef steaks 15 cents a pound.

North of Blossman's was a small home occupied for a time by Dr. Arthur Spohn after he married Sarah Josephine Kenedy. They later moved to the Kenedy mansion on the bluff. The Amusu Theater was built here in 1912.

Past the theater was the home of John Timon, father of the later county judge Walter Timon. The big two-story house was built in 1885 of imported cypress, oak and hard pine. Six years after the house was built, on a February day in 1891, Mrs. Timon and her daughter returned from Beeville to find a wrecked house and the body of John Timon. There were signs of a struggle but no clear indication of how he had died. If it was murder it went unsolved. The old Timon home became the Russell House, which moved from the 300 block. When the house was torn down in 1955 the demolition workers said it was as sturdy as the day it was built.

Mrs. E. D. Sidbury built a new home on the southeast corner with Starr, which was later sold to Robert H. Bingham. His drug store was at the other end of the block.

On the west side of the 600 block, on the corner, the Hatch & Robertson building was constructed in 1891. The structure had many tenants over the years, including Bluntzer

24. In the 1940s Thomas Boucher's Pharmacy was located in a corner of the Furman Building at 600 N. Mesquite at the corner of Peoples Street. The pharmacy included a lunch counter. Next door was the Amusu Theater. The Furman Building was constructed on the site of the old Blossman grocery store.

Hardware on the lower floor and Wheelus Photographic Studio on the second floor. Later, it housed Bingham's Drug Store, owned by Robert H. Bingham. After the 1919 storm, found valuables were displayed in Bingham's windows, a sad display of watches, rings and necklaces of people who lost their lives in the storm. That old building is still there.

Past Bingham's was the B. R. Harris Grocery store. Findlay's Café followed, in the 1920s, and later this building housed the A&G Army-Navy Store. Next door was the post office before it moved to the Federal Building. Afterwards, it housed Oscar Nau's hardware store. The upper floors of several buildings in this block were partitioned for rented rooms.

Near the end of the block was Norwick Gussett's lumberyard, which was wrecked in the 1874 hurricane. At the end of the block was an old blacksmith shop that was rented by the First Baptist Church in 1883, before it moved to a new brick building a block north.

In the 1930s, on the east side of the 600 block, Sun Pharmacy occupied a corner of the Furman Building. This was where Blossman's once stood. Sun Pharmacy moved to Chaparral and Sun Sporting Goods occupied that space for a time then Boucher Pharmacy.

Next door was the Amusu. Inexplicably, for a time in the 1930s, a bowling alley was located above the theater, which must have been unpleasant for moviegoers. The Tulsa Coffee Shop and Russell boarding house followed the Amusu. On the corner, where Barry-

25. *The Hatch & Robertson Building was built in 1891 and first housed the Bluntzer and Robertson Hardware Company. Following the 1919 storm, jewelry and other items found on the bodies of storm victims were displayed in the windows of Bingham's Drug Store in this building for relatives to identify. The house next door was the Matthew Headen home.*

26. *Sailors march down Mesquite, past the State Hotel (far right), Nau's Hardware, Findlay's Café and B. R. Harris Grocery. The occasion was the opening of the new Port of Corpus Christi on Sept. 14, 1926. The parade ended at Cargo Dock No. 1 where a large crowd gathered to watch the first vessels pass under the Bascule Bridge and enter the new turning basin. The sailors were from three U.S. destroyers — the Borie, Hatfield, and John D. Edwards — that took part in the celebration.*

27. The A&G Army-Navy Store at 605 Mesquite was adjacent to Nau Hardware. This brick building was constructed on the site of the Matthew Headen home. It housed the B. R. Harris Grocery and Findlay's Café before the Army-Navy Store and Nau Hardware moved in.

Hendrix Drug Store was located before it moved into the Jones Building, Taylor Brothers Jewelry built a new store.

On the west side of the street in the 1930s was the Lovenskiold Building followed by the A&G Army-Navy Store, Oscar Nau's Hardware, with apartments above, and the Stamms' Jewelry at the end of the block. Dr. Fred Stamm and his wife Maria ran a jewelry store and optometrist's clinic. Stamm's was followed at this location by Ben Stever's Jewelry, before it moved next to the Centre Theater on Chaparral.

Mesquite Street extends for 15 blocks in what was known as the Beach Section. Most stores and businesses were located in the seven blocks from Cooper's Alley to Taylor Street. Mesquite. Except for the Courthouse and a few small hotels, the north end of the street was mostly residential, including the area north of the Courthouse called Irishtown.

28 and 29. The State Hotel, at the corner of Mesquite and Starr, was built in 1907 by V. M. Donigan, an Armenian immigrant. The State was built on the site formerly occupied by Professor J. D. Meredith's Female Academy. Below: a street view of the 700 block of Mesquite in the 1930s shows, at far left, the front of the State Hotel. Texas Motor Sales is just past the State and, across the street, is the Mesquite Street entrance of the Ritz Theater. The First Methodist Church at Mesquite and Mann can be seen in the distance.

30. *The State Hotel on the corner of Starr and Mesquite.*

In the 700 block of Mesquite, on the east side of the street, was Sam Shoemaker's home and blacksmith shop on the corner. Shoemaker was one of the town's first volunteer firemen in 1871. His daughter Libby later lived in the home. Past Shoemaker's was Alexander Kinghorn's wheelwright shop and, later, Mrs. Lillie Rankin's rooming house.

One of the three homes on the east side was that of Sheriff Matthew Nolan, a Confederate colonel, and his wife Margaret McMahon. Nolan fought in the battle of Galveston and brought back two captured American flags and a sword. The Union commander on Mustang Island, Major William Thompson, led a raiding party to reclaim Nolan's battle trophies. Thompson's men surrounded the Nolan home where they found Mrs. Nolan, her mother and sister. Thompson took away the sword and flags. They ended up in Iowa.

Later that year, across from the Nolan home, Mat Nolan was shot with a double-barreled shotgun by the Gravis brothers (Frank and Charles). He died soon afterwards and was buried in Old Bayview.

Sam and Lillie (Mussett) Rankin's home was at 714 Mesquite and his real estate office was at 720. Years later, after his death in 1909, the Rankin home became the office of Port Printing and the real estate office housed the furniture store of C. A. Davis.

On the west side of the block past Starr Street was the Corpus Christi Female Academy run by Professor J. D. Meredith from 1880 to 1896. The State Hotel was built on this site. Armenian immigrant Vartan Manasseh Donigan — V. M. Donigan — built the State Hotel in 1907, considered the city's first modern hotel. Donigan managed the hotel with his children, especially his sons Mesog and Parnot. The family lived in the hotel until Donigan built a baronial mansion on Ocean Drive called Donigan's Castle.

31. *The artesian well that gave Artesian Park its name was drilled by army troops in 1845. The water was heavy with sulphur and deemed unsuitable for drinking. It was later prized as a health tonic and was bottled and sold.*

The original State Hotel in 1907 had three floors and 25 rooms. It was enlarged in 1916 and a fourth floor was added. In 1926, the west end of the hotel was added, which doubled the size of the hotel with 100 rooms, 50 with bathrooms. The State Hotel Café, Billboard Lounge, and Apollo Confectionery were popular venues inside the hotel.

When Ranger Captain Frank Hamer brought a company of Rangers to quell expected disturbances sparked by the Fred Roberts killing in 1922, they stayed at the State Hotel.

At the end of the 700 block on the west side was George Hobbs' wheelwright and blacksmith shop, on a small part of where the Caller-Times parking lot is now.

In the 1930s, on the east side of the 700 block, was Clark's News Stand, run by Wilbur Williams, followed by Port Printing, C. A. Davis Furniture, and the Magnolia Service Station. On the west side was the State Hotel, followed by Texas Motor Sales, and Travis Bailey's Motors on the corner. Despite its name, Texas Motor Sales, owned by Walter Saunders, did not sell cars. The firm's business was to service and repair automobiles, which it had been doing since 1915, making it one of the first service stations in the city.

In the 800 block on the east side corner was the Cheston L. Heath home. Heath and his father owned Heath & Son Emporium on Mesquite. The younger Heath became president of the school board and would spend his own money to buy books for students who couldn't afford them. When he died in 1918 the Mexican Central School on Carrizo was renamed the Cheston L. Heath School. Mrs. Mary Heath's home at Taylor and Mesquite was followed by Mrs. May Clark's home at 810 (later it was the home of Mrs. America Todd).

Down the block was the grassy, shaded Artesian Park, which got its name from a well dug there in 1845 by Zachary Taylor's soldiers. The soldiers wouldn't drink the water because, said one critic, one taste made you want to pull out your hair and run.

The artesian well in the park was plugged and forgotten until 1853. During a drought that year, Henry Kinney, the town founder, had the old well re-drilled. About halfway down, Kinney decided to give the well, and the block around it, to the city provided it would finish the job. When the well was completed, the water was still undrinkable with a strong odor

32. Artesian Park in the 1930s. Friday night dances and Sunday band concerts attracted many to Artesian Park. In the 1930s and 1940s, the park was a favorite hangout for dominos, horse-shoes, and shuffleboard players. During World War II, on Friday, the Naval Air Station Band played in the park.

like rotten eggs. But the mineral water was considered a cure-all and prized by some.

In the 1880s, J. J. Turpin and Thomas Southgate, who operated a drug store, bottled the water and sold it. The label claimed it would cure catarrh, rheumatism, stomach trouble, and would grow hair on bald heads.

One man who believed strongly in the healthful effects of the Artesian Park water was George Washington Grim, who married Cora Rabb, the wealthy widow of rancher Green Rabb. Grim said he came to Corpus Christi to die but was rejuvenated by drinking water from the well in Artesian Square.

Grim built the Natatorium on the bayfront which featured a mineral-water bath, with the water piped in from Artesian Square. The mineral water was so corrosive that it ate away his iron tubs and he had to buy copper tubs. Grim's Natatorium was destroyed in the 1916 hurricane. The last well in Artesian Square was drilled in 1935 and closed in 1953 on orders of the health department.

Artesian Park was the scene of band concerts, horseshoes and domino games, and political rallies. Nueces County Judge Walter Timon often spoke at the park and so did Gov. "Pappy" O'Daniel who held a rally there in 1938.

On the west side of the 800 block of Mesquite was the First Baptist Church, which moved to a new brick building on the corner from an old converted blacksmith shop a block south. A new church was built on Ocean Drive in 1950.

33. A rooftop view of the 800 block of Mesquite Street at the Taylor Street intersection shows the First Baptist Church on the left and Cheston L. Heath home on the right, which was occupied by his widow Mary at the time of this photo in the 1930s.

Beyond the church were several homes and at the end of the block was the residence of E. B. Cole, a real estate developer, who gave the city land along the bay for Cole Park. The Caller-Times was built on the old Cole home site and later expanded to take in the whole block, including the site where the Baptist Church once stood.

On the east side of the 900 block, at 912 Mesquite, was the home of Priscilla Hawley, a heroine in the Civil War. When Union forces threatened a Confederate post on Mustang Island, the soldiers there prepared to retreat but the only men who knew the twisting channel around Harbor Island were gone. A 14-year-old girl said she knew the channel and she piloted the boatload of Confederates to safety. The girl was identified as "Grace Darling" because she didn't want her name told; she thought her actions "unladylike." She was Priscilla Stephenson who married Henry Hawley.

In the 1000 block, between Mann and Aubrey, was the First Methodist Church, built in 1912 to replace an older church built in 1872. The 1912 Methodist church was a landmark until the new church was built on Shoreline in 1955.

On the east side of the 1000 block, second from the corner, was the Martin Kelly home, built around 1857. During the Civil War, when Corpus Christi was bombarded by Union ships, cannonballs smashed through the roof and kitchen wall.

Annie Marie (Kelly) Lewis, who grew up in the home of her uncle, Martin Kelly, said the house was shell concrete with high ceilings that showed wooden support beams. "There were no bathrooms or closets in the original house; they were added later. There was a concrete water cistern in the yard."

34 and 35. The First Methodist Church, at Mesquite and Mann (top) was built in 1912. When the church was under construction, the pastor, Rev. T. F. Sessions would give workers "faith checks" on Saturday and church elders would go to the bank on Monday and sign personal notes to cover the checks. The church building was remodeled (bottom) to replace what was considered a confusion of architectural styles of the original. The building was torn down after a new church was built on Shoreline in 1955.

36. *Nueces County's first courthouse (left, in 1875) was built in the 1850s and designed by Felix von Blucher. The second courthouse sat next to the older structure, facing Mesquite. It was completed in 1875, cost $15,000 to build, and was called the Hollub Courthouse after the designer and builder, Rudolph Hollub. It was replaced by the 1914 Courthouse.*

Next door was the home of John McClane, who came to Corpus Christi as a sheep man in 1856. McClane was a blockade runner during the Civil War, carrying cotton to Matamoros in an old sloop and bringing back supplies and tobacco for the troops. His blockade-running ended when he had to abandon ship and wade ashore to escape capture.

McClane became sheriff of Nueces County in the 1870s during reconstruction. On May 9, 1874, bandits killed four men at Morton's store at Penascal on Baffin Bay. Seven alleged killers were brought to Corpus Christi and a mob gathered at the jail with a rope. McClane was able to back them down and prevent a lynching. Two suspects were sentenced to hang and on Aug. 7, 1874 McClane gave them a drink of whiskey and escorted them to a scaffold on the 1854 courthouse where they were hanged. The following year, when bandits terrorized Nuecestown and the alarm spread to Corpus Christi, McClane rode the streets, shouting, "Close your windows! Bar your doors! Arm yourselves! Protect the town!" McClane died at his home on April 1, 1911.

Across the street were the 1854 and 1875 courthouses, the latter designed by Rudolph Hollub and called the Hollub Courthouse. Hollub, a former officer in the Austrian army, was a mapmaker and aide to U. S. Grant in the Civil War. He came to Corpus Christi as an engineer employed in building the Tex-Mex Railroad. Hollub later moved to Castroville, where he died. In 1913 the county's third courthouse was built next to the older structures, which were torn down. The 1914 courthouse still stands, though it has been vacant since July 1977 when the new courthouse on the bluff was occupied. The 1914 courthouse, a fine ruin of a building, lingers on, with hardy weeds growing in the cracks of the façade.

37 and 38. Top, from left, the Nueces County Jail, the 1854 Courthouse building, and the Hollub Courthouse. Bottom, members of the grand jury sit on the steps of the old 1854 Courthouse, which served as an auxiliary building to the Hollub Courthouse next door. Calvin J. Allen, the founder of Calallen, with his hat between his knees, was on that grand jury.

39 and 40. Above, the Mesquite Street entrance of the 1914 Courthouse. Below, County Clerk Marion Uehlinger was the last to leave when the courthouse was closed on July 27, 1977.

41. Water covered the 1100 and 1200 blocks of Mesquite in the wake of the 1919 hurricane. On the left was the Belden Hotel, past the Belden Street intersection.

42. Shoeshine boys posed for the photographer in Artesian Park.

Mesquite north of the courthouse was mostly homes in an area known as Irishtown. Lillie Anderson Rankin said Irishtown was so-called because so many families were of Irish descent, although there were many of German descent as well, including the Vetters, Shaws, and Fitzsimmons.

In the 1930s and early 1940s, the blocks of North Mesquite past the Courthouse featured the Belden Hotel, at 1201, a restaurant called The Mesquite at 1311, run by Mrs. Bertie

43. The Constantine Hotel was built in the 1890s on the corner of Mesquite and Lawrence. It was renamed the Bidwell shortly after the turn of the 20th Century. The Bidwell Hotel was remodeled in 1940 and used as a furniture showroom for Lichtenstein's next door on Lawrence. It was torn down in 1999.

Shuler, Vernon Armstrong's Little Cash Grocery at 1315, the Mesquite Hotel at 1401, and the old Mew family home at 1424 at the corner of Fitzgerald. The Town Hall wrestling arena was at 1601, the Labor Temple at 1824, and not far beyond that was the end of Mesquite and the entrance to the bascule bridge. Mesquite, like Water and Chaparral, lost many structures in the 1000 and 1100 blocks with the construction of the terminus of I-37.

Mesquite Street has a rich history. In the 200 block, at Frederick Belden's home, Zachary Taylor discussed over dinner his plans for war with Mexico. In the 500 block, at Market Hall, people danced at the annual Firemen's Ball. In the 700 block, at Mat Nolan's home, Union soldiers carried away a flag and sword trophies captured in the battle of Galveston. In the 1100 block, on Aug. 7, 1874, two Penascal raid killers were hanged from a scaffold built out from the older courthouse. Mesquite, like Chaparral and Water, opens a window into the city's past.

Chapter 4. Downtown East-West Streets

Including Taylor, Starr, Peoples, Schatzel, Lawrence, and
William from Lower Broadway below the bluff to the bay.

The 20 streets downtown that run west to east, generally from the bluff to the bay, along with Water Chaparral and Mesquite, comprise the old Beach section of the city. Of those 20 streets, the most important, or most commercialized, include Taylor, Starr, Peoples, Schatzel, and Lawrence.

TAYLOR: like the other cross streets that run from the bluff to the bay, Taylor is a short street, only four blocks, but it has a long history. It was named for Gen. Zachary Taylor, who brought half the U.S. Army to Corpus Christi in the summer of 1845 in preparation for the coming war with Mexico. His soldiers camped along the shoreline and dug a water well in Artesian Park.

When Taylor and the army were here, Corpus Christi was hardly a village. It was a trading post set up to sell goods to Mexican traders. Taylor's soldiers considered it part of Mexico, although it was claimed by Texas.

"We are over the line in Mexico and ready for anything," Lt. John James Peck wrote his wife. Another lieutenant, U.S. Grant, the future Civil War general, described it as "a small Mexican hamlet with an American trading post at which goods are sold to Mexican smugglers."

There was no Taylor Street at the time, but from the top of where the street is today the view from the bluff would have shown hundreds of tents stretching along the shore. The famous Daniel P. Whiting lithograph depicts the scene in 1845, although the perspective of Whiting's sketch was from North Beach (page 280).

Taylor's soldiers dug a deep well at the site of Artesian Park, just north of Taylor Street, but the water smelled like rotten eggs and was undrinkable. For drinking and cooking, army teamsters harnessed mustangs to haul water from the Nueces River 12 miles away.

Six years after the army marched to the border, Taylor Street was named and laid out in the grid of streets by Henry Kinney. That was in 1852, the year Corpus Christi was incorporated. The street in the 1850s included the John Dix home at Taylor and the bay and the Charles Russell home, where Dix's married daughter Mary Eliza lived.

The most famous structure on Taylor went up in 1878. After a long struggle to raise money, the town's Episcopalians built the Church of the Good Shepherd on the corner of Taylor at Chaparral, next to where Taylor's soldiers dug the artesian well. The church's 60-foot-high steeple could be seen far out in the bay. The Sanborn Fire Insurance Map for 1885 shows half a dozen houses, a carpenter's shop and a blacksmith shop on Taylor Street. After the turn of the century, in about 1904, the old John Dix home was converted into the Seaside Hotel, owned by Jack Ennis, a Beaumont oilman. The Seaside was famous for its view of sails and fishing boats and its shady arbor of wind-shaped salt cedars.

1. *The Church of the Good Shepherd was built at Taylor and Chaparral in 1878. Left of the church was the Parish Hall and on the right was the rectory.*

2. *Taylor Street in 1912, looking east, shows the new First Baptist Church on the left followed by the Church of the Good Shepherd a block to the east. Past the end of the street was the Pavilion Hotel, built in 1908 as an adjunct to the Seaside Hotel. On the right was the Central Christian Tabernacle, the E. P. Cooper home, and a blacksmith shop at the corner of Mesquite.*

3. Taylor Street in the 1930s. A vacant lot on the right was the site of the Church of the Good Shepherd which was moved to South Broadway. The two-story home with a gallery on the corner was the Cheston L. Heath residence. On the other corner was the First Baptist Church.

About 1908, the Seaside Electric Theater was built across the street from the Seaside Hotel. Motion pictures had been shown in town for four years, but they were shown in converted storefront buildings. The Seaside Electric was the first in town built exclusively as a theater. It featured an orchestra with four women.

In the 1930s, Taylor Street had seven businesses and one home, according to the 1933 City Directory. David Peel's Funeral Home was at 520 Taylor, on the site where the Caller-Times is today. A block down, on the north side of the Mesquite Street intersection, was the home of Mrs. Cheston L. Heath. Businesses included a tire shop, an electric company, and a restaurant, at the Water Street intersection, run by R. C. Nolte.

STARR: One block south of Taylor is Starr, which runs from Lower Broadway to the bay. It was named by Henry Kinney for James Harper Starr, doctor, land agent and treasury secretary of the Republic of Texas in 1839-1840. Other downtown side streets (Taylor, Peoples, Schatzel and Lawrence) were named for men who had a strong connection to Corpus Christi, but not James Harper Starr. Kinney's reasons for naming the street after Starr are unknown.

A man named Gocher had a windmill used to grind corn and grain off Starr west of where the State Hotel was later built. In the next block, John Riggs' boarding house was past the Mesquite intersection, where Taylor Brothers' Jewelry store was built. Eli Merriman stayed in the Riggs' boarding house while he attended the Hidalgo Seminary in 1864. Ernest Bagnall, an undertaker, had an office at Starr and Mesquite. Annie Schallert, who married him, said their home was down the street past the Chaparral intersection. The Bagnall undertaking office was next to the Corpus Christi Female Academy, run by Professor J. D. Meredith and his wife.

4. The Federal Building was constructed in 1915 at a cost of $125,000 at Lower Broadway and Starr streets. The three-story building served as the post office, on the lower floor, with federal offices and court facilities on the second and third floors. The photo dates from the early 1930s.

Much of the history of Starr Street is linked to that of the Federal Building, on the south side of the street at the junction with Lower Broadway.

The Commercial Club, which existed before the Chamber of Commerce, asked Congressman John N. Garner to push through a bill in Congress to construct a new Federal Building in Corpus Christi. Garner's legislation was passed and Congress authorized the federal courthouse building in Corpus Christi on May 30, 1908.

Congress appropriated $70,000 to purchase a site and construct a building. It was not enough. A site was chosen in 1908 at the upper end of Starr Street next to the bluff, but the project was delayed until 1913 when Garner succeeded in getting Congress to double the amount to $140,000.

The house on the site was that of Timothy J. Dineen, a traveling salesman, and his wife Olive. The site was cleared and construction began in 1915. When work was finished in December 1916, the Post Office, Customs office and federal court offices were moved into the building. The three-story structure of tan brick and white stucco with a red tile roof was finished about the time the bluff balustrade was built and downtown streets were paved.

This was the first building constructed to house federal offices in Corpus Christi. In past years, federal offices were leased. In the 1919 storm, the U.S. Weather Bureau office at Corpus Christi was located in the City Bank Building at Peoples and Chaparral. The following year, it moved to the third floor of the new Federal Building.

In 1929, the Post Office occupied the first floor of the building. On the second floor were the offices of the postal inspector, U.S. attorney, U.S. marshal, law library, federal judge and courtroom. Besides the weather bureau, offices on the third floor included witness rooms, military recruiting offices, IRS and Customs offices, and an immigration office.

5. *The imposing State Hotel, left, dominated the 500 block of Starr, between Mesquite and Lower Broadway, in 1930.*

Because Customs officers worked from the building, confiscated liquor was destroyed at the Federal Building by pouring it down city drains.

On May 19, 1939, Postmaster Gilbert McGloin and Assistant Postmaster Albert Dittmer were found shot to death in McGloin's office on the second floor. Both were shot in the head. A .45 caliber handgun was found near Dittmer's body. Investigators said McGloin was sitting behind his desk when he was shot. Dittmer was shot behind the ear. It was considered an open-and-shut case: one murder, one suicide, one gun, two bullets fired. Investigators said there was an argument leading Dittmer to shoot McGloin and then put the barrel of the .45 behind his right ear. What was the quarrel? No motive was given. Mrs. Gilbert (Ameta) McGloin, a teacher at David Hirsch Elementary, was appointed to succeed her husband as postmaster.

After Corpus Christi gained an appropriation to build a new post office on Upper North Broadway, which opened in 1939, the Federal Building was remodeled to provide more space for federal court and other federal offices.

Soon after the Japanese attacked Pearl Harbor on Dec. 7, 1941, recruiting offices were flooded with volunteers. A group of 135 Corpus Christi men calling themselves the Pearl Harbor Avengers was sworn in in front of the Federal Building.

When German U-boats were taking a deadly toll on shipping in the Gulf, the Federal Building was a beehive of activity. Countermeasures against U-boats were coordinated from Eighth Naval District offices on the second floor.

After Hurricane Celia hit Corpus Christi on Aug. 3, 1970, virtually the entire Federal Building was commandeered by the Office of Emergency Preparedness. A dozen federal agencies set up shop. A radio station was installed on the first floor and law offices were converted into a communication center.

6. *Starr Street looking toward the bay on Aug. 1, 1939. On the right was W. T. Grant with J. C. Penney across Chaparral. On the left was the Mayflower Café and down the street was the Elks building which later was remodeled for the Dragon Grill and now houses the Vietnam Restaurant.*

After a new, larger federal courthouse opened on Shoreline Boulevard on Feb. 12, 2001, the 83-year-old Federal Building on Starr Street was purchased by Thomas J. Henry to house his law firm.

In the 1930s, Starr Street was dominated by the Federal Building, at 523, followed by the State Hotel, at 510, and in the next block, between Mesquite and Chaparral, Biel's Grocery, at 416, and above it the Dallas Hotel. Taylor Bros. Jewelry was on the corner of Mesquite and Starr followed by St. John's Restaurant west of the W. T. Grant building.

At 416 Starr was the Lyric, one of the oldest theaters in Corpus Christi, built in 1910 by H. H. Elliott. After the Lyric came the Liberty in 1919, followed by the Harbor Theater in 1923, and for a short time was called the Palace Theater.

Afterwards there was the Stella Peck Restaurant then a Biel's Grocery Store. The first floor in the 1930s and 1940s was occupied by Biel's. An eye-catching feature of Biel's was a fish tank the length of the front window that was filled with tropical fish. The second floor had rented rooms, called Lyric Flats, and finally the Dallas Hotel.

Biel's Grocery was there from at least 1931 until 1976, when it became a Jr. Food Mart. The Dallas Hotel occupied the upper floor for two decades or more. The structure at 416 Starr Street was renovated by Sparkman Energy in 1981.

In the next block, between Chaparral and Water, there was the Mayflower Restaurant on the corner of Chaparral across the street from J. C. Penney. Down the block there was a bingo parlor, then a taxi stand, and the Elks Club, which was later the Dragon Grill (Chapter 1, Water Street, page 19).

7. *The Dallas Hotel, above the Biel Grocery, was first called Lyric Flats (after the Lyric Theater which had been there), Harbor Rooms, Texas Rooms, and finally the Dallas Hotel. Biel's Grocery occupied the lower floor from 1931 until 1976.*

8. *Looking east on Starr Street at the Mesquite intersection. The Barry-Hendrix Drug Store on the corner (right) was where Taylor Brothers Jewelry was later built. On the left in the middle of the block was the old Lyric Theater, which for a time was called the Palace.*

PEOPLES: One block south of Starr, Peoples Street runs from Lower Broadway at the bluff to the bay. It was named by Henry Kinney for John Peoples, a Mexican War correspondent who became editor of the Corpus Christi Star in 1848. The story of John Peoples is also the story of how the gold rush of 1849 came through Corpus Christi.

In January 1848, gold was discovered in California and, like the rest of the country, Corpus Christi was stricken with gold fever. The town's newspaper, the Star, was filled with news that described the gold fields and the best way to get there. Henry Kinney, the town's founder, placed ads in Eastern newspapers asserting that Corpus Christi was the best route to take to get to the California gold fields.

The route promoted by Kinney was by ship to Corpus Christi then travel across South Texas and Chihuahua and Sonora in Mexico to California. Gold seekers began to arrive in January 1849. They were organized into companies with names such as the Essex Mining Company, the Carson Association, the Kinney Rangers (named for Henry Kinney), and the Mazatlan Rangers. The editor of the Corpus Christi Star, John Peoples, joined the Mazatlan Rangers and departed for California in February 1849. The trip across Texas took 33 days, three times longer than it should have and Peoples wrote a letter to the Star blasting his fellow travelers as lazy loafers. On days when they should have been traveling, Peoples wrote, some refused to stir, forcing the entire company to waste time. On the trip across the arid states of northern Mexico, they ran out of water and suffered dysentery. To cross raging rivers they had to caulk wagon beds and turn them into rafts. In crossing the Gulf of California Peoples was drowned. Word spread that the journey from Corpus Christi across Chihuahua and Sonora was dangerous and the traffic of gold seekers through Corpus Christi ended. We have a reminder of that time in Peoples Street, named for John Peoples.

9. Peoples Street at Lower Broadway (top) with the Greyhound Bus Terminal on the right and the tunnel entrance at lower left.

Peoples Street, like its neighbor to the south, Schatzel Street, were the principal east-west side streets that run from the bluff to the bay and through the heart of the business district. From 1921 to 1940, the west and east ends of Peoples were marked by the bluff tunnel entrance at the west end, above City Hall, and at the Pleasure Pier on the east end, on the bay. In between the tunnel and the pier were some of the city's major structures, from City Hall to the Furman Building, the City Bank Building, the Nueces Hotel, and the Sherman-Jones Building.

The 500 block of Peoples Street begins past the intersection with Lower Broadway. In the 1930s and 1940s, on the north side of the street, at 524, was the Greyhound Bus Lines, followed by the Riggan Hotel, at 516, run by John and May Riggan, then Frank Daugherty's Sandwich Shop. The old Hatch & Robertson Building (known for a time as the Lovenskiold Building), at the corner of Mesquite, housed Bingham's Drug Store. Across the street at 505 was City Hall, built in 1911 to replace old Market Hall.

Across Mesquite, on the north side of Peoples, was the Sun Pharmacy, which occupied the prime corner of the Furman Building. Historically, this was the site of R. G. Blossman's Grocery, which faced Mesquite. In the 1930s Sun Pharmacy, then Thomas Boucher's Pharmacy, was on Blossman's old site.

What could be called the Chapman/Furman corner has a long history. William Chapman, an Army quartermaster stationed in Corpus Christi in the 1850s, purchased three lots from Henry Kinney: two were on the site where the Nueces Hotel was later built. The other was at Peoples and Mesquite. William Blair Chapman, his son, and Helen Chapman, William

Chapman's widow, operated a store on this site after the Civil War. The building later burned.

R. G. Blossman's Grocery was located on that site for many years, fronting on Mesquite. Dr. McIver Furman, a descendant of William Chapman, once said of Blossman's store: "I can see it now, the barrels of lard and, on the top shelf, the bottles of Sunnybrook whisky, at only $1.50 a quart." Blossman's store also burned.

Mrs. Jessie C. Furman, granddaughter of William Chapman, built the first floor of what became the Furman Building. In 1926, a much larger building was constructed above and around the original building. Two additional floors were added, in the business boom that followed the opening of the Port of Corpus Christi. Dr. McIver Furman kept his office in the Furman Building. The 70-year-old building was rehabilitated in 1984 and a four-level parking garage was added on Mesquite Street side behind it.

Next door was the Palace Barber Shop, run by John Kanipe, who could walk out his front door and see his main competition directly across the street, with Warren Shaw's Barber Shop. Past Kanipe's was the McDonald Building followed by the City Bank Building on the corner. The McDonald Building and City Bank Building are still there.

On the south side of the 400 block, on the corner, was the Seeligson Building. Among its tenants was Dr. Carl Haltom, optometrist. After his death his widow, Dr. Ruth Haltom, ran the office and later his daughter, Dr. Kate Haltom. It was followed by Western Union, Jack Bonner's office supplies, and Shaw's Barber Shop. A bar called Clay's Place, across from the McDonald Building, was later converted into a Douglass's Eat-a-Bite. On the corner was Montgomery Ward on the site of the old Uehlinger Building.

In the 300 block, on the north side, was the Nueces Hotel (Chapter 1, pages 16-18). On the southeast corner of Chaparral, in the 300 block of Peoples, was the Sherman (later Jones) Building, built on the site of the Hunsaker Building and Norwick Gussett's store and bank. On the ground floor was the Barry-Hendrix Pharmacy.

11. *Peoples Street, with City Hall on the right, the Riggan Hotel on the left, and three tall buildings down the street were the City Bank Building, the Nueces Hotel, and the Jones Building on the right. The bluff tunnel entrance is not visible in the right foreground.*

The H. G. Sherman building was constructed in 1929. The building that stood on that site was the old Hunsaker Building, which was built in the 1850s, a twin to the Ohler Building on the north side of Peoples. A story in the Times on Sept. 22, 1929 said the old Hunsaker Building was bombarded by Lt. Kittredge's Union warships in August 1862.

"A cannon ball tore through the roof of the building, killed a dog on the floor of the saloon which occupied the ground floor, crossed the street taking off the horn of a saddle of a passing horse, and burst on the building opposite."

The six-story Sherman building was constructed with a foundation and frame to support an additional six floors. The building was constructed for a price of $215,000. H. G. Sherman sold the building to W. W. Jones, pioneer cattleman and real estate man who also purchased the Nueces Hotel across the street. Shortly after Jones purchased the building he added four stories to the structure, in 1937. The Jones family sold the building in 1979 and the name was changed to the Nueces Building.

Past the Sherman-Jones Building was George Plomarity's Manhattan Café. There was a private club on the second floor that, accounts say, sold illegal whiskey during Prohibition, catering to the guests at the Nueces Hotel. The club was owned and operated by Linn K. "Doc" Mason, originally from Monongahela, Pa. Mason later opened the Dragon Grill (Chapter 1, page 19). His business partners were Bob Shoop, F. Wilbert Garton and Clyde Jennings. A customer said they bought pure grain alcohol from Kansas City in five-gallon cans, added flavorings to "age" it and sold it in pint bottles. Bob Shoop later opened the popular Shoop's Grill. After Prohibition was repealed in 1933, the Wonder Bar, with a billiard parlor, opened in a two-story brick building next to the Manhattan Café.

12. *The Jones-Sherman building stands on the south side of Peoples, the Nueces Hotel on the right, and the Robert Driscoll Hotel on the bluff, shown in 1942, the year the Driscoll opened.*

Past the intersection with Water Street was the Pier Café and the iconic three palms of the Nueces Hotel, called Tres Palmas. The Pleasure Pier stretched out from the end of Peoples Street into the bay.

The 1,000-foot Pleasure Pier was built in 1922 off Peoples Street, with landing places for boats and a pavilion on the T-Head part of the pier. The pier, said to be the longest of its kind in the South, became a favorite place to stroll.

The newspaper reported that the pier was one of the first places visited by tourists "who want to get out over the water and watch the activities of boats and boatmen."

The Pleasure Pier lived up to its name. Like the old Central Wharf had been in its time, the Pleasure Pier was ideal for an evening stroll, for air and exercise, with the stars reflected in the waters of the bay.

An old fisherman's shack at the foot of the north side of the Pleasure Pier was remodeled to become the Pier Café, which extended out over the bay. It was operated by John Govatos. The Pier Café was moved into a new building on the south side of the pier in 1932. In January 1939, the city warned the tenants on the Municipal Wharf and along the waterfront to move out to make way for the seawall improvement project.

The Pier Café was still on Water Street, past the end of Peoples, but the water was a block away. The once-popular cafe did not thrive in its new landlocked location.

"When they filled in the waterfront," John Govatos said, "it made a mess of the Pier Café. The water was gone, and the glamour was gone."

13. A construction worker at the Robert Driscoll Hotel had a good view of Peoples Street in 1941. The hotel opened in May 1942.

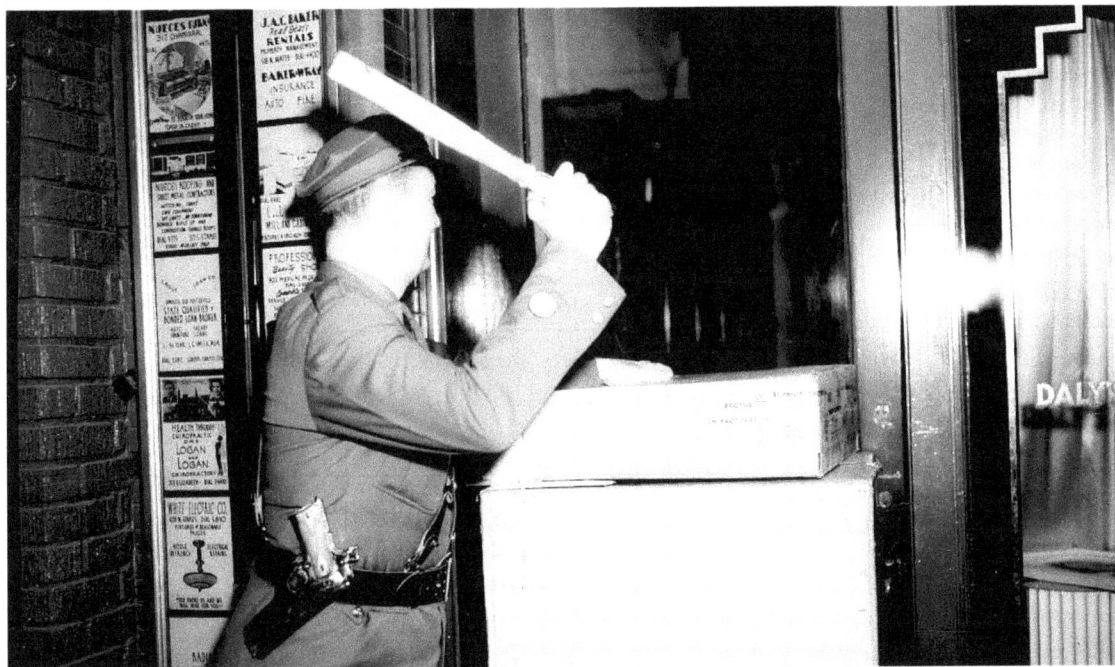

14. An air-raid warden made his rounds during a citywide blackout on Jan. 29, 1942, after U-boats were sighted near the Aransas Pass ship channel. The warden stopped to check on a light in the window of Aubrey Daly's Camera Store, at 415 Peoples.

15 and 16. Schatzel Street looking east toward the bay in 1897 (top) with Market Hall on the left. The street in 1935 (below) shows City Hall on the left, followed by the State National Bank, the Gugenheim-Cohn Building, Corpus Christi National Bank and Lichtenstein's.

SCHATZEL: One block south of Peoples Street, the misspelled Schatzel Street was named for John Peter Schatzell, a wealthy merchant engaged in the Mexican trade who was the honorary U.S. consul at Matamoros.

Henry Kinney, the founder of Corpus Christi, was a close friend of Schatzell's and persuaded the elderly gentleman to retire to Corpus Christi. After Schatzell moved to Corpus Christi in 1850 he built a fancy home on the south bluff called Mansion House, where the First Presbyterian Church stands today.

When Kinney was busy promoting and financing his Lone Star Fair in 1852, it was with $45,000 that he borrowed money from his friend Schatzell.

17. *The city's oldest and newest fire trucks were displayed in front of the main fire department at City Hall on Schatzel Street in 1941. The fire truck on the right was a 1913 LaFrance and the other truck was bought for the North Beach Fire Station when it was new. The city in 1941 had four fire stations, five pumper trucks and one hook-and-ladder truck. The four stations were located on Schatzel, Leopard, Morgan and Bessie on North Beach.*

When Schatzell died in 1854, the executor of his estate, Capt. Samuel Fullerton, pressed Kinney to repay the loan. Kinney was forced to mortgage his ranch holdings, including two-thirds of Mustang Island. One account of Schatzell's generosity came to light after his death. Any army of Texas volunteers were captured in the raid on Mier, Mexico, in 1842. Imprisoned in Mexico at Rancho de Salado, they were forced to draw beans in a lottery of death to decide who would live and who would face a firing squad. Seventeen men drew black beans and were executed. Schatzell pleaded with Mexican authorities to free the survivors. When the last of them were freed in 1844, Schatzell loaned them money to buy clothes and pay for their passages home. He never collected, or perhaps never intended to collect, his debts from the Mier prisoners. Of all the people for whom Henry Kinney named Corpus Christi streets, John Peter Schatzell was most deserving. The name has been perpetuated, though the man himself is not often remembered.

From 1911 to 1950, the 500 block of Schatzel was dominated by City Hall, with the City Police Department and the Central Fire Station. Across the street was one of the oldest businesses on the street, William DePuy's sheet metal shop. The J. W. Leatherwood Building, at 509, for a time housed the First State Bank until its new building was constructed. In that block in the 1930s and 1940s were Dave Wilkins Electric Company, the Blueprint Shop, and Western Auto on the first floor of the Weil Building.

Past Mesquite, in the 400 block, was the First State Bank (later the State National Bank) followed by the Gugenheim-Cohn Building, at 416 Schatzel. When it was built in 1907, it was a three-story building. A fourth floor was added in 1912 and leased for use as the federal court while the Federal Building on Starr was under construction.

18. *The Eidson-Meehan Department Store (later it was Eidson's) was located on the corner of Schatzel and Chaparral across from the Corpus Christi National Bank. Businesses on this corner over the years included Gugenheim & Cohn Department Store, Eidson-Meehan, Limerick's Furniture, Lerner's, and Zales Jewelry. There's an empty lot there now.*

The Gugenheim-Cohn Building was built by Simon Gugenheim and Herman Cohn, who also owned the Gugenheim & Cohn Department Store. One of the tenants in the building was Dr. P. G. Lovenskiold, the town's first dentist who served as mayor for 10 years, from 1921 to 1931. Past the Gugenheim-Cohn Building was the Corpus Christi National Bank, which fronted on Chaparral.

On the east side of the 400 block, on the corner with Mesquite, was the two-story brick Citizens Industrial Bank, built on the site of the old Cheston C. Heath's Emporium. Later, in the 1940s, Charles Hale's typewriter business was on the ground floor with Lewis Ingram's Palace Hotel on the second floor.

At 421 was Eldon Belk's Barber Shop; his brother Bige was a barber on North Beach. The Belk Barber Shop was later sold to William Knox. It was followed by John Doan's Crystal Café, William McCurdy's Jewelry Store, Helen Graves' Music Store. On the corner was Eidson's Department store across from the Corpus Christi National Bank.

Only two businesses were located in the 300 block of Schatzel in the 1930s: On the north side of the block was Lichtenstein's, which fronted on Chaparral (Chapter 2, pages 62-64) and on the south side of the street was Jack Nelson's Electric Company. The Sun Pharmacy was on the southeast corner, but its address belonged to the 400 block of Chaparral.

The triangle of blocks between Schatzel and Peoples is fan-shaped, with the small end under the bluff and the large end on the bayfront. Schatzel slants to the right, away from Peoples. City Hall, the State National Bank, the Gugenheim-Cohn Building, the Corpus Christi National Bank, and Lichtenstein's third store were all wedge-shaped, apparently designed to conform to the unusual angle. It gave the street, from above, an odd appearance.

19. *Lawrence Street on July 2, 1933, facing east, shows the St. James Hotel on the left and across Chaparral was the Doddridge Building which housed the Texas State Bank & Trust.*

LAWRENCE: South of Schatzel is Lawrence Street, which runs from the bluff to the bay. It was named for Dr. David H. Lawrence, Corpus Christi's first doctor. He came to the United States from England in the early part of the 19th Century. He lived at Dayton, Ohio before coming to Texas shortly after the Revolution. He arrived in Corpus Christi in 1840, the year after Henry Kinney founded the town.

After the death of his wife, Dr. Lawrence married Ellen Pettigrew of Corpus Christi, considered a local beauty. On Feb. 16, 1846, she led the opening dance at the Annexation Ball with Gen. Zachary Taylor. Dr. and Mrs. Lawrence had twins, a son named Marion, and a daughter named Mary.

When Nueces County Sheriff Mat Nolan was shot on Dec. 2, 1865, he was carried to the nearby home of Dr. Lawrence, on Mesquite Street (where the Caller-Times parking lot is now). Lawrence told Nolan his wound was fatal.

During the yellow fever epidemic of 1867, it was said that the doctor's treatment consisted of having the patient's feet soaked in a bucket of hot water mixed with ashes and mustard, then the patient was wrapped in blankets and sweated to discharge the fever.

Dr. Lawrence had an office in the St. James Hotel before he died on March 14, 1879. He was buried in Bayview Cemetery. Mary Sutherland in "The Story of Corpus Christi" said Lawrence was a much-beloved doctor of the old days. (Another city street, Buddy Lawrence Drive, was named for the doctor's grandson, a longtime county commissioner.)

From the eastern end of Lawrence Street was the old Hiram Riggs' pier, the first built in Corpus Christi. It was followed later by the Staples Wharf. At the end of Lawrence was a large wool warehouse. There were two dominant buildings on the street. One was the St. James Hotel, though its address was on Chaparral, built in the 1870s. The other was the Constantine Hotel (renamed the Bidwell), which faced Mesquite.

20. In the late 1930s, Lawrence Street shows the Frank Sparks Insurance Building (left) in the old Southwestern Bell Building. The Bidwell Hotel stands at the corner of Mesquite. The Doddridge Building can be seen at the corner of Chaparral.

In the 500 block of Lawrence, on the south side of the street, was a vacant lot. On the north side of the street, at 520 Lawrence, was Southwestern Bell, until 1938 when it moved to a new home on North Broadway. Frank Sparks' insurance agency moved into the old Southwestern Bell building. Past Mesquite was the Constantine/Bidwell Hotel, fronting on Mesquite. On the east end of the block was the St. James Hotel, facing Chaparral. Between the Bidwell and the St. James, in 1933, was James Barker's Barber Shop, followed by Darl Elliott's trading shop; he later worked at Nau Hardware. Next was Charles Mitchell's Battery Service, Weldon Knowles Plumbing, and a boarding house run by Anna Costello. On the south side of the street were several residences.

Past Chaparral, in the 300 block, there was the Gulf Hudson-Essex auto dealership owned by Walter Elmer Pope, followed by the Margaret Grant Dancing Studio, which was gone by the 1940s and Corpus Christi Business College moved into that building. The Kenedy Pasture Company had an office building at 312-314 Lawrence and there were several land agencies and real estate offices in that block. Except for the corner locations, the south side of Lawrence consisted of empty lots, from Lower Broadway to Water Street.

WILLIAM: One block south of Lawrence Street is William which runs from the bluff to the bay. In the 200 block, in 1914, was the home of Adolph Anderson, at 212, next to Blucher's ice factory (listed on Water). In the 400 block was T. J. Noakes' blacksmith shop, at 414, and the Masonic Hall at 418. In the 1930s, only two addresses were listed for William: R. R. Williams Body Shop at 316 and Horace Conway's Conservatory of Music at 520.

The Conway Conservatory was advertised as "the largest and most modernly equipped exclusive violin conservatory in the state." By the 1940s Conway's had moved to Six Points and Bertha Lacey's Dance Studio occupied the building.

132

21. *The Kenedy Pasture Company Building at 312-314 Lawrence. Sign over the doorway notes that the Commercial Club, forerunner of the Chamber of Commerce, was in this building, which survived the 1919 storm. In the 1890s, Mifflin Kenedy's office was in a frame building at Chaparral and William, below his home on the bluff. He died in 1895.*

22 and 23. Above, looking east toward the bay, William Street at the intersection of Mesquite presented a scene of destruction in the wake of the 1919 storm. Below, looking east on Laguna past the Mesquite intersection after the 1919 storm. The downtown, a shallow bowl between the bay and the bluff, was devastated by the storm.

134

Chapter 5. North & Lower Broadway

*From the arroyo at Cooper's Alley north to the terminus
(today's I-37), crossing Blucher, Lipan, Mestina, Leopard,
Antelope, Buffalo, and Winnebago streets.*

Upper Broadway on the high bluff, or plateau, was where Henry Kinney built his home in 1839 and where other pioneer merchants, such as William Mann and Henry Redmond, chose to build their homes. The higher elevation provided a clear view of the bay and the town below.

Henry Kinney named the street Broadway after New York City's great avenue. This was at a time when Corpus Christi had only a few stores and perhaps a hundred citizens, which shows the reach of Kinney's ambitions. He laid out the town's early streets and on an 1852 street map grid he spelled Broad Way as two words and proudly noted that it was 166 feet wide.

The arroyo that ran from Chatham's Ravine to the bay — also known as Blucher's Creek — served as the dividing line between north and south addresses. South of the arroyo was South Broadway which later became an avenue of fine homes. After the bluff was terraced and the balustrade was built, beginning in 1915, a new street was created at the bottom of the bluff called Lower Broadway.

North Broadway was where Martha Rabb, Mifflin Kenedy and Henrietta King built their magnificent mansions, standing aloof on the high bluff, in a display of the wealth of the cattle empire. When the cattle barons built their homes on the bluff, North Broadway became Corpus Christi's most stylish address, long before there was an Ocean Drive.

Henry Kinney was the first. He built his home on the bluff in 1839 when he founded the town. Henry Lawrence Kinney was born in Pennsylvania in 1814, the son of Simon and Phoebe Kinney. When he was 18, he got into a fight with a man who accused him of seeing his wife. Kinney left home and traveled to Illinois where he opened a store and bought a farm.

Kinney contracted to build a segment of the Illinois and Michigan Canal. The project collapsed in an economic downturn in 1837 and Kinney departed from Illinois, leaving canal workers unpaid. He arrived in Texas and opened a store on Live Oak Point. He called himself "Colonel" though he had no military credentials. In 1839 he moved his trading post to a site overlooking Corpus Christi Bay.

Kinney was engaged in the Mexican trade. Traders bought in wool, hides and other products from Mexico and were sold leaf tobacco, calico cloth, and manufactured goods. This trade was illegal in Mexico which made Kinney and the other Corpus Christi merchants smugglers in a technical sense.

The trading post was first called Kinney's Rancho and then, by 1842, Corpus Christi, after the bay. The settlement was six years old in 1845 when the first units of Gen. Zachary Taylor's army landed on July 31, 1845. Kinney rented buildings to the Army and set up several businesses, including the Kinney House hotel.

1. The Southwestern Bell telephone building was erected on the site of Kinney's home in 1938. After Kinney, the homes of Gen. Hamilton Bee, John S. Givens, and Atlee McCampbell all stood on that site.

When Taylor's army departed Kinney left with it and served as a quartermaster during the war in Mexico. At war's end, Kinney returned to Corpus Christi and set about trying to improve the town's fortunes. When gold was discovered in California, Kinney encouraged the traffic of emigrants heading West to start from Corpus Christi. The gold-seekers purchased wagons, mules and horses Kinney had acquired as Army surplus. The traffic stopped when emigrants discovered that the route across northern Mexico was both arduous and hazardous.

In 1852 Kinney borrowed money to hold a fair at Corpus Christi. He hoped to attract visitors who might buy land and settle in South Texas. The fair was a failure, for Kinney's purposes, and he was forced to mortgage his ranch holdings. He left Corpus Christi in 1854 for the Mosquito region of Nicaragua, where he proposed to establish his own empire in Central America.

This filibustering effort failed and Kinney returned to Corpus Christi in 1858. He was elected to the Legislature but resigned in March 1861 in protest of secession. He was shot to death in Matamoros in March 1862. There are conflicting accounts of his death but the most reliable indicate he went to visit his former lover late one night and was shot by her husband. He was buried in Matamoros in an unmarked grave.

Twelve years after his death, on Jan. 4, 1874, the City Council discussed the unsightly

2. Forbes Britton built "Centennial House" on North Broadway in 1848-1849.

condition of the old Kinney home on the bluff, at the corner of Broadway and Blucher streets. It was dismantled not long afterwards.

Hamilton Bee, called Hamp, was a Confederate general known more for retreating than fighting. He built a two-story home on the old Kinney site. Anna Moore Schwien, a former slave, said Bee and family lived there until they moved to San Antonio. Behind the Bee home was Charles Lovenskiold's place on North Carancahua.

Alice Lovenskiold Rankin said, "East of us was where Kinney lived. The Bees built a house on that corner. It was brick in the lower part and lumber in the upper." She recalled a brick wall between their home and the Bee place. Some thought it had been built in Kinney's time but she thought it was put up by Hamp Bee.

John S. Givens, an attorney from Oakville, bought the Bee home and added a second story. Givens was the prosecutor in the Chipita Rodriguez trial. He sold the home to Atlee McCampbell. Coleman McCampbell, author of a history of Corpus Christi, was born in that house. It was turned into apartments then the building was torn down to make way for a Southwestern Bell Telephone building in 1938.

Next to the Kinney site was Forbes Britton's house, built in 1848-1849. Britton was at Corpus Christi with Zachary Taylor and fought in the Mexico War. Britton returned to Corpus Christi after the war and engaged in the wool, hide and commission business.

Anna Moore Schwien, born a slave in 1856, said the Britton house was under construction when her mother arrived with the Baskin family from Mississippi on Jan. 1, 1849. "She said she could see the holes in the side of the bluff where they dug out the clay to make the shellcrete bricks" for the Britton home. Britton, elected to the Texas Senate,

3. Mifflin Kenedy's mansion was built in 1885. After his death in 1895, his daughter, Sarah Josephine Spohn and husband, Dr. Arthur Spohn, lived here. The house was torn down in 1937.

traveled to Austin for a special session in February 1861. He died of pneumonia on Feb. 14, 1861.

The Forbes Britton home acquired several owners, including Judge Pat O'Docharty, Maurice Levy, J. M. Howell, James Bryden and George Evans. Evans had it the longest, from 1882 to 1936, and it was known as the George Evans home.

Evans, a wool merchant, was mayor in 1884 and 1885. On Sept. 6, 1885, the Caller reported that a meeting of the Reading Club, held at the George Evans' home on the bluff and hosted by Mrs. Evans, was poorly attended. The paper couldn't understand why so few showed up to listen to a reading of Nathaniel Hawthorne's "Marble Faun" since there was nothing else going on — "no free concerts in town or cat hunts in the country." Beginning in 1949 the Britton-Evans home was called the Centennial House to recognize its 100th anniversary. It is still there, one of the city's rare historic structures.

North of Britton's was a house owned by the Cook family. Anna Moore Schwien recalled that "Mrs. Cook died there and soon after Mr. Cook died, leaving two children, Cora and Jack. They were taken in by Mr. and Mrs. Richard Power, who lived across the street and had no children. Cora Cook taught school here after the Civil War."

The Cook property on the corner of Lipan and North Broadway was sold to Mifflin Kenedy, where he built his home in 1885. It was described as an Italianate villa painted in three shades of olive green, with a 65-foot tower rising above the roof line. The house had alternating projections and recesses of windows to reflect the shifting patterns of light and

4. *Dr. Arthur Spohn in his new Cadillac in front of the Mifflin Kenedy mansion, in about 1905. In the back seat is his wife's niece from Brownsville.*

and shadow. It was designed by English architect Alfred Giles. The interior was finished with walnut, oak, mahogany, cherry and cypress. The trim on the grand stairway was polished mesquite that came from the Kenedy ranch. Acetylene gas was produced in a small building in the back for the 200 gas lights in the mansion. Maston Nixon, who built the Nixon Building down the street, said that Mifflin Kenedy's house "was as strong as a ship. He wanted it storm proof."

The house was completed only three weeks before Mifflin's wife Petra died. She moved into the house on Feb. 26, 1885 and died on March 16. After her death, Mifflin Kenedy's adopted daughter, Carmen Morell Kenedy, the daughter of a Monterrey merchant, moved into the mansion. Almost to the day, ten years after his wife's death, Kenedy died in the mansion following a heart attack on March 14, 1895.

After Carmen Morell Kenedy died in 1899, Mifflin's daughter, Sarah Josephine, and her husband, Dr. Arthur Spohn, moved into the house. Dr. Spohn had the trees in the yard wrapped in barbed wire to keep stray cattle from rubbing up against them.

In the late 1930s the 400 block of North Broadway, between Blucher and Lipan, featured Southwestern Bell at 401 on the old Kinney site, followed by the Britton home, at 411, and the Mifflin Kenedy mansion at 423. The Kenedy mansion was torn down in 1938 and the salvaged materials taken to the ranch at Sarita and used to build a church.

Across Lipan Street, in the 500 block, were two cottages owned by Judge Richard (Dickie) Power. The judge lived in the corner cottage. Eli Merriman said Dickie Power wrote poems and that many of them "were just splendid." His home on the bluff, Merriman said, "had little bitty windows on account of the Indians." On the site of the second cottage was where Martha Rabb built her home.

When John and Martha Rabb moved to town from their ranch at Banquete, they first

5. Martha Rabb's Magnolia Mansion on North Broadway soon after it was built in 1875.

lived at the south end of the bluff in a house they bought. This was about 1857. During the Civil War, while the family was at the ranch and Rabb commanded a Confederate cavalry unit, the house was used as a military hospital by Dr. E. T. Merriman.

John Rabb, born in 1825, was related to the Rabbs around LaGrange. When he was 21 he joined Zachary Taylor's army and was wounded in the battle of Monterrey. John met Martha Ann Reagan in school near LaGrange. They married in 1848 and moved to Banquete in the 1850s.

Rabb bought 400 acres on Banquete Creek, built a home, and began a free-range cattle operation. During the Civil War, Capt. Rabb's company of volunteers served to protect remote ranches throughout South Texas, but mostly in the lower Rio Grande Valley.

John Rabb died on April 15, 1872 and he was buried in Banquete Cemetery. He left 10,000 head of cattle and 3,500 sheep on the open range. His widow Martha began to buy land and increased the size of the ranch from 400 to 30,000 acres. She gained the nickname of "Cattle Queen of Texas." She built a palatial home on the bluff in Corpus Christi which she called the Magnolia Mansion.

In 1879 Martha married Rev. Curran M. Rogers, a Methodist minister, and sold the ranch and home on Broadway. David Hirsch, a merchant and wool dealer, bought the Magnolia Mansion. He later sold it to Mifflin Kenedy, who bought it for his son John G. Kenedy.

The house was used as a temporary hospital after the 1919 storm destroyed the Spohn hospital on North Beach. Dr. Harry Heaney helped convert the Kenedy home into a temporary hospital. In 1925 the Kenedy home was given to the Catholic Church and used as a parochial school. When Mifflin Kenedy's home was torn down in 1937, the old Magnolia Mansion was moved across Lipan to that site. It was dismantled in 1952 and the timbers used to build the chapel for the Holy Family Parish.

Richard King, the great cattleman, died in San Antonio of stomach cancer on April 14, 1885. Eight years after his death, widow Henrietta King built a home just north of Martha

6 and 7. The John G. Kenedy home (the Magnolia Mansion) was moved in 1938 from its original site north of Lipan (above) to where Mifflin Kenedy's mansion stood (below).

Rabb's Magnolia Mansion. The turreted and gingerbread-trimmed King home was built on the site of the old William Mann house.

In front of the King mansion were wooden steps with a hand railing that led down the bluff. Amelia Daimwood recalled "climbing the old wooden steps in front of the King-Kleberg home to get to the original wooden church (Presbyterian) on the bluff." The stables in the rear of the mansion burned in March 1896, but the mansion itself was undamaged. The Charles and Sarah Weil family lived next door and Carrie Weil recalled coming home from a dance when the stables were burning. When the fire was out, one of her younger brothers was missing. He was found behind a tree trunk where he had fallen asleep.

8 and 9. Henrietta King's home on North Broadway was built in 1893. The mansion was pulled down in 1945. Below, a buggy travels down Broadway around the turn of the century. At far left was Mifflin Kenedy's home followed by John G. Kenedy's home.

Living with Mrs. King in the mansion were her daughter and her husband, Robert J. Kleberg Sr., and their five children. One reason for building the house was so the Kleberg kids could attend school in town. When President William Howard Taft visited Corpus Christi on Nov. 22, 1909, Henrietta hosted a lunch for him. Knowing his reputation for enjoying a good meal, she had a 60-pound turkey sent from Cuero for the main course.

10. *Henrietta King in her favorite rocking chair. She was an austere woman who dressed perpetually in black after her husband's death in 1885. She took diamond earrings he gave her to a jeweler to have covered with black enamel so they would be less ostentatious.*

Henrietta King was an invalid in her last years. She died at age 92 on March 31, 1925. As the matriarch of King Ranch, her accomplishments were many. She controlled the ranch her husband founded longer than he did. He ran it for 32 years; she controlled it for 40 years. She doubled the size of the ranch after King's death, assisted by Robert J. Kleberg.

At the time of her death, she was said to be one of the richest women in the world. She owned a ranch of 1.2 million acres, served by 300 windmills, and grazed on by 125,000 cattle. She promoted the growth of Corpus Christi and Kingsville with generous gifts of land for schools, for Spohn Hospital, for the First Presbyterian Church. Some of the Kineños at the far end of the ranch rode two days to get there in time for the funeral. When her casket was lowered into the earth, horsemen waiting at the edge of the crowd rode forward and then galloped around her grave with hats held aloft in a final salute.

Richard King Sr., the banker and grandson of the original Richard King, had moved into Mrs. King's house on Broadway after his own place on North Beach was destroyed in the 1919 hurricane. He later built a new place on South Broadway.

11. The Corpus Christi Cathedral was built on the site of the Martha Rabb home on the corner of Lipan and North Broadway.

After fire damaged St. Patrick's Cathedral on Carancahua on Nov. 28, 1938, the John G. Kenedy family donated land on North Broadway for the site of a new church. Ground was broken for the cathedral in March 1939 and the building finished the following year. The name was changed from St. Patrick's to Corpus Christi Cathedral.

It was located on the site of Martha Rabb's Magnolia Mansion. The King/Kleberg mansion next door to the north was dismantled in 1945 after the Corpus Christi diocese acquired the site.

North of the King/Kleberg mansion and past the Mestina intersection was Charles and Sarah Weil's home, where they raised 11 children. The Weil family owned a general mercantile store and later a grocery store and ranch in Starr County. They first lived on Chaparral then moved to the bluff. The Weil children went to school by crossing through their back yard to the school buildings on Carancahua. The boys played baseball and flew kites on the empty lot where the Meuly house once stood.

After the turn of the century the Weils moved into a new home on South Broadway, near Park. The old Weil place at 529 was sold to Leonard M. Thomas, who owned Thomas' Model Pharmacy. Thomas came to Corpus Christi from Missouri in 1901 and opened the Thomas Drug Store across from Market Hall. His pharmacy was damaged in the 1919 storm and gutted by fire two years later. He eventually settled in the 500 block of Chaparral next to the Corpus Christi National Bank. The Thomas Model Pharmacy was the first drugstore in town with a soda fountain. He died in 1950.

The next house to the north was the A. M. French home which had become the residence of J. A. Barnes, a real estate agent. On Nov. 13, 1923, a package was delivered to the Barnes home and when he opened it a bomb exploded, killing him and his seven-year-old son. Theodore Fuller described the event in "When the Century and I Were Young." "I was living with the Wrights at the top of the hill on Broadway, a block from the arroyo. We

12. *An empty lot on North Broadway was the site of the J. A. Barnes' home, where a package bomb killed Barnes and his seven-year-old son on Nov. 13, 1923.*

were home for lunch when the big boom came. 'That engineer must be drunk,' someone said. 'No reason ever to couple cars that hard.' We were still talking about the rough handling of freight cars when a phone call told the family that there had been an explosion in a home on North Broadway near the high school. We dashed from the house and ran for North Broadway. At the crest of the hill we could see that a small crowd was milling about in the street south of the Leopard intersection. As we stood there we heard that a package had come in the mail and had exploded when the man opened it. I could see something that froze my tongue. A black spot alongside a red splotch high on the side of the house next door. The black spot was a clear imprint of the rubber heel of a shoe. The explosion had not been a small one."

Three years after the bombing, Frank Bonner, a student at the University of Texas who was dating Barnes' daughter (and later married her) was charged with the crime. He had taken out a life insurance policy on his future father-in-law and had experimented with explosive material. He attended class near a site where 40 sticks of dynamite and blasting caps went missing. The jury could not reach a verdict on Bonner and he was acquitted.

A new building built on the site where the Barnes home had been housed Montgomery Ward until 1933 when it moved to a new location on Chaparral. The Show Room of Finer Furniture was there in 1949 and the Wilson Building parking lot is on that site today.

In the 19th Century, the Fitzgerald home on corner of Leopard and North Broadway was bought by Conrad Meuly. His original home was in the 200 block of Chaparral. The Meuly house on the bluff was sitting vacant at the end of the Civil War. The house was vandalized, with window frames and doorways ripped out, by Union troops when Corpus Christi was under occupation at the end of the war. A newspaper report at the time said the soldiers

13. The 12-story Nixon Building (left) and the 14-story Plaza Hotel (right) changed the city's skyline and led to irrevocable changes on North Broadway as palatial homes were cleared to make way for tall commercial buildings.

pulled out furniture and fixtures, including a rosewood piano, to use as firewood. Margaret Meuly filed a claim for damages with Union authorities.

One of the more sensational murders of the 1860s occurred in this house. Mary Sutherland in "The Story of Corpus Christi," and John Dunn in "Perilous Trails" wrote about this crime. Two drifters were living in the Meuly place. One, an ex-soldier, found work on the docks and the other, an old man from Mexico, cooked for him in return for part of his wages. They had a falling out and the ex-soldier was brutally stabbed to death, his body left in a closet. The killer died in jail before he could be hanged.

The Fitzgerald/Meuly house was torn down in 1871. This was the site chosen by Maston Nixon for a high-rise office building. When the port opened in 1926, with the city growing like a boomtown, office space was at a high premium and Maston Nixon planned to build a multi-story office building on the bluff to fill the need.

Nixon grew up in Luling. His first job was to harness a mule that pulled the ice wagon. He served as an artillery captain in World War I and after the war moved to a cotton farm near Robstown. Nixon and wife Hallie moved to Corpus Christi in 1925 and soon afterwards Nixon became interested in property at the corner of Broadway and Leopard. Nixon got options on the site, which included two cottages and an empty lot.

Nixon brought in H. L. Kokernut as a business partner with plans to construct the largest office building in the city. The 12-story Nixon Building opened on April 2, 1927. It was soon filled with tenants, mostly cotton brokers.

Across Leopard from the Nixon Building was the Redmond home. Henry Redmond, from England, was involved in the Mexican trade and moved to Corpus Christi in the early 1840s. He became a partner of William Mann and in 1849 he married Louisa Baskin, the

14 and 15. *Henry Redmond's home (left, above) was moved to clear the site for the Plaza Hotel. The First Presbyterian Church was torn down when the Plaza was built. The Driscoll Hotel was built on the site of the church and the Seaton home (right). Below, North Broadway after the balustrade was built and before the Plaza and Driscoll were constructed.*

sister of Mann's wife Esther. Redmond, it was said, bought the first town lot sold by Kinney and built a home on the bluff, at Leopard and Broadway, before he moved to the border. The house was purchased by railroad builder Uriah Lott. It was eventually sold to Dr. Henry Redmond, son of the original owner.

Maston Nixon said his business partner, H. L. Kokernut, looked across Leopard at the Redmond house and said, "Maston, we need a hotel on that corner." Nixon began to take steps to see that it happened. He formed a Corpus Christi company to finance building a hotel and found a San Antonio company to run it. The site was purchased and the Redmond

16. *The Plaza Hotel (left) reflects a shadow of the Nixon Building while the Driscoll Hotel on the right was under construction in 1942.*

house was moved to the Spohn Hospital to be used as a dormitory for student nurses. Palms in the yard were replanted in the Nueces Hotel garden and became known as the three palms, Tres Palmas.

The Plaza Hotel opened in 1929, giving Corpus Christi two tall buildings on the bluff. The 14-story hotel, towering over Broadway, was known for its Pullman Coach lobby furniture and a roof garden resembling a ship's deck, called the Plaza Deck View.

Robert Driscoll Jr., rancher and banker, was a major investor in the Plaza. He died soon afterwards. After his death, Jack White, who was operating the hotel, bought out the other investors who were eager to sell during the Depression. Clara Driscoll, Robert's famous sister who inherited the family fortune, refused to sell. A court suit resulted, which White won. He changed the name to the White Plaza. The feud between Clara Driscoll and Jack White was not over.

Next to the Plaza was the First Presbyterian Church. The original church on this site was built in 1867, during the yellow fever epidemic. Dressed lumber on the site was diverted to make coffins, according to church history.

A new church was completed in 1902. Beginning in 1929, a new church was built on South Broadway. North of the Presbyterian Church was the Mildred Seaton home which, long before, had been the Rube Holbein house. In 1936 the Seaton home housed Cage-Mills Funeral Home.

Clara Driscoll, known as the woman who saved the Alamo, bought the Presbyterian Church property and the Seaton home and planned to build her own hotel next to the White

17.*Clara Driscoll. After the turn of the 20th century, liquor-warehouse owners of the Alamo property made a deal to sell the old mission in San Antonio to prepare a site for a hotel. Clara Driscoll and the Daughters of the Republic of Texas began a desperate campaign to raise $75,000 the owners wanted for the property. Clara and the DRT came up with $25,000 for a down payment but did not have the remaining $50,000 by the deadline. Clara signed five notes for $10,000 each, after which she was called, "The Savior of the Alamo." She managed the Driscoll family ranch after her brother's death and built the Driscoll Hotel on the bluff in Corpus Christi in 1942. She died at age 64, on July 17, 1945. Her bequest was to use the Driscoll wealth to create the Driscoll Foundation Children's Hospital.*

18. Three homes on North Broadway, from left, include the old Ohler home occupied by Jack and Nellie Grant, Mrs. Thomas Hickey's home, and Norwick Gussett's. The Gussett home was built by Edmund J. Davis. The Grant and Hickey homes were torn down and the Davis-Gussett home was moved to make way for the U.S. Post Office that was built on the site.

Plaza. She named the new hotel after her late brother. The 20-story Robert Driscoll Hotel opened on May 25, 1942. Clara Driscoll occupied a penthouse from where she could look down on the White Plaza.

The Driscoll Hotel catered to famous guests during the war. Tyrone Power kept a room there while he was stationed at the Naval Air Station. Mary Pickford stayed there while her husband trained to be a Navy pilot. A decade later, Elvis Presley had a room at the Driscoll when he performed at Memorial Coliseum. Clara Driscoll occupied her 20th floor penthouse (with 12 bathrooms) until her death on July 17, 1945.

The Driscoll Hotel was converted into a bank building, which later became Wells Fargo. The White Plaza was demolished in 1962 to make way for the 600 Building. The Nixon Building was sold to Sam Wilson, who changed the name to the Wilson Building.

Across Antelope on the corner at 703 North Broadway was Jack and Nellie Grant's home. William Adams recalled that this was the Ohler place, built sometime in the 1850s. "The Ohler family — Edward Ohler, wife and two sons — had a house where the new post office is now being built." William's brother Robert also recalled the Ohler place. "The Ohlers lived on the hill. One day I went up there and they were making soap. I saw him cooking it in a large cast iron pot. It was yellow and was sold in the town."

Mrs. Delmas Givens (Elizabeth Manly) said in an interview the nicest looking place in the city, when she arrived in 1876, was the Allen M. Davis home, just past the Ohler home, at 711 North Broadway. This house was later known as Mrs. Thomas Hickey's place.

19. *The U.S. Post Office on North Broadway at Antelope opened in September 1939. It was torn down in 1983 to make way for the Texas Commerce Plaza (later Frost Bank).*

The house next door was the home of Gov. Edmund J. Davis, which was later sold to Norwick Gussett. In 1937, the house was moved to Carancahua to become the Hennessey Apartments. The post office was built on the site of the Ohler, Allen M. Davis and E. J. Davis homes. Four decades later, the post office was torn down to make way for the Texas Commerce Plaza. When the post office was built in 1938 it sat next to Mrs. Delmas Givens' home, at 719. Her late husband had been a longtime city attorney. Mrs. Givens' home was torn down for the Vaughn Petroleum Building, built in 1959.

At 723 was the home of Horatio Gussett, son of Norwick Gussett. He had the house built when he married Mary Henrietta Barnard in 1898. The Gussetts' home had nine rooms with galleries on both floors. The bluff then was clay and treacherously slippery when it rained. Horatio had a boardwalk erected on the side of the bluff in front of their house. "Nettie" Gussett said their home overlooked a mesquite thicket and blacksmith shop below the bluff. She sold the house in 1953 to make way for the Oil Industries Building.

In the next block, at 819, was the James F. Scott home. Scott, a cattle rancher at Alice, was the son of John Wesley Scott and Charlotte Scott, who later married E. D. Sidbury. Scott had the nine-room home built shortly after the turn of the century. After he died in 1916, the home was operated as a rooming house by his daughter Clara. It was demolished in 1946 to clear the site for a Greyhound Bus Terminal.

North Broadway was transformed between 1926 and the 1950s with fine homes giving way to high-rise hotels and office buildings. The Kenedy, Rabb and King mansions were dismantled. The E. J. Davis, Delmas Givens, Horatio Gussett and James F. Scott homes were demolished. You wonder about the stories they had seen and the lives that were lived inside their walls. Gone with the old houses are the ghosts of the people who lived in them.

20. The bluff below North Broadway about 1910, before the balustrade and bluff improvement project transformed that natural division between downtown and uptown.

LOWER BROADWAY: This street was created when the bluff balustrade was built. The concrete balustrade and landscaped terrace represented the city's first big civic development in the second decade of the 20th century. The side of bluff separating downtown from uptown was like an ugly scar. Gullies washed out on the slope and runoff deposited mud on the streets below. Raw dirt roads straggled down the bluff at Peoples, Schatzel and Lawrence streets. In wet weather residents struggled through mud to the bluff approaches. Wooden steps were built to carry pedestrians up the slope. In some places, makeshift boards were laid to help people ascend the side of the bluff.

Mayor Clark Pease asked Alexander Potter, a New York engineer, to devise a way to convert the bluff from an eyesore to an attractive feature. Potter drew up plans for terracing the bluff and building a retaining wall topped by a concrete balustrade. In 1913, after Roy Miller was elected mayor, work began on the bluff beautification project. The bluff was terraced to prevent erosion and leveled in some places and raised in others, to create a uniform height. Retaining walls were built and highlighted with an elegant balustrade. Grand stairways led from the downtown to uptown.

The first section was completed in 1915. It eventually stretched from Mann Street to where Mesquite and North Broadway join. As the bluff was being terraced and the balustrade built, Daughters of the Confederacy hired sculptor Pompeo Coppini to design a Confederate memorial fountain. His fountain on the side of the bluff, above the terminus of Peoples and Schatzel streets, depicts Corpus Christi as a young woman flanked by Father Neptune and Mother Earth. Coppini's fountain was completed in 1915.

Alexander Potter's original plan called for a pedestrian tunnel to link downtown and uptown. The tunnel was built more than a decade after the bluff improvement project was completed. The tunnel entrance was behind City Hall between Schatzel and Peoples. It came out at the basement of the newly built Plaza Hotel. The tunnel eventually connected to the basements of the Plaza Hotel, the Nixon Building and the Driscoll Hotel. Several

21 and 22. A large crowd turned out in February 1929 (left) when the city's bluff tunnel was opened. The tunnel in 1975 (right) when the city debated whether to keep it open or close it. The city closed it in 1977.

shops opened adjacent to the tunnel exit below the Plaza Hotel, including a barber shop, a beauty shop, and a furrier. The decrease in pedestrian traffic using the tunnel began in the late 1950s. By the 1960s, trash and broken beer bottles littered the floor and the walls were splashed with urine and obscene graffiti. In 1977, the City Council ordered that steel gates be erected to close the tunnel. The main entrance between Schatzel and Peoples was sealed. The three exits on the bluff were closed.

Only a few businesses and homes were located on Lower Broadway in the 1930s and 1940s. They were on the east side of the street since the west side was the slope of the bluff. At the south end of the street, near the intersection with Lawrence, was the Gregory Apartment Building, run by Bonnie Jean Gregory, the widow of Dr. George W. Gregory. Across the Lawrence intersection was Southwestern Bell Building, which became Frank Sparks Insurance Company headquarters in 1938.

At the Starr intersection, on the south side, was the Federal Building and on the north side was the Eagle Loan Company. Karl Swafford's photo studio was in a two-story brick building at 718 Lower Broadway, between the Peoples and Taylor intersections. Swafford's studio was later used by photographer George Seitter.

Past the Taylor intersection was the David Peel Funeral Home. Past Peel's was the home of Mrs. Hester McLean, who owned a clothing store on Chaparral. In 1935, on the site of the McLean home, the Caller-Times built a new structure. The four-story building was designed by architect Nat Hardy. It fronted on Broadway and extended down the side of Twigg Street. Pete Pompa, a pressman, recalled when the move was made from Mesquite Street to Lower Broadway. They went to press with the Sunday edition on Saturday night

23. *The David Peel Funeral Home at Lower Broadway and Taylor on Sept. 10, 1931.*

24. *The Caller-Times' new building at Lower Broadway and Twigg in 1935.*

25. *The C.A. Craig home was a boarding house when it was demolished in 1956.*

and when the press run was finished, they began moving the equipment. They worked 40 hours without a break and by Monday morning the new press was ready to roll in the new building on Lower Broadway. "They gave us a $10 bonus," Pompa recalled.

Past Twigg were two homes — Julia Cooper's and the Craig place.

Julia Cooper's house, with a wide porch with columns, was built in 1907 on Upper Broadway. During the bluff balustrade work the house was moved down to Lower Broadway, north of the Twigg Street intersection. The property was purchased in 1956 for right of way to build the Harbor Bridge approaches. The Cooper home was moved for a second time, out to Brewster Street.

Next door was the 20-room C.A. Craig home, at 924 Lower Broadway. When it was built in 1906, the house had 12 rooms. Eight more were added later. The 1919 storm knocked down the palm trees in the yard but the house was undamaged.

Craig, a retired dentist, was also an agent for the San Antonio and Aransas Pass Railroad. Craig's Rooming House became a popular boarding establishment, known for its six-foot-long bath tub.

The Craig house was torn down in 1956 when the city moved to demolish or relocate the homes displaced by the Harbor Bridge project. Lower Broadway today ends with the intersection with Twigg. Beyond is the network of streets leading to Harbor Bridge and north of that is the 1914 courthouse.

26 and 27. As the balustrade was being built, Daughters of the Confederacy hired sculptor Pompeo Coppini of San Antonio to design a Confederate memorial fountain. His fountain on Lower Broadway depicts Corpus Christi as a beautiful young woman flanked by Father Neptune and Mother Earth. Pompeo Coppini's fountain was completed in 1915.

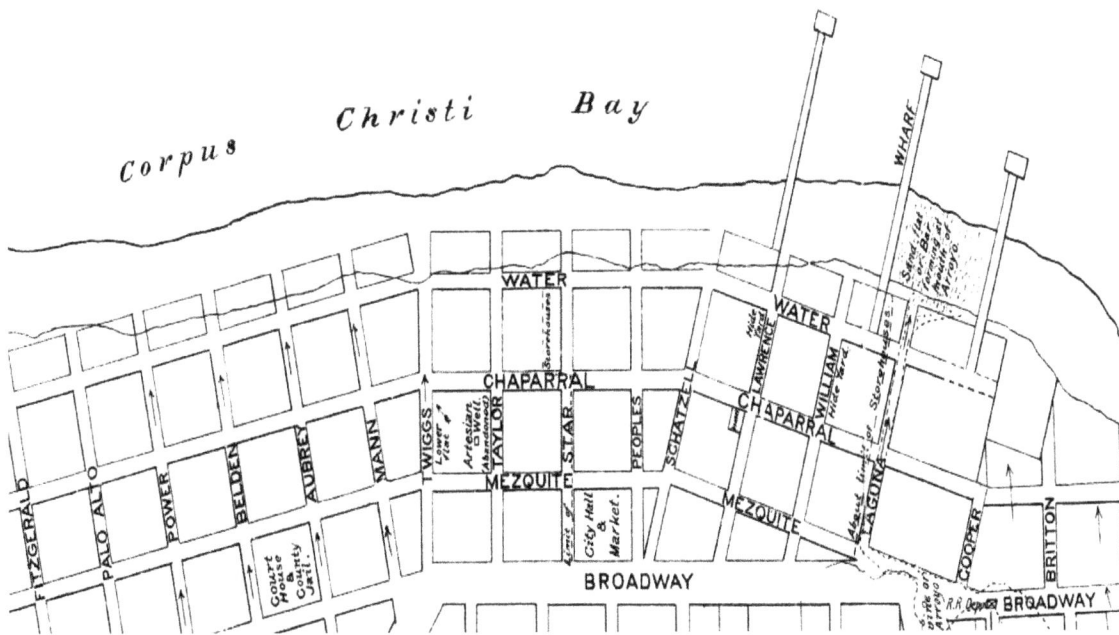

28 and 29. Above, detail from 1875 map shows the downtown's principal north-south streets, Water, Chaparral and Mesquite and its connecting east-west streets. Below, map shows north-south uptown streets Broadway, Carancahua, Tancahua, Carrizo (misspelled), Artesian, Waco, and Black and east-west streets Comanche, Lipan, Mestena, Leopard, Antelope, Buffalo and Winnebago. Section in the middle of the lower map described as an area occupied "almost exclusively by Mexicans living in jacals," which reflects the prejudicial realities of the time.

157

Chapter 6. South Broadway

From the arroyo south past the Tex-Mex Railroad and Mesquite Street intersection, on south to the intersection with Park Avenue and on down to Coleman.

South Broadway was a residential street where homes of the well-to-do were built in the 19th and early 20th Century. The stately structures featured Corinthian porticos, wide balconies, spacious lawns, and carriage steps by the street. These homes had a high, wide, and splendid view of the waterfront, which was closer in those pre-seawall days. The residents on Broadway could walk out on their columned porches and watch sailboats tacking across the bay.

The arroyo, which ran from where Blucher's Park is today down to the bay, was the dividing line between north and south addresses. Both North and South Broadway represented the city's most stylish residential street.

At 223 South Broadway was the home of Mr. and Mrs. G. R. Scott, across the street from the W. K. Shepperd home at 222. The Scott mansion was built in the 1880s. In 1908, Ella Scott held a reception in her home for William Jennings Bryan, on vacation in Corpus Christi after he lost the presidential race to William Howard Taft. Ella Scott told a reporter that she invited a few people but that some 30 or 40 uninvited guests showed up. A reporter for the Caller wrote that their house on South Broadway "was surrounded by the finest display of horses and buggies seen here in years."

Mrs. Scott's daughter Lucille married Walter E. Pope, a young lawyer in the Scott law firm, Pope was elected city attorney, state legislator and ran for governor. The Scott mansion, later known as the Pope-Scott home, was torn down in 1958.

William Rankin's home was at 313 South Broadway. Rankin, born in 1856 to parents who immigrated from Scotland, established a thriving grocery business. After his marriage in 1885 Rankin built a new home on South Broadway in 1894. Dan Reid, who built the home, looked at Rankin's building plan and complained, "There's enough lumber in it for two houses." It was copied from a house Rankin admired in New Orleans.

The buildings on South Broadway were mostly on the west side of the street. There were a few homes and a church in the 200 and 300 blocks built on the east side. Most prominent was the home of Edwin and Winifred Flato home at 316. The house was two stories in front and four stories in the back.

Edwin Flato was born in Flatonia, which was named for his grandfather. He moved to Corpus Christi in 1906 to work as a bookkeeper for Corpus Christi Hardware. Within a year he was named president of the company. After the 1919 storm the business was separated, with the retail operation on Chaparral renamed Nueces Hardware while the wholesale operation moved to South Broadway. In World War II the Flatos held dances and their home was often filled with officers from the Naval Air Station. Flato's gardens were famous for their flowers, including a variety of hibiscus registered as the Edwin Flato Hibiscus. Flato's wife died in 1958 and after his death, in 1971, the house was torn down.

1 and 2. The G. R. Scott home with the round turret (top) was at 223 South Broadway, built in the 1880s. The 11-room Pat Dunn home (bottom) was at 317, built in 1907.

The Patrick F. Dunn home, at 317, was on the west side of the street across from the Flato home. Dunn owned a cattle ranch on Padre Island for more than 50 years. He built the home in 1907 for $10,000. The Dunn family spent summers on the island and lived in town in the winters so the children could attend school.

The house in town was not the center of Pat Dunn's life. It was the island, where he began his unique cattle ranch in 1879. His cattle fed on sedge grass, waded in the surf and knelt to drink water from seep tanks dug in the sand. Dunn's ranch house and the corrals nearby were made of driftwood and his ranch hands became adept beachcombers. Dunn, in a joking way, called himself the Duke of Padre Island.

He grew up on a farm five miles from Corpus Christi on the way to Nuecestown. His father Thomas died when Pat was seven, during the Civil War.

In the drought year of 1879, when Pat was 21, he moved cattle to Padre Island where he had acquired grazing rights. He called the island the greatest cattle ranch in the world. In the next few years Dunn established what he called "El Rancho de Don Patricio."

Dunn built four stations with corrals and holding pens a day's ride apart down the length of the island. The number one station was called Owl's Mott, two was Novillo station, three was at Black Hill, and four was at Green Hill. During roundups Dunn's hands moved cattle up from the southern end of the island. They used traps and cutting chutes to reduce the need of roping, which Dunn thought cruel.

In 1884 Dunn married Clara Jones, a widow, and adopted her daughter. The Dunns moved down the island to the old Curry Settlement. They had a small house at the Settlement; some of the Curry family members still lived there. In 1890, Dunn moved the family to Corpus Christi and eventually built a spacious home on South Broadway. But Dunn spent his days on the island, except when he served in the Legislature and lived in Austin during legislative sessions.

In 1907 Dunn built a two-story house facing east on Packery Channel. The unpainted house was built of driftwood and furnished with door hinges from ship refrigerators, chairs from a wrecked steamer; a wooden cask with Japanese letters served as a washbasin, and whisky barrels were used to catch rainwater.

Dunn said the house was two-story because the lumber that washed up was too long and he didn't have a saw to cut it. Some of Dunn's tall tales may have been partly true. He said that one Christmas one of his hands picked up oranges and lemons that had washed up on the beach. Dunn sent him back to look for a coconut.

"He went down to the beach and came back a few minutes later with some coconuts," Dunn said. "We had some of the finest ambrosia you ever tasted." Dunn said that at another time they were craving sausage and, as if by order, they found a sausage grinder on the beach. They rounded up a wild pig and soon had pork sausage with sage.

After the 1916 hurricane destroyed the two-story ranch house on Packery Channel, Dunn built a one-story house a mile and a half away. He didn't live there long. In 1926, he sold the island to Albert Jones and Col. Sam Robertson, who planned to develop it into another Miami Beach.

Dunn moved into town and stayed at the Nueces Hotel. His daughter May, who married Jack Chilson, lived in the mansion on South Broadway.

Dunn soon came to regret selling the island and told a reporter, "If the Lord would give me back the island," he said, "and wash out a channel in Corpus Christi Pass 30 feet deep, and put devilfish and other monsters in it to keep out the tourists, I'd be satisfied." In another interview he said, "I want to find another island, one that no one can reach."

The self-proclaimed Duke of Padre Island died of a heart attack on March 25, 1937, in his room at the Nueces Hotel. He was 79. You wonder if, in death, that Pat Dunn found that private island that no one else could reach.

3. *The Joseph Hirsch home was built at 411 South Broadway in 1910. The house was moved to Carancahua in 1946 to make room for a YMCA expansion. It was razed in 1956.*

Nine years after Pat Dunn's death, the house on Broadway was sold in 1946 to Walter Foster, owner of the Princess Louise Hotel, and used to house his art and antique collection. The house was demolished in 1955.

Past the Dunn home was one of the city's oldest structures, the home of William Chapman, an Army quartermaster stationed at Corpus Christi after the Mexican War. Chapman was a business partner of Richard King, Mifflin Kenedy and Charles Stillman. He imported some of the first Merino sheep to Nueces County. Chapman purchased a four-acre lot from Henry Kinney for $900 and the Chapman home was built in the 1850s with lumber shipped from New York. Chapman died at Fort Sumter in 1859 but his son William and his widow Helen returned to Corpus Christi after the Civil War.

Andrew Anderson recalled a school operated in the Chapman house about 1869. "Mr. and Mrs. (J. B.) Carpenter ran a school for boys and girls, having at times as many as a hundred scholars. This was in the Chapman house. The rules of conduct were framed and hanging up inside the door. Mr. Carpenter did not whip or slap anybody; if a pupil would not obey the rules he had to go home."

In 1930 the Chapman house was moved to the back of the lot facing South Carancahua. There was major disruption in that area when the state in 1965-'67 built the Midtown Traffic Exchange, so-called, which extended Agnes and Laredo (State Highway 44) into the downtown. It cut across Tancahua, Carancahua and South Broadway. The Chapman house was sold for $825 and moved to the Westside. Others were knocked down.

162

4. Herman Cohn's Greek-Revival mansion was built in 1914 at 425 South Broadway. The house was destroyed by a fire set by an arsonist on June 8, 1976.

The home of Joseph and Sadie Hirsch was built in 1910 at 411 South Broadway. The house was moved to Carancahua in 1946 to make way for a YMCA expansion. It was demolished in 1956.

South of the Hirsch home was Herman Cohn's residence at 425. The Greek-Revival-style mansion was built in 1914 for Cohn, a partner in the Gugenheim & Cohn department store. The Cohn house was noted for unusual features. One was a system of vents that relied on natural drafts to keep the rooms cool. The house had one of the first hot water systems in the city and it had a vacuum-cleaning system in the basement with air tubes in the walls connecting to the rooms. The Cohn house was destroyed by a fire set by an arsonist in 1976.

The Perry Doddridge home was at 435, although the numbers were changed later and the address became 501, which it is today. The house was built for John Peter Schatzell in 1849 and originally known as Mansion House. Schatzell was a merchant in Matamoros who became friendly with Henry Kinney and chose to retire here. When Schatzell died in 1854, Samuel Fullerton, executor of the estate, acquired Mansion House, where he and wife Mary and daughter Rachel lived.

A young wool merchant named Perry Doddridge married Rachel Fullerton in Mansion House on June 12, 1862. Perry Doddridge worked as a clerk in Brownsville for the riverboat line owned by Richard King and Mifflin Kenedy. He moved to Corpus Christi and started a wool and hide business. He later opened a bank, in 1871, and was elected

5. *The W. W. Jones mansion at 511 South Broadway was sold to the city for use as a library.*

mayor in 1873. During those years the Doddridge home was one of the town's social centers. Every Thursday evening was open house where "old and young amuse themselves brilliantly and feast on the best fare," wrote Maria von Blucher. E. H. Caldwell said the Doddridge home "was a frequent gathering place for many of us young people. We attended dances, played games, conversed, and generally passed happy times."

The Doddridge Bank went under in 1893 and Doddridge spent his personal fortune repaying the depositors 60 cents on the dollar, which left him bankrupt. He died on June 11, 1902. Rachel Doddridge died the following year and left the property on South Broadway to the First Presbyterian Church. The old Mansion House was dismantled to make way for a new First Presbyterian Church, which was built on the site in 1929.

The stately colonial-style home of W. W. Jones was built in 1907 at 511 South Broadway. While it was being built, the Jones family rented the Doddridge-Fullerton home next door. William Whitby Jones was one of the richest cattlemen in South Texas. He was also a banker, real-estate broker and later owned the Nueces Hotel. W. W. Jones was born in Goliad in 1858. His father, A. C. Jones, was a prominent merchant in Beeville. About 1890 W. W. Jones bought much of the land that became Jim Hogg County and in 1905 he moved to Corpus Christi. He invested in building the Nueces Hotel, which opened in 1913, and later bought out the other investors. In 1937 the Jones' mansion was sold to the City of Corpus Christi for use as a public library. The city paid $26,000 for the property, although it was valued at $35,000. The library opened in its new quarters on Oct. 11, 1937.

6. *The Clark Pease home was built at 521 S. Broadway in 1905. It was torn down in 1962.*

La Retama occupied the Jones mansion until 1955 when it was moved to the old City Hall building on Mesquite. The Jones home was torn down in 1957 to make way for a parking lot for the First Presbyterian Church.

The Clark Pease home was built in 1905 at 521 South Broadway, the year after Pease came to Corpus Christi from Wisconsin. He established the Clark Pease bank which became the City National Bank. He was elected mayor and served from 1909 to 1913. The home was built with a carriage house which was converted into a garage for Pease's Maxwell. Pease died in 1929 and his wife in 1940. The house was sold to Herbert and Gertrude Guy, who moved from their home on Carrizo. The house was torn down in 1962.

The original home of Charles and Sarah Weil was on North Broadway north of Henrietta King's mansion. The Weils built a new home on South Broadway sometime after the turn of the 20th century. The area became the Weil neighborhood when the adult children of Charles and Sarah built or bought their homes nearby.

The site at 611 was purchased by Richard King Sr., a banker and grandson of the great King Ranch cattleman. After King's home on North Beach was destroyed in the 1919 hurricane, he moved his family into the King-Kleberg mansion on North Broadway before he built a new home on South Broadway. The two-story red-brick home, built in 1926, became the home of King and wife Minerva Pierpont Heaney King, daughter of Dr. Alfred G. Heaney. The Kings lived in their stately home on Broadway until Mrs. King died in 1966 and he died in 1974. The King home was converted into law offices in 1990.

7 and 8. The Carrie Weil Lichtenstein home (top) was built in 1913. The Giles-Farenthold home next door (bottom) was built by Dr. Clyde O. Watson. Both are still standing.

Next door to the King mansion was the one-story home of Julius Lichtenstein and wife Carrie (Weil) Lichtenstein, at 615 South Broadway. Julius was three years old when his father moved his department store from Indianola to Corpus Christi, in 1874. Julius married Carrie Weil in 1902 and in 1904, with the death of his father, he became the head of Lichtenstein's & Sons. In 1905 he built a house on North Chaparral and in 1913 he built a larger house at 615 South Broadway.

9. *The Carrie Weil Lichtenstein home (left) followed by the homes of Richard King Sr., Charles and Sarah Weil, Clark Pease, and W. W. Jones next to the First Presbyterian Church.*

Julius Lichtenstein died in 1923 and his widow Carrie in 1958. The house was sold to Howell and Hortense Warner Ward. After Mrs. Ward died in 1978 the house was sold and, at this writing, serves as offices for Durrill Properties.

On the corner with Park Avenue is the Giles-Farenthold home, built by Dr. Clyde O. Watson, though it is usually identified with Dr. H. R. Giles, who served as mayor, owned the Giles Hotel on Chaparral, and practiced medicine for 50 years. Dr. Giles died in 1948 and the home was sold to George and Frances Tarlton "Sissy" Farenthold, state legislator and candidate for governor. It became known as the Farenthold home and then gained the hyphenated name of Giles-Farenthold. It has been restored at 625 South Broadway.

South of Park Avenue, on the corner lot, was the Church of the Good Shepherd. It had been moved from its old location at Taylor and Chaparral in 1926. On its new site on South Broadway the old church building was enlarged and remodeled, given a new roof and brick front while the original nave and chancery were preserved. A new church was built in 1950.

Across from the church, on the east side of South Broadway, was a large building constructed by the church in 1938. It was the Corpus Christi Civic Center. It was privately operated, though the church owned it.

The Civic Center was an all-purpose community building where a variety of civic functions were held. Dances were held every Saturday night. During the war years the Civic Center became a popular center for servicemen, where canteens were open and dances were held three times a week. The Civic Center was remodeled and renamed Munds Hall in 1956.

South of the church was the home of former mayor Roy Miller and wife Maud Heaney Miller. Their first home at 1224 North Chaparral was destroyed in the 1919 storm. Miller purchased the house at 703 South Broadway.

Dale Miller recalled that his mother was always entertaining, especially young folks. "When I was young there was always a gathering on the lawn in the summertime. The bay

167

10. *The Church of the Good Shepherd in 1936. The original building at Chaparral and Taylor was moved to Broadway in 1926. A new church was built on the site in 1950.*

was only about 75 yards away. People would drop in and play games. She loved young people and she would always be the ringleader in the fun, dancing and gaiety."

Roy Miller came to Corpus Christi from Houston to work as a railroad publicity agent in 1907. He married Maud Heaney, daughter of Dr. Alfred G. Heaney, became editor of the Corpus Christi Caller and was elected mayor in 1913. After three terms as mayor, Miller led the campaign for a deepwater port and worked in Washington as a lobbyist. He died on April 28, 1946 when he was 62. Maud Heaney Miller died in 1965.

Two Caldwell brothers built their homes at the south end of Broadway, the first homes built south of the Doddridge-Fullerton place. At 711 South Broadway was the home of William Herbert Caldwell, son of a Presbyterian minister and brother of E. H. Caldwell. W. H. Caldwell built his house on South Broadway in 1884. Originally it had five rooms but he added a second story in 1906 and planted palm trees in the yard. He surrounded the house with flowers which were given to the neighbors and then he opened the city's first floral shop from a stable next to the house. All the flowers sold by Caldwell were grown in his yard.

After Caldwell died his daughter Julia operated the floral shop into the 1950s. A year after Julia Caldwell died, in 1970, at the age of 87, the old Caldwell home was dismantled for scrap lumber.

The next house south at 715 was the home of Edward Harvey Caldwell. He was 21 when he came to Corpus Christi from Tennessee. He came to join his father, pastor of the First Presbyterian Church, and his eight brothers and sister. He arrived on the mail boat on March 24, 1872. It was Sunday so he went to church where he played the organ and taught Sunday school.

11. The E. H. Caldwell home at 715 South Broadway was demolished in 1964.

Caldwell studied law in the McCampbell law office but that didn't suit him. He got a job as a bookkeeper for wool merchant and banker Perry Doddridge.

In his memoirs, Caldwell said that one day a yellow dog spooked his horse and Caldwell took out his pistol and shot the dog dead. A district court judge fined him $50 for carrying a concealed weapon. "I thanked the jury and added the observation that I had no doubt that more than half of them at that very moment were carrying concealed weapons."

In 1875, Edward Harvey Caldwell and his brother William leased the Borjas Ranch west of San Diego and bought 1,200 sheep.

On Caldwell's first night at the ranch he and a herder were in camp. By firelight they saw men ride up on horseback. One man who was presumed to be the leader asked to be shown where to water their horses. Caldwell refused. He believed they were bandits. After the men left to water their horses, the leader returned and Caldwell kept his rifle pointed at his heart. He again demanded that Caldwell lead the way to water but Caldwell could hear their horses splashing in the water tank.

"I told him they knew very well where the water was," Caldwell said. "He insisted I show him. I said I wouldn't. He asked why. I replied 'porque' (because)." Caldwell kept his gun pointed at the man's heart until they departed. As Caldwell suspected, he discovered next day that the men were bandits. They had raided Nuecestown and burned Thomas Noakes' store the day before. This was the famous Nuecestown Raid.

Caldwell's ranch house, built of caliche rock with loopholes for defense, became headquarters of other sheep men in the area. Caldwell was elected to the county commission of the newly formed Duval County. The Borjas Ranch became a mail stop and Caldwell was named postmaster, with a salary of $12 a year. In 1880, he married Ada Lasater, the sister of Ed Lasater, later the famous rancher at Falfurrias. Caldwell met her during a game of croquet at her parents' ranch in Atascosa County. She was home from school in Ohio.

12. *Edward H. Caldwell owned a sheep ranch near San Diego and a hardware store in Corpus Christi.*

Caldwell decided to get out of the sheep business. A parasite was killing the sheep flocks and the price of wool plummeted after the tariff on Australian wool was lifted. Caldwell and two men drove 5,000 sheep to San Angelo and then on to Abilene where he sold them at a heavy loss.

In 1884, Caldwell returned to Corpus Christi, invested in the J. B. Mitchell hardware company, and built a home at 715 South Broadway. E. H. bought part of the R. W. Rayne tract, an area then known as the South Side. Caldwell's lots extended from the water's edge up to Staples Street. He said in his memoirs it was a perfect place to build a home. Caldwell said the family stayed in Mrs. Merriman's boarding house while their house was being built. They moved in in March 1884.

In 1895 he started his own hardware firm, the Caldwell Farm and Ranch store. Caldwell's hardware store was a prosperous concern until it was wrecked in the storm of 1919. On the morning after the storm, the store was in ruins. Caldwell kept the business going long enough to pay off his creditors.

Edward Harvey Caldwell, sheep rancher, hardware merchant, civic leader, longtime elder of the First Presbyterian Church, died at his home on South Broadway on March 14, 1940. He was 89.

After E. H. Caldwell died, his daughter Sarah operated a tea room and antique shop in the old home before it was torn down to build the Cliff House in 1964.

The E. A. Born house was built on the corner of Coleman at 723 South Broadway in the mid-1890s. It was said to have been the first house in town equipped for electric lights. The Born house was converted into apartments in 1941 then razed in 1965 to make way for a parking lot for Cliff House apartments.

One of the oldest houses in the city was built in 1851 at 801 South Broadway. This was the Walter Merriman house. Merriman, a lawyer, was married to Henry Kinney's sister. Anna Moore Schwien said Walter and his wife lost their children in a yellow fever epidemic in 1854. Afterwards, the Merrimans moved to Indianola.

The three-gabled clapboard house was purchased by Banquete cattleman John Rabb in 1859 as a town home for his family. It was used as a hospital during the Civil War by Dr. E. T. Merriman (not related to Walter Merriman). After the war, the home was occupied by Martha Rabb's daughter Lulu, who married Wade Hampton. It was called the Hampton Place. In the 1930s the house was purchased by a retired physician, Dr. Ernest Bobys, and it became known as the Merriman-Bobys house; it was later moved to Heritage Park.

Except for a few survivors like the Giles-Farenthold and Merriman-Bobys houses, the old Broadway homes, built in times long past, were demolished, seen as they were as the enemy of progress.

Chapter 7. Leopard Street

From the intersection with North Broadway to the city limits, crossing Carancahua, Tancahua, Carrizo, Artesian, Waco, Staples, Last (later Alameda) and other streets out to the city limits and Highway 9.

Henry Kinney told Ethan Allen Hitchcock, one of Zachary Taylor senior officers, that when he arrived at Corpus Christi in the fall of 1839 he shot at a spotted tiger on the hill above the beach. It may have been a cougar, which people once called leopards or panthers, but that incident likely gave Leopard Street its name.

Leopard was one of Corpus Christi's first streets, named by Kinney, and shown on his 1852 grid of streets. All the area around Leopard Street was referred to as the Hill and it became a euphemism for the town's Hispanic population which dominated the western area of the high bluff.

In 1875, following the Nuecestown Raid, a wounded bandit who had been shot at Thomas Noakes' store was brought into town on an oxcart. They came down Leopard Street looking for a place high enough off the ground to hang him. They began to loop a rope over the steeple of the old St. Patrick's Church on Tancahua.

Cattleman Martin Culver, who was in town on business, stopped them, telling them they should be ashamed of themselves for attempting to defile and desecrate God's premises. The mob went on down Leopard Street to a gate with a cross pole. There the bandit was hanged, and left hanging until the next morning when priests from St. Patrick's came to take it down. It was on Easter Sunday.

Leopard was one of the city's heaviest traveled streets. Kate Smith (later Mrs. Adolph Anderson) recalled walking up the hill to Leopard Street to go to school at the convent. "There were so many ox-carts I couldn't even cross the street until all the wagons and teams passed. They came from King Ranch and from up country."

A former slave named Hattie Littles recalled that Leopard, when she was young, was a white shell road used by farmers and ranchers coming to town. Much of Leopard was either dirt or shell until 1930 when the city paved it out to Palm Drive.

Mrs. Angie Westbrook once recalled when her family first came to Corpus Christi in 1900. They came in on Leopard Street by wagon and when they reached the slope going down the bluff, "We had to lock all four wheels of the wagon and then we could hardly hold the horses it was so steep."

The 600 block of Leopard runs from North Broadway to Carancahua.

Old city directories reveal that the first block of Leopard was lined with family homes. In the 1913-14 directory, five residences are shown on the south side of the 600 block. Among those, at 621, was the home of H. G. Sherman, a realtor who was one of the major investors in the Nueces Hotel and the builder of the Sherman Building across the street. Three homes were listed on the north side of Leopard in the 600 block.

1. The 12-story Nixon Building on the left and the 14-story Plaza Hotel on the right were two tall citadels that framed the eastern end of the street at North Broadway.

2. *The 12-story Nixon Building on the left and 14-story Plaza Hotel marked the entrance to Leopard Street. Construction was underway on the Robert Driscoll Hotel, just visible on the far right, which opened in 1942.*

Then Corpus Christi began to grow after the port was opened for business and Leopard Street began to change. Old homes were knocked down or moved and trees uprooted as new buildings were erected. The residential character of that block changed beginning in 1927 and what had been an old street became a new one.

Maston Nixon, a former Robstown cotton farmer, bought the old Meuly site at the corner of Leopard and Broadway. There were two buildings on the site known as the Daimwood cottages and an empty lot where youngsters went to fly kites. On this site Nixon built the city's largest office building, the 12-story Nixon Building.

The Nixon venture set off a building boom for the east end of Leopard. Robert Driscoll built the Corpus Christi Bank & Trust at Leopard and Tancahua and Perkins Brothers built its store at Leopard and Carancahua. The Plaza Hotel was built in 1929 across from the Nixon Building.

Corpus Christi's first radio station, KGFI, broadcast from the Plaza Hotel. It did not have a transmitting tower but used wires strung across Leopard from the Plaza to the Nixon Building. When the city scored some commercial triumph, a green flag was flown from between the Nixon and Plaza. This was a focal point of town, between the city's two tall buildings on the bluff.

By 1930, the first block of Leopard, the 600 block, included the two bookend buildings, the Nixon Building and the Plaza Hotel. "Leopard always had a unique character," said William Radeker ("Corpus Christi Recollections"). David Bickford's Drug Stores, No. 1 and No. 2, were on the south side of the street at the corner of Upper Broadway (at 601) and at the Carancahua intersection (at 625). The Nixon Café was behind Bickford No. 1

175

3. *The Nixon Café was run by John Nicols and the Govatos brothers, John and Clem. It was established in the Nixon building in 1927.*

and Boyd Morrow's New England Cafeteria was behind Bickford No. 2.

The Nixon Café in the Nixon Building was established in April 1927. The café, first called the Nixon Coffee Shop, was started by John Nicols who was joined in the business by a cousin Clem Govatos. John Govatos, who owned the Pier Café, joined Nicols and Clem Govatos in 1940. The name was changed to the Nixon Café.

The Nixon Café stayed open all night, except during the World War II years. Morris Lichtenstein said he liked to go to the Nixon Café after dancing to get the K.C. Sizzling Sirloin, for which it was famous. Many others, he said, preferred the café's steak-and-egg combo called Weaver's Special.

Listed on the 1938 menu under "Steaks and Chops" were Clem's Special Beef Tenderloin, 70 Cents, Small Sirloin Steak, 95 cents, Lamb Chop (2), 50 cents, Pork Chops (2), 50 cents, Veal Chops (2), 50 cents, Brookfield Sausage, 35 cents, Boiled Ham or Bacon, 35 cents, Calf Liver with Bacon, 40 cents.

The 700 block of Leopard runs from Carancahua to Tancahua.

In the 19th Century, on the south side of the 700 block of Leopard, was the home of Mr. and Mrs. Charles Schallert. Their daughter Annie married Ernest Bagnall, a carpenter who

4. *The Perkins Brothers Department Store at the corner of Carancahua and Leopard on Nov. 22, 1940. It was sold in 1955 to become Lichtenstein's Uptown Store. It closed in 1968.*

became one of the city's first undertakers. This home was later sold to James Field and then J. W. Marshall.

It was on this site that Perkins Brothers Department Store was built. It opened in October 1929 about the time the stock market crashed. The newspaper reported that the Perkins store was erected at a cost of $150,000 and represented "one of the most modern buildings in the city." The building was designed by Fort Worth architect Wyatt Hedrick. A noted feature of the structure was its terrazzo floors.

The store in Corpus Christi was part of a chain established in North Texas by Sam B. Perkins. The local store was managed by his son, Willard Perkins, who married Mabel West, the daughter of South Texas cattle rancher George West.

Perkins Brothers' Corpus Christi store was sold to Lichtenstein's in 1955. Janice Edison, who lives in San Miguel de Allende, Mexico, wrote a letter to the author about that sale.

"My father was Nathan Friedman," she wrote, "the last president of Lichtenstein's. I remember the night he came home and told my mother that they had just bought the old Perkins store on the bluff. Mom said she always thought it was such a pretty building. We got in the car and drove up the bluff to see it that night. Dad went into the store and started flipping on light switches and going through the stockrooms. He would pull stuff out for us to see, laughing, amazed to find very old merchandise still in the stockrooms. He found a treasure trove of old shoes, still in their boxes, in the Perkins' stockroom. Some of the merchandise was more than 50 years old. Too bad we did not have hindsight to save it and preserve it as a department store museum."

Lichtenstein's closed its uptown operation, the old Perkins Brothers store, in 1968 and the building was torn down to make way for a bank parking garage.

5. *The end of the 700 block, at the Tancahua intersection, in the 1930s. On the left was the Mountjoy Auto Parts and Machine Shop, with the Corpus Christi Bank & Trust across the street. On the opposite corner was Thomas McGee's Eagle Pharmacy.*

Past Perkins in the 1930s was Slim's Coffee Shop, run by Rollie Easterling, followed by Cecil Hampsten's Paint and Body Shop and Mountjoy Auto Parts at the end of the block. Across the street was the Incarnate Word Academy, although its address was 701 North Carancahua. The academy took up most of that block except for St. Patrick's Cathedral. The academy included a three-story building, facing Carancahua, a playground, and two wooden frame buildings that were part of the original convent built in the 1880s.

When the circus came to town, William Radeker recalled, it paraded down Leopard Street and passed the Incarnate Word Academy on its way out to the carnival grounds on Port Avenue. "For students that was a special day because they were allowed to leave classes and go outside and watch the parade."

The 800 block runs from Tancahua to Carrizo. On the south side of the street at the corner was the Corpus Christi Bank & Trust. It was built on the site of the Michael Thomas Gaffney home, which was moved to Buffalo Street. Rancher Robert Driscoll Jr. started the banking firm in 1928 and became its first president. It was first located in a rented building on Schatzel but moved into a new building on Leopard at Tancahua.

What became known as the Hill Bank was established to handle wills, trusts, and real estate but it was ready to open as a full-fledged bank when Robert Driscoll Jr. died in 1929. His sister Clara, famous as the savior of the Alamo, became the bank's president. She managed the Driscoll estate from an office in the building. She died in 1945.

Nearby, in the 1930s, was the Little Mexican Inn, at 811 Leopard, run by Mrs. Reyes Ibarra. The business was later moved to Buffalo, at the Carrizo intersection. At the end of the 800 block, at 825 Leopard, was Rose Baggett's Rose Café. This was later occupied by Slim's Coffee Shop, which was moved from the 700 block.

178

6. *The Corpus Christi Bank & Trust at 801 Leopard, at the Tancahua intersection. Clara Driscoll had an office in this building. The bank was founded by her brother Robert.*

7. *The Little Mexican Inn at 811 Leopard, past the Corpus Christi Bank & Trust, was operated by Mrs. Reyes Ibarra.*

8. On Saturdays on Leopard the entire street seemed to be in movement. It was the most picturesque street in the city, and the most often photographed by "Doc" McGregor. The two tall buildings on the left were Braslau's Furniture and Braslau's Dry Goods.

Across the street from the Corpus Christi Bank & Trust was Thomas McGee's Eagle Pharmacy, at 800. It was followed by Corpus Christi Shoe Hospital, run by Harry Applebaum, and Abraham Wolfson's Furniture Store, at 814 Leopard. Wolfson, from San Antonio, moved to Corpus Christi in 1927 and entered the furniture business. In 1934, he founded Wolfson Furniture on Leopard, where he was joined by his sons Sylvan and Maury. At the end of the 800 block was Piggy Wiggly No. 3, which later became an HEB store.

The 900 block of Leopard runs from Carrizo to Artesian. In the early part of the century, Conrad Uehlinger ran a beer garden on the corner. After that was the Urbano G. Meza blacksmith shop; he later moved to the 2200 block of Leopard, past Leary, and opened an auto repair shop with his sons. Past Meza's blacksmith shop was Harry Holbein's photo studio, Dr. W. E. Wills' office, and Dr. H. H. Segrest's office.

Segrest, a dentist, was the manager of the Corpus Christi Kids baseball team in the 1890s. He and his son, Dr. David Segrest, practiced dentistry in town for 50 years. Across the street was Jacob Reuthinger's home and grocery store and Sexto Gutierrez's barbershop.

By the 1930s, Uehlinger had moved to the middle of the block, at 910, where he operated a café and confectionery. Uehlinger's was known for its hamburgers, made from fresh beef supplied by the Taft Ranch.

In that same block, on the north side of the street, was Eber Bessett's Spark Plug Chili Parlor, followed Joe Simon's Grocery, J. L. Welch's Bluff Drug Store, with a cigar factory above it, Braslau's Furniture and Braslau's dry goods. Braslau's first furniture store at 918 Leopard was on the site of Meza's blacksmith shop. Sam Braslau was born in a village near Kiev, Russia in 1895. When he was 17 his family pooled their resources and gave him 100 rubles, about $50, to pay his passage to Galveston. He chose Galveston because it had a Russian immigrant aid society at the time. That was in 1912.

9. In 1950, past the Artesian intersection, at 904 Leopard was the Spark Plug Chili Parlor. At the end of the 800 block was an HEB food store; it had been Piggly Wiggly No. 3.

Braslau moved to San Antonio and worked in a furniture store for $6 a week and attended night school to learn English. He came to Corpus Christi in 1914 to work for the Sugarman brothers who owned a furniture store on Leopard. He was a salesman for the firm, operating from a peddler's wagon, selling furniture, wood stoves, and blankets.

After he served in the army in World War I, he owned a grocery business in Newport News, Va., but returned to Corpus Christi in 1926 and with his brothers Frank and Morris established Braslau Furniture Company. The store was located in the same 900 block where the Sugarman brothers had their first store. The three Braslau brothers operated the store until 1943 when Sam left to establish a real estate business. The firm continued under the management of Morris and Frank Braslau.

The Braslau brothers sold their dry goods store in 1942 and concentrated on their furniture business, which they moved one block west. David Stein's Dry Goods moved into the old Braslau furniture store and the Blanck Brothers Dry Goods, run by Jacob Blanck, moved into the old Braslau dry goods store.

On the south side of the 900 block, in the 1930s, were Harry Knowles Repair Shop and home, at 911, followed by Claude Ferrell's pool room. Sykes Furniture, operated by Plumel Sykes and his son, was at 917. San Jacinto Hardware was at 921-923. The San Jacinto Hardware site had once been a grocery store owned by the Reuthinger brothers.

The 1000 block runs between Artesian and Waco. In this block was Edward and Simon Grossman's department store on the corner, at 1002. The Grossman brothers, like the Braslaus, were natives of Russia who emigrated to the United States in the early part of the 20th Century. Eleven Grossmans came to the U.S. and eight settled in Corpus Christi.

"I came to America to be a free man," Edward Grossman once said. "My father was prominent in the grain business in Russia. I had $10 in gold when I landed in this country. Business was in a critical condition. I walked the streets several months looking for work. My first job was in a shoe factory in Derry, N. H. I made $3 a week. I became ill while

10. *The Ben Grande Saloon building shortly before it was torn down in 1950.*

working in the shoe factory and was advised to move to a warmer climate. I went to Galveston and from there came to Corpus Christi. I heard it was a growing city."

Edward Grossman operated a clothing store on Chaparral Street in 1916. After it was destroyed in the 1919 storm, he and his brother Simon founded Grossman Brothers Department Store at 1002 Leopard. The Grossmans sold out in 1948 and moved out to Port Avenue. Next door was Sam Salem's Grocery, where sugar and lard and other staples came in barrels and coffee was ground in the store.

Past Salem's Grocery, at 1016, was Henry Stevens' hides and furs. The Melba Theater was built on this site. When the Melba opened in 1927 it was initially called the Leopard Street Theater and the foyer featured a tile mosaic of a crouching leopard. The Melba was followed by the Success Café, run by George Tahinakos. The Nueces Drug Store (later, in the 1940s, the Economical Drug Store) was on the Waco corner at 1024. This was on the site of the old Cavazos' Saloon. Across the street in the 1000 block, early in the century, were homes, with one barbershop and the Grande Saloon on the corner.

In 1909, Sam Dunnam moved his bottling plant from Water Street (where the Nueces Hotel laundry building was later constructed) to the corner of Artesian and Leopard, at 1003. Dunnam moved to Corpus Christi from Corsicana in 1904 and bottled and sold fruit juices. He used steam power because the city had no electricity at the time. He obtained the Coca-Cola franchise in 1908 and moved his operation to Leopard. He moved again, out to Lester, in 1929.

The Sugarman brothers had a furniture store on this site. Sam Braslau, who worked for the Sugarman firm as a salesman, built his own new store on this site. At the other end of the block was the Grande building.

11. *On the corner of Leopard and Waco, in the 1000 block, was the Nueces Drug Store, just past the Melba Theater and across the street was the Grande Theater.*

Francisco Grande's saloon was on the corner with Waco, a landmark on the street dating back to the 1880s. The roof line and overall shape of the building was almost identical to that of the St. James Hotel on Chaparral. Hattie Littles said people would give directions by saying "that's out by Pancho Grande's."

The city's greatest saloon was the Grande. The family lived upstairs, over the saloon. In time, there was a whole Grande complex — the Grande Hotel, the Grande Restaurant, the Grande Pool Hall. The Grande Saloon had cockfights and it was said that a man could ride up on his horse and a drink would be brought out to him. Francisco, sometimes called Frank, died in 1905 and his son Ben took over. The saloon became known as the "Ben Grande".

Theodore Fuller, when he was a boy, was wandering around while his father conducted some business. He heard music coming from the door of a big two-story building. It was the Grande Saloon. "Some men came out laughing and talking in a jovial mood," Fuller wrote. "A female voice from the inside called goodbye a couple of times. I peeked in and saw the long shiny bar. The smell of whisky and beer was strong. A man at the bar turned, saw me, and yelled a good-natured hello. I scampered back toward Papa and his friends. It was my first sight of the famous or infamous Ben Grande."

After Nueces County voted "dry" on March 10, 1916, the Grande building housed a grocery store, hotel, and other businesses. The building was torn down in 1950.

In the 1930s, two of the most prominent structures in the 1000 block of Leopard were the Grande Theater, at 1015, and the Melba Theater, facing each other from across the street. The Melba showed second-run features and westerns, mostly westerns. The Grande showed movies from Mexico on weekday evenings. On Saturdays at the Melba and the Grande, admission prices were a nickel for the balcony and 10 cents for the main seats

*12. Braslau's Furniture anchored the Artesian Street end of the Grande block, at 1001.
Across the street was the Grossman Brothers' Department Store and the Melba Theater. Out
of the frame on the right was the Grande Theater.*

downstairs. There was no segregated seating at the Melba or the Grande, as there was at the downtown theaters like the Palace and the Ritz. After Southern Alkali located in Corpus Christi in 1934, the company each year held a Christmas party for its employees. The party for the Anglos was held at the Ritz downtown while the party for blacks and Hispanics was held at the Grande Theater.

The 1100 block runs between Waco and North Staples.

The old Blaine store was on the corner of Staples, which was known as the Blaine corner. The store was 1123 Leopard; the Blaine family lived upstairs. The store was later converted to Brennan's Bakery. Ernest Page, who moved to Corpus Christi in 1890 with his carpenter father, recalled one day, as a boy, when he was skipping toward a butcher shop on Leopard and heard gunshots. He saw a man grab his stomach, fall to the ground and die. This occurred at the Johnny Blaine corner.

In the 1930s, on the south side of the 1100 block of Leopard, there was the Alamo Service Station, at 1101, which was later Jacob Nieman's Dry Goods store. Next door was Charles Joseph's watch repair shop and Manuel Cortez's photography studio. At 1107 was the Leopard Street Bargain House run by Abraham Golff and next door was the office of Dr. J. M. de la Garza. Frances Nelson's Café was 1121, followed by a barber shop, and on the corner, at 1129, was the drug of Juan Galvan Jr., on the site where George Zamary's grocery store once stood.

13 and 14. *The Grande Theater (above) was known for showing movies made in Mexico.*
Young women dressed in Western outfits (below) pose in front of the Melba Theater on March
14, 1941. The Melba Theater was across the street from the Grande.

15 and 16. The Melba Theater in the late 1930s.

17. The 1100 block of Leopard, on the south side of the streets, shows the Ben Grande Saloon at the end of the 1000 block, at Waco. On the right was the Galvan Drug Store on the former site of George Zamary's Grocery Store.

On the Waco corner on the north side of Leopard, in the early 1930s, there was the Shapu & Frelich Department Store at 1102, a large store owned by Isi Shapu and Isadore Frelich. It opened in 1930 and closed after a few years. It was built on the site of the old Davis-Orcutt Mercantile Company, which was there shortly after the turn of the century. The Shapu-Frelich building later housed Morris Five Cents to One Dollar Store. There were three other Morris stores on Agnes, Alameda, and Water. Still later, this was the site of Woolworth's Five & Dime. It was followed by the Texas Café at 1106, which was later Bill's Liquor Store. Sam Ferris's grocery store was at 1108 and the Eagle Store, a dry goods business run by Israel Goltzman, was at 1110. The Fenix Café at 1114 later became Adele Allen's Grocery and still later the Leopard Street Bar, with billiards upstairs. Next door was Mercedes Grocery followed by the Lamar Café at 1120. On the corner was Henry Grossman's Department Store. His brothers, Edward and Simon, ran the larger store in the 1000 block. The Grossman store later became Joseph's Economy Store, a pawn shop.

The 1200 block of Leopard runs from North Staples to Last, changed to Alameda.

Early in the 20th Century there were a few houses in the 1200 block, most of them on the south side of the street, and no businesses at all. That changed by the 1930s, after the port was opened, as the town was growing and Leopard Street was growing with it.

In the 1930s on the north side of the 1200 block there was a service station at the Staples intersection followed by Victor Moses' grocery store. He later moved to the other end of the block and Star Tire moved to that site. The Fair, a dry goods store run by R. D. and Frank Rossi, was at 1210, which was later moved to the 1100 block and Fletcher Furniture moved into the building. The Flores Café, run by Plar Flores, was next door, at 1212. Louis Maldonado operated the San Antonio Barber and Beauty Salon at 1214. It was followed by La Amistad Bakery at 1218, the Modern Department Store at 1220, and the South Texas Candy Company at 1222.

18. *The 1300 block of Leopard. On the right was Sears (where City Hall stands today) past the Cudd Supermarket. Across the street was Chat 'N Chew Restaurant and Bunk's Café.*

On the south side of the 1200 block was Frank Amin's Fruit and Vegetable Market, which later was converted to Oregon Holman's Café. Romulo Lopez's barber shop was at 1203 and the Herro Brothers Second Hand Store, run by Mrs. Mamie Herro, was at 1205. There was a shoe and harness repair business at 1207; the NuPort Coffee House later moved into this building. Next door was Jay and Frieda Ransom's café at 1209, which was later Van Dohlen's Candy Company. James Riggle's Photography was at 1213 and Ray Dye's Five Cent Eats was next door, at 1215.

The 1300 block of Leopard ran from Last (Alameda) to Sam Rankin.

On the south side of the 1300 block was Cudd's Supermarket followed by Sears Department Store, where City Hall is today. On the northeast corner, at 1302, was Mike Dunn's Grocery in the early part of the century. After Dunn, it went through a succession of occupants: Leo Gunderland, who later moved to Water Street, then Thomas Whelan, who moved from his store down the block at 1320. It was later a Goodyear tire store.

In the 1930s, on the north side of the 1300 block, past Mike Dunn's, was the Chat 'N Chew, which opened in 1935. The owners, Maudie and O. V. Jackson, got the name from a café they ate at in Alhambra, Calif. When it first opened, the Chat 'N Chew was a diner with 10 stools. "I paid a man $75 for the place," said O. V. Jackson in 1984. When we started out, it was just me, my wife, and the dishwasher. I did the cooking, Maudie washed and cooked. We did whatever needed to be done. We catered to oilfield workers and their families. A T-bone steak cost 35 cents, a hamburger 15 cents, a bowl of chili was 10 cents, and we paid the dishwasher $7 a week."

Past Chat 'N Chew was Bunk's Café owned by B. J. (Bunk) Spence. When it opened in 1937 it was first called the Quality Sandwich Shop but it became known Bunk's Café. A former customer, Adam Ronan, wrote, "My grandfather would take the whole clan out to

19. *O. V. Jackson's Chat 'N Chew Café at 1312 Leopard on Oct. 25, 1938.*

Bunk's on payday. Bunk's place had the best chicken-fried steak anywhere."

The 1400 block runs from Sam Rankin to Josephine. In the early part of the century only one home was located on this block of Leopard and no business firms. In the mid-1930s there were two fruit stores on opposite sides of the street, Hatoum Hamauei's Waco Fruit Store at 1403 and Sied Karam's Sunkist Fruit Store at 1404. The Olegario Fernandez Meat Market was at 1412 and next door was Juan Gonzalez's Funeral Home. The Mirabal Printing Office was nearby on Sam Rankin.

The 1500 block runs from Josephine to Mexico. In the early part of the 20th century, only one residence was on that block, the home of H. E. Linney. By the 1930s there were several homes, a Humble station on the northeast corner, and John Bassous' Garden Food Market in the middle of the block. There was nothing on the south side of the street.

In the remaining nine blocks going west, from the intersection with Mexico to Peabody, there were several residences but the street was dominated by service stations, garages and auto parts stores. In the 1700 block was Jesus Chavez' Grocery Store. In the 1900 block there was S. R. Dunn's Veterinary Clinic and fire station number two. (The other three, in the late 1930s and 1940s, included the main fire station at City Hall on Schatzel, one at Morgan and 11th, and one on North Beach on Bessie.)

In the 2000 block between Doss and Lester was the English Barbecue Stand and Walter Vetters' Restaurant. In the 2100 block was Cage Implement, Modern Food Store, and Chaz's Place, a café run by C. F. Bates; it was later Lois & Jack's Café then C. D. Staves' Coffee Shop. In the 2200 block was Urbano Meza's auto shop. In the 2500 block was Griggs' Pig Stand. A vacant lot at the southwest corner of Leopard and Port was where carnivals and circuses set up. This later became Spudder Park, named for a baseball team called the Spudders. William Radeker said if you drove north on Port past Leopard, "it was not uncommon to be delayed by tractors pulling as many as 20 trailers, each containing a 500-pound bale of cotton being hauled from the gin at Port and Agnes to the docks."

20 and 21. Bunk Spence's café (above) was down the street from Chat 'N Chew and across from Sears. A horse-drawn wagon was double-parked in the 1300 block of Leopard, west of Thomas Whelan's Grocery.

22. The Nueces Coffee Company, shown on Feb. 9, 1935, was off Leopard at 707 Lester.

23. Oil Company Row on North Port shows the 700 block past the Comanche Street intersection, in August 1936. Corpus Christi at that time listed 45 oil-field supply firms in the vicinity of Leopard and Port. At the beginning of 1937, 30 new oil fields were brought into production in the South Texas area adjacent to Corpus Christi.

24. Corpus Christi High School (center right) in 1932 between Leopard and UpRiver Road. At the bottom right is Holy Cross Cemetery at 3015 UpRiver. Palmer Street by the school did not connect Leopard and UpRiver then; it was later extended and renamed Fisher Street and then Battlin' Buc Boulevard. Not visible in the photo is Rose Hill Cemetery at the end of Comanche adjacent to Holy Cross.

The Nueces Coffee Company on Lester Street, off Leopard, was founded by the Yarborough brothers, W. O., J. L., and D. B., who had learned the coffee business as salesmen with the San Antonio Coffee Company. When the Port of Corpus Christi was opened in 1926, the three brothers pooled their assets of $40,000 and started the Yarborough Coffee Company in Corpus Christi. The name was soon changed to the Nueces Coffee Company. Their company became a major importer of green coffee beans. The Nueces Coffee Company dominated the coffee trade in the Coastal Bend region of South Texas for the next three decades.

City limits in the 1930s extended to Palm Drive by Holy Cross and Rose Hill cemeteries. People driving to Robstown turned left at Palm Drive, skirted Holy Cross and took Shell Road to the Old Robstown Road. Then, at the end of Leopard was the countryside. Now, it's just more suburbs and Leopard goes all the way to Calallen.

25. Corpus Christi High School and the original football stadium behind it on Oct. 26, 1937. Corpus Christi High School was built in 1929 to replace the old Brick Palace on Carancahua, which was converted into a junior high school. What was usually called the senior high school near the end of Leopard was named for Roy Miller in 1950.

26. *Nine graduates in the 1950 class show their legs in a class photo. The girls included (left to right) Wanda Hull, Frances Zoch, Sharie Willingham, Barbara Airheart, Becky Scott, Janet Howard, Juana Lee Kuenstler, Virginia Warren, and Nancy Cairns. They were members of the last graduating class of Corpus Christi High School. The name was changed to Roy Miller High School in 1950.*

At the edge of town, off Leopard Street, Corpus Christi High School was built in 1929 at 515 Palmer Street, which connected Leopard and Shell Road. Palmer was later changed to Fisher and still later to Battlin' Buc Boulevard. The new high school in 1929 replaced the old Brick Palace on Carancahua. What was usually called the senior high school was named for Roy Miller in 1950.

North of the senior high school, where Shell Road (UpRiver now) crossed Leopard, was the Fred Roberts Memorial Hospital. Fred Roberts, a reputed Klan leader, was shot to death on Oct. 14, 1922 by Sheriff Frank Robinson. It was a sensational case that resulted in the Texas Rangers being dispatched to restore law and order in Corpus Christi. Sheriff Robinson resigned and was later found not guilty in a trial moved to Laredo (Chapter 9, page 198).

27. *Flag-lowering ceremony at Roy Miller High School on an unknown occasion in the 1950s.*

28. *The Fred Roberts Memorial Hospital, past the junction of Leopard and UpRiver Road, opened in 1928 and closed in 1946. It is shown on March 17, 1937.*

The Fred Roberts Memorial Hospital opened at the end of Leopard Street in 1928. It closed in 1946. Dr. W. C. Ghormley opened the Ghormley Clinic in the old hospital in 1947. When it closed in 1956, the building was converted into a nursing home, which closed in 1969. It houses Catholic Charities today.

In the 1940s, a dirt road connected the end of Leopard to Highway 9, where road-house bars and dance halls were located outside the city limits. One was the Continental Tavern and Dance Hall, operated by M. J. Frangos, who also owned the Ship Ahoy Grill, and another was Good Time Charlie's Dance Hall, owned by Charlie Sciba. Both were on Highway 9, which was later renamed Leopard.

In the 1960s some businessmen lobbied to change the name of Leopard to Main Street, but the city, without any heavy lifting, decided to keep Kinney's historic name but to extend Leopard Street all the way to Calallen, replacing the name of Highway 9 within the city.

Chapter 8. Staples and Six Points

South Staples from Kinney to 15th Street past Six Points. South Alameda from Booty to Del Mar Boulevard. Ayers from Six Points to 17th Street. North Staples from Kinney Avenue past Leopard to Ramirez Street.

Staples Street got its name from Waymon N. Staples who came to Texas from Alabama in 1857 with his brother William. Waymon established himself in the grocery and produce business in Corpus Christi while William turned to ranching in Live Oak County.

The Ranchero newspaper reported in October 1859 that merchant W. N. Staples advertised the arrival of a large lot of hoopskirts very cheap, choice family groceries, whisky, and said he would accept wool, hides, silver and gold in exchange. Staples added that he would not object to a few hundred-dollar bills on New Orleans banks. The Ranchero reported six months later, in March 1860, that "Our merchants, E. Ohler and W. N. Staples, received supplies of groceries and merchandise yesterday per steamer Mexico."

Waymon Staples served as vice president of the Walker Mounted Rifles, a local militia formed in 1859, and was elected to the City Council in 1860. He was appointed mayor after the war and held the position in 1866 and 1867.

When Market Hall was built in 1871, the City Council passed an ordinance prohibiting the sale of fresh meat and produce within the city except at Market Hall, giving the builders of that facility a monopoly. Staples had moved his store from Chaparral to the edge of the city to Last Street, north of Leopard, but the Market Hall monopoly hurt his business. He sold his property within the city and moved to Alice, where he died in 1893.

In the early years, Black Street ran from Leopard to Kinney Avenue where it merged with Staples Street. In 1929, the City Council changed the name of Black Street to North Staples. It also changed the name of Last Street, north of Leopard, to North Staples and Last Street south of Leopard to Alameda. South Staples extended from Kinney Avenue south to the far reaches of the city, where there is an intersection today called Six Points.

South Staples begins at Kinney Avenue, what used to be known as Railroad Avenue. Going south, the street crosses Laredo, Agnes, Marguerite, Mary, Coleman, Furman, Hancock, Buford, Craig, Morgan, Elizabeth, Booty, and Ayers.

The first block, between Kinney and Laredo, starts with 200. In the first block past the Tex-Mex tracks was the Frederick Miller Restaurant in 1914. By 1919, Blake's Drug Store was there and in 1925 a new two-story brick building was built on the site. Charles Kardell's Pharmacy occupied the lower floor with office space above. (Kardell's later moved to the 400 block.) Rayford McNabb's liquor store, the Old Mill Package Store, was in that building, which still stands today, though vacant and decrepit.

In the middle of the block, at 207, 209, and 213, were the Alamo Café, the Alamo Bar and the Alamo Grocery. The Alamo Bar was operated in the late 1930s and early 1940s by Frank Kucera and Louis Regmund. The Alamo Grocery was run by Albert Regmund and

1. KC Barbecue at 302 S. Staples was operated by Lucille Kohrman. Prices on the signs read: Plate Lunch, 25 cents, Hamburgers, 5 cents, Cigarettes 15 cents a pack.

Louis Marek and the café by Henry Chambers then Mrs. Beulah Harris. At the end of the block, at 221, was the Meuly Building, constructed in 1925. It first housed the Brown Meat and Grocery Company on the first floor and the Independent Order of Odd Fellows hall on the second floor. By the 1940s George Jarrott's grocery store and John Hrchek's meat market were on the first floor and the Odd Fellows hall was still on the second. This building was later the home of Guess Lighting.

Across the street from Blake's Pharmacy was the G. E. Warren Grocery Store. It was the corner facing Railroad Avenue (later Kinney). In front of this store was where reputed Klan leader Fred Roberts was shot and killed by Sheriff Frank Robinson.

It happened on Oct. 14, 1922. a Saturday. Sheriff Robinson and deputy Joe Acebo stopped at Warren's grocery store. Warren was said to be a Klan member. After some words between the sheriff and storekeeper, the sheriff slapped Warren, who shouted, "Don't hit me. Get out of here." The sheriff and deputy left and crossed Staples to Blake's Drug Store. Warren called his friend Fred Roberts, who came to the store, talked to Warren, then went out to his car. As he started the engine, Sheriff Robinson reached in, turned off the ignition, then fired three shots at Roberts from his .45 caliber Colt revolver. Two deputies also fired. Roberts was killed instantly.

Sheriff Robinson resigned after the shooting. He and three deputies were indicted for murder and the trial was moved to Laredo on a change of venue. The former sheriff testified that he shot Fred Roberts because he thought he was going for a gun. The jury found the defendants not guilty. After the Fred Roberts killing, the power and influence of the Ku Klux Klan in Corpus Christi began to ebb and had mostly disappeared by the 1930s.

The 200 block on the east side in the 1930s and 1940s included a junk yard that sold used auto parts, and Household Furniture, run by Edwin Motel, which was later Benjamin's Furniture, operated by Benjamin Roach.

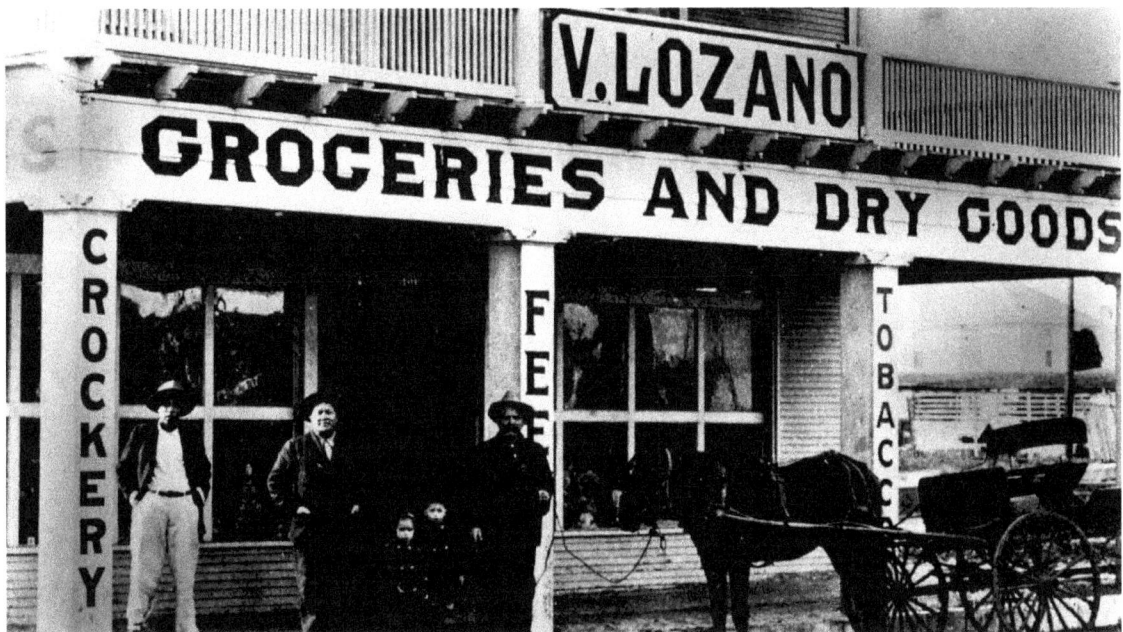

2. *Vicente Lozano's grocery and dry goods store was on the corner of Agnes in 1913.*

The 300 block of South Staples runs from Laredo to Agnes. On the northwest corner at Laredo was the Eastern Seed Company, founded by Curtis Clark, whose father was known as "Farmer" Clark. His farm was off Ocean Drive at Airline. Curtis Clark was known as a pioneer grain and seed dealer. He established his first store on Leopard in 1919. He moved to the 300 block of South Staples in 1929. He called it Eastern Seed because he obtained his stock from Eastern states. He died in 1968.

The rest of the 300 block on the west side included Miller Hardware, operated by Bernie and Monroe Miller, Ed Johnson's City Mattress Company, Isom Watkins' restaurant, and the A&S Café. Watkins' restaurant was gone by the 1940s and the building converted to Joe's Bicycle Shop run by Elias Martinez. The A&S Café was operated by J. W. Smith in the late 1930s and Henry Eckerman in the 1940s.

On the east side of the street was KC Barbecue Café in an old home. The next store south, at 306, was one of the first businesses on the street, the Behmann Grocery Store owned by John and Elise Behmann opened in 1907. Two sons, Arno and Herman, took over the business in the late 1930s. South of Behmann's was the home and business of William Holland and his wife Tennessee who sold used furniture. Past Holland's was Suniland Furniture which later moved to the 500 block.

The 400 block of South Staples runs from Agnes to Marguerite. The dominant business on the northwest corner was that of Vicente Lozano, whose first business was a grocery store on Mesquite. He relocated to South Staples in 1913 and opened a grocery and general merchandise store. He joined Behmann's as one of the only businesses on the street. The 400 block became known as the Lozano block.

The Lozano family moved to Corpus Christi from Bagdad, Mexico in 1891. In Corpus Christi, Vicente worked as a fisherman and would sell his catch to the chef at the St. James Hotel. He opened his store on Mesquite in 1902 with $20 worth of borrowed stock. Lozano

3. Charles Kardell's Pharmacy, at 401 S. Staples, was located in Lozano's old store in 1941 before a new building was constructed on the site.

4. High Hat Drive-In at Staples and Marguerite opened in 1937. It was torn down in the 1950s and Suniland Furniture was built on the site.

5. Entrance to Furman Avenue from South Staples. The Furman Avenue Church of Christ is on the extreme right. That building, as of this writing, is still standing.

built a new store on Staples in 1913. The Lozano building, constructed on the site of the old store, opened in 1941 and housed Doctor's Pharmacy. Corpus Christi's first TV station, KVDO, began broadcasting in 1954 from the Lozano building. Down the street was the Pla-Mor Billiard Parlor and the Lozano Café, which was run by Maria Lozano after her husband Manuel died. Shield Brothers' Electric was at the end of the block. In later years, KRIS TV broadcast from its facility in the Lozano block.

Across the street the east side included a service station, residence, and Corpus Christi Cleaners.

The 500 block, from Marguerite to Mary, included a mix of homes, with a few older residences subdivided into apartments, and businesses. On the west side of the block, past Marguerite, was a service station, apartments, and in the middle of the block Louis Motal's blacksmith shop. Rush Guy's NuWay Grocery store was near the end of the block, at 521, and the Blue Bonnet Café was at 525. The Blue Bonnet was run by Julius Bush in the 1930s and later by Leo Braun, a former salesman for the J. C. Blacknall auto dealership.

On the east side, on the corner, at 502, was High Hat Drive-In where young women car-hops sometimes wore top hats. It opened in 1939 and lasted into the 1950s when it was torn down and the Suniland Furniture building was constructed on the site. Suniland was run by Abraham Braslau and his son Isaac. Down the street was the Hugh Sutherland Jr. residence; his mother Mary wrote "The Story of Corpus Christi". The Nueces Printing office was next door and Pearl Distributing Company was at the end of the block.

The 600 block of South Staples runs from Mary to Coleman. The west side of the block contained mostly businesses while the east side consisted of homes and apartments, with service stations on each corner. The dominant business on the west side of the street in the 1930s and 1940s was Guy's New Market Grocery on the corner, followed by Charles Bertch's Pharmacy at 605 and Irene Holly's Beauty Salon at 607.

6. *Superior Ice Cream, at 819 S. Staples, stood next to a Piggly Wiggly store which was later converted into the City Bowling Parlor.*

There was another fruit stand down the block, followed by Frances Wilson's Jumbo Hamburger Hut, which was short-lived. Oklahoma Barbecue, run by Willliam Young, and Joe Hamlett's Staples Street Fish Market were down the street. In 1911, a wood-frame building at 617 South Staples, next to the William Petzel home, was used as a temporary high school while the "Brick Palace" was being built on Carancahua. Students called the Staples Street building the chicken-coop school.

The address numbers on South Staples jump from 600 to 800, skipping the 700s, with the short block between Coleman and the end of Furman Avenue. In the 1930s and early 1940s, the west side of the block included a beauty shop, apartments, a Piggly Wiggly supermarket. The Piggly Wiggly building at 817 was converted into the City Bowling Parlor, run by John Black, and much later, in the 1960s, Mack Matheny operated an auto-repair garage there.

The 900 block runs from Furman to Hancock. On the west side of the street was the Superior Ice Cream business across from the Church of Christ. By the 1940s, Currie's Nurseries was located 909 and in later years took in much of that block. Across the street, on the east side past the church, were homes, apartments, E. A. Medford's Central Shoe Shop and Biel's Self-Service Grocery. The Furman Avenue Church of Christ was built in 1920. Forty years later, the congregation moved out to Weber Road and the old church was occupied by several businesses. The decrepit old building was recently demolished.

7. *The Oriental Laundry and Cleaners moved from Third Street to 1236 South Staples, at the Morgan intersection, in 1947. That building was later converted into a recording studio.*

The 1000 block runs from Hancock to Buford. The dominant business on the west side of the block was the Bonham Food Store at 1019. The business was owned by two brothers, J. Forrest Bonham and Otha. Forrest also owned a service station in the 1100 block. Their father was killed when he was struck by a taxi on Staples in 1938. The Bonham store by the 1960s was Clarence Edwards' Grocery and by the 1980s it was Joe Martinez's Meat Market. North of Bonham's was Biel's Grocery and Borden's Heap O' Cream.

On the east side of the street, at 1002, Charles Payne, who owned the Mayflower Café on Chaparral, opened a Mayflower Junior. After its demise, Kyle Dowdy opened a restaurant in the building. The rest of the block included a real estate office, apartments, and a service station on the corner with Buford.

The 1100 block runs from Buford to Craig. On the corner on the west side in the 1930s was T. V. Cobb's Southend Drug Store, which was sold to Leonard Beyer in the 1940s. Past the drug store was Sam Cimo's Grocery followed by the Armstrong Barber and Beauty Shop, run by Clarence Armstrong. By the late 1930s, that building housed Nurge Parks' barber shop. It was followed by the OK Cleaners, which became the OK Bakery, and then, in the 1940s, J. K. Browning's paint store.

On the east side, on the Buford Street corner, was Bonham's Service Station, followed by homes and apartments.

The 1200 block, from Craig to Morgan, is a short block. In the 1930s and early 1940s, there were mostly homes and apartments on both sides of the street. Exceptions were Sam Cimo's Busy Bee Fruit Stand, at 1209, and George Garrett's Grocery at the end of the block, next to Morgan. There was also Fred Buxton's Monuments in the middle of the block. The Charles and Charlotte Lehman home was on the corner, at 1201. On the east side were homes, a service station, and J. R. Reeves' Snacks Chicken Village at 1224.

The Oriental Laundry built a huge new facility at 1236, on the corner of Staples and Morgan, in 1947. The operation was moved from its location on Third Street. The Oriental Laundry was closed and the building sold in 1978 and converted into a recording studio. The building still stands, although dilapidated and broken down.

8. *Six Points Grocery, owned by the Cudd family, was at 1657 S. Alameda between Booty and Ayers next to the Del Mar Drug Store. The building earlier housed the Edgar Wooten Grocery Store and later housed Six Points Hardware.*

The 1300 block, from Morgan to Elizabeth, was mostly residential in the 1930s on both sides of the street. One home, at 1305, was that of Louis L. Harris, who owned a wholesale grocery firm. By the 1940s, some homes in the 1300 block had been converted into small businesses. The former Harris home housed Clarence McVay's Waffle House (he had another one on Chaparral). This was later John Doan's Waffle House. Lining the west side of the 1300 block were Howard Tire Service, Nueces Electric, Christine's Beauty Shop, Lee Baking, run by Wade and Woody Lee, Bell Ice Cream, and Kuhn Paint Store.

On the east side, homes gave way to Cutler's Bicycle Shop, Peerless Cleaners, and the Taxco Café, which was operated by Celso Guzman, who previously worked at Nau Hardware and Nueces Coffee Company.

In the 1500 block (no 1400s), from Elizabeth to Booty, the Sunflower service station on the corner was followed by several homes, the Samuel J. Blythe residence, and the Blythe grocery store. When Blythe retired his son, S. J. Blythe Jr., ran the store. By the 1960s Knolle Jersey Milk was in the old Blythe store. In the 1940s, the Keener Market Grocery and Auto Serv Grocery were established in the middle of the block.

The west side of the street was mostly commercial. Businesses included Frank Dawson Plumbing, P. H. Dunn's Physician Supplies, Mrs. Clara Belle Carter's Beauty Shop, a pottery shop run by Walter Magness, who had been the manager of Fehr Baking Company.

The 1600 block runs from Booty to the Six Points intersection. In the 1930s that block consisted of homes with two service stations and the Del Mar Drug Store on the west side of the block. The E. B. Wooten Grocery Store became the Six Points Grocery, owned by the Cudd family. By the 1960s, the old Del Mar Drug Store building was occupied by Corpus Christi Piano. On the east side was the Midway Service Station followed by the Orchard Building, which housed Del Mar Cleaners, owned by E. A. Orchard. At 1618 was the Electro-Mechanical Company which by the 1960s was the location of Luciano's Restaurant. At 1614 was Cap's Place Drive-In run by Louis Simmons.

9. Road work on South Staples in the early 1940s, past the Six Points intersection, with Limerick's grocery store on the right, followed by Joe McInnis's Drug Store.

10. Joe McInnis operated a drug store in the State Hotel in the 1930s. He moved to South Staples past Six Points by 1941. He later opened McInnis Book Store at 1704 S. Alameda.

Next door at 1620 was the Higginbotham-McCord Lumber Company which eventually became McCord's. In the front of McCord's a cross-section of a large redwood tree was displayed as a curiosity.

The 1700 block, past the Ayers intersection, included the Triangle Service Station at 1701, in 1933. It became Southmore Service Station by 1937. By 1942, Limerick's Foods was listed at 1701-1706 South Staples. It opened for business in 1937 but the address was first listed on Ayers.

11. *Alameda Pharmacy at Six Points in the 1940s. That building still stands.*

Limerick's was the major business at Six Points. Pat Limerick once recalled that he came to Corpus Christi in July 1937 on vacation and while visiting made arrangements for a building to be constructed at Six Points. He returned to Moline, Ill., and resigned his job with Shell Oil. "By the time I got back here in October, the building was nearly finished and we opened that month." Limerick said people told him he was crazy to build a new store so far out of town. "Why put a grocery store out there?" they asked. He said it did seem remote in the first year or two. In the early morning he could hear coyotes howl and ducks would land on a nearby puddle. But the area grew quickly. When the store was closed in 1959, Limerick said, "It's breaking my heart to close it. It's the oldest store at Six Points."

Past Limerick's on the north side was McInnis Drug Store at 1711 and Ed White & Sons, a uniform firm, at 1713. On the south side, past Six Points, was Vernon McKinney's Alameda Pharmacy, the Tower Package Store at 1714, owned by Albert Kurtz, Biel Grocery No. 6, at 1718, and the Kleberg Post Office substation at 1728, named for Congressman Richard Kleberg.

AYERS: This street was probably named for businessman David Ayers. Though it has been attributed to Thomas Carlton Ayers, a former principal of Solomon Coles School, the street is shown on maps from the 1890s which predates T. C. Ayers. A third candidate for the honor is Nelson Ayers, who was principal of the colored school on Carancahua in 1874.

The street was thinly populated west of Six Points, with only half a dozen homes between South Staples and 14th Street in 1933. That changed greatly within 10 years as the city grew to the south and west. Wynn-Seale Junior High was completed in 1936 and Richter's Butter Krust Bakery moved into a new building two blocks away, at 2001 Ayers, in 1938.

Pick's Drive-In was opened across the street in 1938 by J. B. Pickens, who gave it its name. The drive-in was sold to "Pop" Salvo. The Salvo family eventually owned four Pick's Drive-Ins, besides the original across from Butter Krust.

12. *Richter's Bakeries opened its new Butter Krust plant at 2001 Ayers in 1938.*

13. *Pick's Drive-In across from Butter Krust on Ayers was the first of four Pick's Drive-Ins.*

near South Padre Island Drive, one downtown on Water Street, and one on South Staples near King High School. In the 1940s, there was another drive-in on Ayers closer to Six Points, the Wynn-Seale Inn at 10th Street.

ALAMEDA: This street originally was known as Chamberlain Street. It ran south from Kinney to Booty. In 1941 the City Council made a concerted effort to clear up confusing street names and Chamberlain Street was renamed Alameda. Most of the street was single-family dwellings until it reached the Six Points area.

14. *Paul Harwell's Wynn-Seale Inn was at 1319 Ayers, near the 10th Street intersection.*

In the 1600 block of South Alameda past Booty in 1942 there was Holland Henderson's radio repair shop, followed by a service station on the east side of the street. On the west side was an RC Bottling Plant, Dainty Maid Sandwiches, the Six Points Amusement Club, Bob's Café, run by Robert Day Jr., Morris 5c to $1 Store, the Tower Theater, Tower Pharmacy, Foster Case's Jewelry, Warehouse Liquors, the Del Mar Barber and Beauty Shop, and Six Points Hardware.

South Alameda, past the Ayers-Staples intersection, in 1942 included 1700 and 1800 addresses. On the east side, at 1700, was the Crippled Children's Hospital, followed by Crystal Water (later it was McInnis' Book Store), the Elite Beauty Shop (later Cage's Hardware), Graves Music, Anna Burke's Barbecue. Price's Chef, owned by J. Daniel Price, followed by Jon Von Shoes, owned by John Vaughn, Dabney Cleaners, Gulf Security Life and Creel Gates Bakery, Cactus Beauty Salon and the Conway Conservatory of Music, which moved to Six Points from Blucher Street.

Alameda Pharmacy was on the west side of the street, along with Jitney Jungle No. 2, the Medical-Dental building offices, Sportsman's Man Shop, Fenner's Ladies Wear, and Piggly Wiggly No. 7 (later HEB) before the intersection with Del Mar Boulevard.

Beyond the busy intersection of Six Points was mostly open country. West on Ayers, southwest on Staples, and south on Alameda was where the cows grazed and the cotton grew. Limerick's Food Store was squeezed between the triangle created by the junction of Ayers and Colorado Avenue. In 1942 the City Council changed the name of Colorado to South. Out from Colorado was the road leading out of town, the old Chapman Ranch Road, which was usually called Dump Road. It got that name from the Ropes boom in the early 1890s when E. H. Ropes planned to build a railroad to the south and railroad ties were trucked out past Colorado Avenue and dumped. The railroad plans died when the Ropes boom fizzled but the road was known afterwards as Dump Road. Now it's South Staples.

15. *"Dago" Bob's Fruit Market was at 117 N. Staples next to Sammons Lumber Co. The name was changed in 1937 to Doc & Bob's Fruit Stand.*

NORTH STAPLES: From the 100 block north to the 1300 block past Ramirez, North Staples consisted mainly of small homes with stores, garages, lumber yards, in the mix. Going north, the 100 block of North Staples runs from Kinney Avenue to Mussett and Blucher. Blucher Street ended at North Staples and became Mussett Street going west.

One of the old businesses on the street was at 102 North Staples, past the Kinney intersection on the east side of the street. This was the Tex-Mex News Stand next to the Tex-Mex Railroad tracks. It was started in 1901 by Constancio Rodriguez. The business was later moved to the 300 block of North Staples and sold to Mr. and Mrs. Orea Velez. The Pioneer Flour Mills built a facility on the site of the old Tex-Mex News Stand. On the northeast corner of this block was a vacant lot where traveling carnivals would set up their operations for a short time.

On the west side of the 100 block in the 1930s was "Dago" Bob's Fruit Market at 117 North Staples. The firm name was changed in 1937 to Doc & Bob's Fruit Stand. It was operated by Robert Wilson and Huber Carr. The business next door was Cleveland Sammons' lumberyard, at 127.

In the 200 block, past the Blucher-Mussett intersection, on the east side of the street, was Frank Sovey's produce market followed by several small homes. Across the street was the C. W. Johnson Lumber Co.

The 300 block of N. Staples runs between Caldwell and Comanche streets. On the east side of the street in the 300 block, in the 1930s, was the Texas Laundry, owned by J. E. Smothers, and a Sinclair Service Station. The Tex-Mex News Stand moved to 316 from the 100 block. Across the street was George Wartell's Grocery, at 305, and several small homes. The 400 block, from Comanche to Lipan, consisted mainly of residences. One exception was the Safety Glass Company and another was Frank Cech's millwork shop.

16. *Jose J. Gonzalez built this structure in 1911 on North Staples. He operated a furniture store and a theater on the second floor until the building was damaged in the 1919 storm.*

On the southwest corner of the 500 block, which runs from Lipan to Mestena, once stood the J. J. Gonzalez Building. It was built in 1911 and included a furniture store on the lower level and the Juarez Theater on the second floor.

The building was damaged in the 1919 storm and razed afterwards. J. J. Gonzalez moved to Laredo but returned to Corpus Christi to establish the Gonzalez Oil Company on the site of his old store. He later owned the Avalon Theater and Avalon Drug Store on Brownlee. His son, Alonso Gonzalez, later operated the company. In the 500 block was a planing mill established by Ernest W. Page. In the 600 block was James Pons' Staples Street Furniture Company followed by the Hollywood Beauty Shop, run by Mrs. Charlotte Wilson. After the Staples Street Furniture store closed, in the 1940s, the building housed Dr. Jose A. Barrera's dentist office and residence.

North of Leopard, including the 700-1300 blocks, consisted mostly of residences. Ideal Cleaners was in the 700 block and Ideal Bottling in the 800 block. C. W. Gibson's Lone Star Fish & Oyster Company was in the 900 block. In the 1000 block, past Winnebago, was Eleno Garza's Grocery, which had been the Joseph Carranza Grocery. The 1100 block, on the west side of the street, was dominated by the Holy Cross Church, school and convent. In the 1300 block, past Ramirez, was the M&M Café, which was later renamed the Hollywood Café, run by Willie Govan, and the longshoremen's union hall.

What was first called Corpus Christi Church, built in 1903, was sometimes called Our Lady of Guadalupe Church. It was moved to Last Street in 1915 and renamed Holy Cross Church in 1923. Its address became North Staples in 1929 when members of the City Council contracted a name-changing fever.

Chapter 9. Uptown Streets

Carancahua, Tancahua, Carrizo, Artesian, and Waco, running north-south, and Winnebago, Buffalo, Antelope, Mestina, Lipan, Comanche, and Blucher, running east-west. Broadway and Leopard are treated separately.

Uptown streets west of Broadway comprise the older Hispanic section of the city that in the earliest years, in the 1840s and 1850s, was known as Little Mexico. It later gained the nickname of "the Hill" which was used interchangeably as a geographic reference and a euphemism for the Hispanic population. A common phrase was "As the Hill goes, so goes the election."

The uptown area also included the homes of some of the earliest pioneers who built on Broadway and on the streets just west of Broadway. Many of these were the finest homes in the city. More people chose to build on high ground after hurricanes in 1874 and 1880 flooded downtown, the "beach section" of the city.

NORTH CARANCAHUA: This was one of the original streets named by Henry Kinney, shown on the 1852 street map grid. For a short time Carancahua was known as Liberty Street after the City Council changed the name on April 5, 1912 because, said one councilman, few people in town could correctly spell or pronounce Carancahua. The council also changed the name of Tancahua to Pleasant Street.

People didn't like the altered names and persistent complaints forced the City Council to change the names back to their original nomenclature. Old tile inlays with the names of Liberty and Pleasant on them could still be found on Carancahua and Tancahua in recent times.

On North Carancahua between Blucher Street and Lipan were several homes and apartment structures. One residence was that of Mrs. Alice Lovenskiold Rankin.

"We lived where North Carancahua and Blucher streets intersect. Our house was built by a Frenchman named Aldurette, who gave it to my mother for taking care of his two boys and letting them go to school while he was away. East of us was where Kinney lived. "

The Rankin home was at 417, on the west side of the street. Across the street, at 406, was the home of Atlee McCampbell. Coleman McCampbell was born in this house. He was the author of a history of Corpus Christi, "Saga of a Frontier Seaport." The McCampbell home was later converted into an apartment building and was torn down to make way for a Southwestern Bell Telephone building in 1938.

The west side of the 500 block of North Caranchua has been a school site for nearly a century and a half. In 1872 two school buildings were constructed on Carancahua, one for white students and one for blacks, on land donated by Richard King. That site between Carancahua and Tancahua has been connected to public education ever since. The first public schools opened in 1873. "A two-story building, with four rooms on each floor, was

1 and 2. Above, students gather in front of the Central School on the school grounds between Carancahua and Tancahua. The school, built in 1872, contained four classrooms on each floor. A wooden fence extending from the front porch separated the boys' and girls' playgrounds. Below, Corpus Christi High School, built on Carancahua in 1911, was widely known as the Brick Palace, for the extravagant expense of its design and construction. The "Brick Palace" was replaced by a new Corpus Christi High School built off Leopard in 1929, later renamed for Roy Miller.

built for the white children and a two-room building south of this was built for the colored pupils," Anna Moore Schwien, a former slave and school teacher, said in her memoirs. The school for black children opened in January 1873 with W. B. Lacy as principal. The white school, called Central School, opened in May. Four teachers were hired for the two schools. A census in 1874 recorded 763 students – 340 white (Anglo and Hispanic) males, 325 white females, 51 colored males and 47 colored females. The city's first high school was constructed in 1892 next to the two elementary schools. It was a two-story building painted yellow. There were three classes in high school, for juniors, sub-seniors, and seniors.

In 1911 a substantial new high school building was constructed on the school grounds. People called it the New Brick Palace. When the school district built a new high school out on Leopard, the "Brick Palace" was converted into Northside Junior High. It was torn down in 1961 and the property sold. The board of education building was erected next door to the old Northside location.

Across the street was the R. R. Savage home, a large two-story house with a white picket fence. Savage, who owned a ranch near Alice, came to Corpus Christi in 1874. He sent many cattle herds up the trail to Kansas. The story of the Savage family is intertwined with that of the Scotts.

John Wesley Scott and his bride, Charlotte Matilda Cook Scott, came to Nueces County in 1857 from Burleson County. He bought a ranch near Santa Margarita (later called Bluntzer) which was called Rancho Seco. After he died in the yellow fever epidemic of 1867, his widow married Edward Sidbury, who owned a lumber company. Sidbury built a two-story house on Carancahua, at the corner of Leopard.

After Sidbury died in 1881, he left his estate to his widow, who continued to manage the ranch from her first husband, Rancho Seco, and the Sidbury lumber business. Her daughter, Mary Margaret Ann, called Mollie, married R.R. (Robert Russell) Savage and they had seven children. Two were lawyers, Russell Savage, who became a state representative, and Linton, who as elected county attorney.

When Charlotte Matilda Cook Scott Sidbury died in 1904, she left the house built by Edward Sidbury to her grandson, Rayburn Russell Savage. By the 1930s, the east side of the 500 block of Carancahua, across from the Northside Junior High School, was the Savage corner. Mary Margaret, the widow of R.R., occupied the original Savage house at 524 Carancahua and her son Rayburn occupied the house next door built by Edward Sidbury. The Sidbury house was moved to 1402 North Chaparral in 1946 and from there to Heritage Park, where it was known as the Sidbury-Savage house and occupied by a law firm. (The other Sidbury house in Heritage Park was built Mrs. Charlotte Sidbury on North Broadway in 1893. It was built as a rental property).

Across Leopard, on the west side of North Carancahua, in the 700 block, was the Incarnate Word Academy. It shared this block with St. Patrick's Cathedral.

Incarnate Word Academy was founded by the Sisters of the Incarnate Word in 1871. In the first years of the school, classes were conducted in the old Hidalgo Seminary building at the corner of Lipan and Tancahua. In 1885, a three-story building was erected at the corner of Tancahua and Leopard. In 1925, a three-story brick building was erected past Leopard on Carancahua. The old two-story wooden structure built in 1885 was still used for classrooms. The school and convent were moved to new facilities on South Alameda in the 1950s.

CONVENT OF THE
INCARNATE WORD

3. *Incarnate Word Academy building was constructed on Carancahua in 1925. The building behind it was the original Incarnate Word Academy, built in 1885, the Catholic successor of the Hidalgo Seminary which flourished in the 1860s and 1870s.*

Past the Incarnate Word Academy was St. Patrick's Church, built in 1882 at a cost of $18,000. The building was designed by Charles Carroll, father of Mary Carroll, a longtime teacher who became superintendent of the Corpus Christi school system. Carroll went to New Orleans to select the lumber for the new church and when the structure was completed, he climbed the church tower to place a gold cross atop the steeple. Mifflin Kenedy donated money, murals and pews to the new church; his wife Petra gave bells, pipe organ, and windows for the sanctuary. Mayor J. B. Murphy and wife donated side altars and statues. St Patrick's Church was designated St. Patrick's Cathedral in 1912.

After a fire in 1938 damaged the building, a fund drive began to build a new cathedral. The John G. Kenedy family donated land on North Broadway for the site. Ground was broken for the new cathedral in March 1939 and the building finished the following year. St. Patrick's was pulled down in 1951 and the material salvaged to build Our Lady Star of the Sea on North Beach.

Across from Incarnate Word, on the east side of the street, was the Plaza Garage. Past Antelope and Buffalo streets were several homes and the Hennessey Apartments, at 814. This apartment building was once the home of Gov. Edmund J. Davis.

Edmund Jackson Davis, a federal judge in Corpus Christi, was an outspoken opponent of secession, along with his father-in-law Forbes Britton, a former army officer and state senator. During the war Davis was appointed a brigadier general and led Union forces on the border. In one incident, he was almost hanged after he was captured on the Mexican side of the river by Confederates. But he was released with apologies to Mexico for the violation of Mexican territory. After the war he returned to Corpus Christi and opened a law practice. In 1869, with Texas under military rule, Davis was elected governor in what was called the most fraudulent election in state history.

4. St. Patrick's Cathedral on the corner of Carancahua and Antelope was built in 1882. It was designed by architect Charles Carroll, father of Mary Carroll, a longtime teacher who became superintendent of the Corpus Christi school system. Carroll went to New Orleans to select the lumber for the new church. It was replaced by Corpus Christi Cathedral on North Broadway.

5. The 20-room Bagnall home at 1003 Jones before it was demolished in 1956 to make way for roadway access to the new Harbor Bridge.

Davis in office, between 1870 and 1874, assumed powers that former Confederates considered dictatorial and his regime was seen as corrupt. He was defeated for re-election by Richard Coke, a former private in the Confederate Army.

Despite losing the election, Davis barricaded himself in his office and sent a telegram urging President U.S. Grant to send federal troops to keep him in power. Grant refused. Davis never returned to Corpus Christi. He sold his house on North Broadway to Norwick Gussett, a wealthy merchant.

In 1937, when construction was scheduled to begin on a new post office on North Broadway, the Davis-Gussett house was moved to 814 Carancahua and sold to M. F. Hennessey, who converted it into the Hennessey Apartments. When the Driscoll Hotel was built, the building was moved again to 815 Carancahua.

In the next block, past the Buffalo Street intersection, was the home of Justina Bluntzer, at 909. Her father Nicholas was one of the county's pioneer ranchers. He served as a scout for Col. Robert E. Lee when he was stationed on the border in the late 1850s. Her brother John was a Nueces County sheriff, her brother Joe was a county tax assessor, and her brother Vincent organized the State National Bank.

Justina Bluntzer later married Chilton J. Stevens, but still resided at her home on Carancahua. The house was built in 1887. It was moved in 1956 to clear the area when the Harbor Bridge was built. It was moved to 3025 Huisache.

JONES: Past the intersection of Winnebago was an extension of Carancahua that angled northeast one block to Broadway. This was Jones Street. In the 1930s and 1940s there were three buildings on the street. One was the home of Annie Bagnall, built by her husband Ernest Bagnall in 1883. Bagnall came to Texas from Prince Edward Island, Canada. He

216

married Annie Schallert, whose family lived where Perkins was later built. Bagnall, a carpenter, made coffins and then became an undertaker.

Bagnall built the 20-room house at 1003 Jones himself. Mrs. Bagnall once said that when they married they planned a small house but as the family grew (they would have 11 children) additions were made to the house. The house was demolished in 1956 to make way for the network of roads leading to the new Harbor Bridge.

NORTH TANCAHUA: In early years of Corpus Christi's history, Tancahua was often spelled as "Tankhua." The name of Tancahua Street was changed to Pleasant Street in 1912 by the City Council. After a year of public opposition, the Council changed it back.

In the first block of Tancahua going north, past Kinney Avenue, there was Blucher Park on the left, or west side of the street, followed by the Frank C. Allen home on the corner, just north of the arroyo where Blucher Park is today. Before Allen built his house on the site, Mamie Hawley Jones once said, there was a small cottage where a man named Juan Meza lived.

Frank Campbell Allen, born in Lavaca County, came to Corpus Christi in 1912. He and his brother Clyde went into a partnership with John Jordt, who owned a furniture store on Chaparral Street. The Allens bought out Jordt in 1923.

He built the two-story house at 305 North Tancahua in 1912 for $7,500. He once said, "I built that house for cost plus 10 percent. Most of the purchases were wholesale and I bought the lumber at the mill. An old German built it. It had double floors and ceilings and rested on cantilevered pilings. You could walk on the stairways and they didn't creak." He sold the house in 1975 and the city later purchased the property as the site for a new library building. La Retama Central Library stands on that site today.

One long-time resident recalled that across the intersection of Comanche and Tancahua on the corner of the 400 block stood a two-story white house where a bootlegger lived during Prohibition.

Near the northwest corner of Tancahua and Lipan, at 423, was the home of Mamie Hawley Jones. She was the granddaughter of Thomas S. Parker and his wife Rachel, who came to Corpus Christi in 1845 from Fort Smith, Ark. Parker got a contract to supply Zachary Taylor's army with beef while the army was encamped at Corpus Christi in 1845 and early 1846. He followed the army in the war with Mexico.

After the war, the Parkers lived for a short time in Brownsville. Richard King, the future rancher, boarded with the Parkers and taught Rachel to read. They returned to Corpus Christi and Parker was elected sheriff; he served two years from 1850 to 1852. Afterwards, he held several positions at the courthouse. He died in 1887 and Rachel died in 1906. Both were buried in Old Bayview.

The original Parker house was a two-story concrete building past the arroyo. Two of the water wells in that arroyo, Mamie Hawley Jones once said, were called the Parker wells. "All this part of North Tancahua Street was very different then from what it looks like now (1940)," she said. "The street was nothing but an arroyo up at least as far as the block north of Lipan."

Frank Gay, whose father was the gardener at Mifflin Kenedy's home on Broadway, said that North Tancahua, south from Mestena, "was nothing more than an arroyo, with foot paths worn through and across it in various directions. It was not possible to pass through it in a carriage."

6. *The Philip Scott home was located at 907 Tancahua, past Buffalo. It was torn down during the Harbor Bridge disruption when scores of historic homes on the bluff were demolished or moved.*

In the early years the arroyo was known as Chatham's Ravine. Later it was called Blucher's Creek. It was a natural watercourse, what the Spanish call "rambla," that meandered between Tancahua and Carrizo. It ran from where today's Courthouse stands past where La Retama Library is today and on through a low swale of Blucher's Park. At Kinney it turned east and ran down the bluff between Cooper's Alley and Laguna to debouch into the bay. This explains why some of the buildings constructed over this old watercourse have experienced persistent flooding problems.

Near the Parker house was the Edward Grant home, at the corner of Lipan. Mamie Hawley Jones said that J. O. Moore, a city official, bought the salvaged lumber from Market Hall when it was demolished in 1911 "and moved it up to the bluff where it was used to build the front part of the Grant home. It was good seasoned lumber."

Past the corner of Lipan, in the 1860s and 1870s, was the Hidalgo Seminary. Starting in 1863 the Catholic Church operated the Hidalgo Seminary on a site given to the church by Henry Kinney. The school was under the leadership of Father John Gonnard. The students at the Hidalgo Seminary were taught academics and moral and spiritual lessons. They came from all over South Texas; most of them boarded with families in the town. When Father Gonnard died in the yellow fever epidemic of 1867, the Hidalgo Seminary was operated for a time by Robert Dougherty, then Professor William S. Campion. The Hidalgo Seminary closed in 1877, with the establishment of a public-school system.

In the 1930s, several homes were located in the 500 and 600 blocks of Tancahua Street.

Mestina came to an end at the Tancahua intersection. To the east, the public-school square, with the Northside Junior High, occupied the entire area between Lipan and Leopard. On the west side of the streets were the homes of Mrs. Pete Whelan, at 509 and Ray Kring, city secretary, at 515. Past Mestina was the home of James Blossman, a bookkeeper, and on the other side of Leopard, in the 700 block, were more homes and apartments on the west side of the street. On the east side of the street, Incarnate Word Academy extended back from Carancahua.

In the 800 block, on the west side of the street past Antelope, were the homes of William S. Campion, at 811, Thomas B. Southgate, at 815, and Ernest Uehlinger, at 823. Uehlinger was the manager of the properties in the Uehlinger estate.

William Shakespeare Campion, who was a teacher and headmaster of the Hidalgo Seminary, built the one-story frame structure in 1880. He operated a boys' school in the building. In later years it became the family home. His daughter, Margaret Campion (later Cahill) was born in the house. She died there in 1952. The Campion-Cahill house was moved out to UpRiver Road near Calallen in 1955.

Thomas B. Southgate was a pioneer insurance man. He came to Corpus Christi from Kentucky in 1881. He first worked as a salesman for a drug store and in 1887 he formed an insurance company under his own name. He also founded a real estate company, Southgate & Timmons. He married Emilie Lovenskiold in 1886. Southgate helped to organize the Herdic Transportation, the first such streetcar operation in South Texas, and he also organized a company that built the city's first cotton gin, on Water Street. He died Oct. 1, 1940, in his home and was buried in Holy Cross Cemetery. Where Southgate's home stood was a parking lot by the 1960s.

In the 900 block, past Buffalo, was the home of Phil Scott. Scott, who owned and operated the Auto Laundry on Water Street in the 1930s, purchased a five-room cottage on Tancahua and added a second story. It was torn down in the bridge upheaval.

MEDIA: Past Winnebago was a short block-and-a-half street named Media, which connected Tancahua and Broadway, as Jones Street also connected Carancahua and Broadway. The City Council changed the name of Media to North Tancahua. Several businesses operated in the 1000 block of Tancahua, past Winnebago, in the 1940s, including George Bratton's Pleasure Spot, a beer saloon, a poolroom owned by Thomas Blackshear, the Texas Package Store, and the Simpson Hotel owned by J. W. Simpson. The Brown Skin Café, run by Mary Graves, was there in the 1930s but was gone by the time the street name was changed to North Tancahua in 1941.

NORTH CARRIZO: On the name of Carrizo Street, it's not clear if it was named for the Spanish word for "cane" or "reed." That would fit with Henry Kinney's other plant names, like Mesquite and Chaparral. Or it could have been named for a band of Coahuiltecan Indians along the Rio Grande that was often called "Carrizo." Since the street is in the same area of town as Carancahua, Tancahua, Lipan, Comanche and Waco, it may well have been named for the Indians.

The first block of Carrizo, between Kinney (formerly Railroad Avenue) to Comanche was called Treptow, a name that had some historical connection to the Blucher family's connections in Germany. City directories in the early part of the 20th Century show the various Blucher homes being on Treptow Street.

7. *A self-sketch of Felix Anton von Blucher, who brought his young bride from Germany to settle at Corpus Christi, on the Texas frontier, in 1849. He was an educated and talented man, but the responsibility of being a husband and father was not one of them.*

The Treptow name was changed to North Carrizo in January 1913 to make that one block conform to the rest of the street. The first block of Carrizo was the heart of what came to be called Blucherville. It was where Felix von Blucher brought his young wife, Maria Augusta Imme, in 1849.

Anton Felix Hans Hellmuth von Blucher's name figures prominently not only in the history of Corpus Christi but of South Texas. He dropped the aristocratic designation of "von" soon after his arrival in this country.

Felix Blucher was born in Poggelow, Germany in 1819. He was the grand nephew of Field Marshal Blucher of Waterloo. He was educated as a civil engineer at the University of Berlin and could speak five languages: German, French, English, Spanish and Italian. He left Germany in 1844 and landed in New Orleans, where he worked as a draftsman in a shipyard. In 1845 he joined Prince Karl Solms-Braunfels and helped survey and lay out the town of New Braunfels. He served as an interpreter in peace negotiations between German immigrants and Comanches.

In July 1846 Felix Blucher joined a Texas regiment of volunteers for the Mexican War. He eventually acted as an interpreter for Gen. Winfield Scott.

After the war he returned to Germany where he married Maria Augusta Imme, a young Berlin woman known for her good looks. Eight weeks after they left Hamburg, they arrived in Corpus Christi on July 11, 1849, a Wednesday evening. It wasn't the end of the civilized world that Maria had expected. She found the town larger than she had imagined it would be, with a dozen pleasant-looking houses along the shore and others on the bluff heights. The town had a church, three doctors, and two hotels. She was thankful, as she wrote her

8. *Maria and Felix von Blucher's wedding portrait. Two months later they arrived in the frontier town of Corpus Christi. Felix bought an eight-acre tract of land west of town and hired two carpenters to build a small home. While he was gone for long periods of time, doing surveying and other work throughout South Texas, Maria learned to cope with a harsh environment that was alien to her.*

parents, that, "I have the pleasing prospect of not getting Felix's mother (back in Germany) for a neighbor in Texas."

Felix Blucher bought an eight-acre tract from Hiram Riggs, who built the city's first wharf and started a farm west of town. The farm included the eight acres surrounded by a brush fence. He bought a small house and put two carpenters he had brought from Germany to work enlarging it, which gave it the feel of permanence and stability.

Maria in a letter to her parents said that the house was on a hill with a view of the sea. They had to haul water up from the pond below them. They killed rattlesnakes by the score in her garden, which she preserved in alcohol and planned to send to her mother in Germany. She had studied music under Franz Liszt and brought with their belongings the first piano in Corpus Christi.

9. Painting of the first Blucher homestead. From "Maria von Blucher's Corpus Christi," on page 33. Original in the Blucher Family Papers at Texas A&M-University-Corpus Christi.

Felix Blucher was a multi-talented and gifted man. He was much in demand as a surveyor, engineer and linguist. He was appointed county and district surveyor and he surveyed the original land purchase of the Santa Gertrudis grant in 1853, which marked the beginning of King Ranch. He designed Nueces County's first courthouse, built in 1854, served as an interpreter in court and practiced land law. He traveled throughout South Texas and was known for his extended drinking bouts. One writer said he had command of five languages, but no command of an alcohol problem.

Eli Merriman related the story of one Blucher trip to Austin in his capacity as county surveyor. Going on his way one night he saw a light and thinking it was a camp of white men he rode into it. It was a camp of Lipan-Apaches. Chief Castro, coming up and taking charge of Blucher's horse, spoke in Spanish to him, saying that his tribe had just had a fight with Tancahuas and killed one of their brave men and had him in the pot, boiling. He said that while they were not cannibals, they believed that if they ate the flesh of a brave foe their descendants would inherit his bravery. Merriman said the chief intimated that it would be wise for him to join them in the feast. Getting out his penknife, Blucher fished out one of the man's fingers and ate. After this the chief embraced him and at daylight Blucher found his horse saddled and ready for him to ride on into Austin. Merriman wrote that Blucher found the flesh tough and chewy. There was no mention of any side dishes.

In the Civil War, Col. John S. "Rip" Ford asked Gen. John Magruder to place Maj. Blucher under his command. "He has been a surveyor for many years in the country between the Nueces and Rio Grande and is thoroughly acquainted with the geography and topography of this section." Blucher designed defenses at Pass Cavallo, Mustang Island, and Corpus Christi. He was in the battle of Corpus Christi and fired a cannon that hit one of the Union warships. William Adams said, "We went down on the beach in front of the courthouse, where there was an 18-pound cannon and an old cast-iron cannon. Maj. Blucher was there. He said, 'I believe I'll take a pop at it.' He sighted and fired. It looked

like the ball hit the water to the right of the ship. He said, 'I believe I'll take another one.' He fired again and we didn't see the ball hit the water. The ship moved from there, so we were satisfied that we had hit her."

After the war Felix Blucher surveyed many of the towns, roads, ranches of South Texas. He was a consulting engineer for the Corpus Christi & Rio Grande Railroad (the Tex-Mex).

In their years of marriage, while Felix was away Maria took care of their home and children. She learned soon after their arrival in Corpus Christi that, with Felix's drinking and long absences, the burden would fall on her to make and keep the home. She wrote in one letter, "Felix has been very rough toward me" and in another she said, "I am quiet and content when Felix is away." And he was away for weeks, even months at a time. (From "Maria von Blucher's Corpus Christi.")

She learned to make do. She spent her days caring for the children, doing housework, cooking, cleaning, sewing, washing and ironing clothes. She spent her free time in the garden or reading Alexandre Dumas or playing the piano. She sold eggs and vegetables from her garden to make extra money. She was greedy for the packages from Germany that contained things she couldn't find, or afford to buy, in Texas.

Felix Blucher died at the ranch of Henry E. Woodhouse in Cameron County on Feb. 6, 1879. Funeral services were held for him at his home in Corpus Christi nearly three weeks later. Maria had rarely seen Felix in the four years before his death; he lived mostly on the border or stayed at the King Ranch at Santa Gertrudis. Despite his personal flaws, Felix Blucher was an important figure in the early history of Texas. But it was Maria who was the long-suffering and steady mainstay of the Blucher family. She died at her home on Sept. 28, 1893.

The Bluchers' children included Mary, Julia, Charles, Richard and George. The oldest

11. Charles Blucher's home at 123 North Carrizo was built in 1880. A major renovation was done in 1908, with electrical wiring and modern plumbing installed. The second and third floors and widow's walk were added. This is one of three Blucher homes that have survived.

daughter, Mary, married James Downing, deputy customs collector and later city marshal in Corpus Christi. Her second husband was Charles Meuly, who owned the Las Animas Ranch near Hebbronville. Their second child, Julia, never married. Their third child was Charles F. H. Blucher, who married Mary Meuly, the sister of his brother-in-law. He followed his father Felix and was the county surveyor for 50 years. He built a stately home in 1880 at 123 North Carrizo. Richard, the fourth child, became a rancher and married Julia Rooney. George, the youngest, eventually became president and owner of the Lone Star Ice Company. He married Alice Crawford of Iowa.

Three Blucher homes on North Carrizo survived and have been restored, including the Charles Blucher home at 123 Carrizo, built in 1880. The Richard Blucher home at 205 was built in 1901. It was sold to Herbert and Gertrude Guy; they later bought the Clark Pease home on South Broadway. The George Blucher home at 211 was built in 1904. That these magnificent old homes have endured is a tribute to the city.

North Carrizo in the 1930s and 1940s, from Comanche to Leopard, listed several homes and apartment buildings on the east side of the street. One apartment building, at 514, stood across the street from Cheston Heath School.

Obreros Hall, at the corner of Carrizo and Lipan, was where the Mexican-American movement for social and political equality began, a distinction it shared with Allende Hall. Obreros Hall was also where many Mexican-American social activities took place. One historically important meeting was held at Obreros Hall on Feb. 17, 1929, a Sunday.

The man who organized that meeting, and emerged as one of the leaders, was Ben Garza, owner of the Metropolitan Café on Chaparral. The delegates who attended the meeting included representatives from separate Hispanic civil rights organizations, from Corpus

12. *Obreros Hall at Carrizo and Lipan was where a meeting was held on Feb. 17, 1929 that resulted in the merger of Mexican-American civil rights organizations. Obreros Hall was torn down in 1974 when the new Nueces County Courthouse was built on that site.*

Christi, San Antonio and the Valley. These included the Council No. 4 of the Order of Sons of America, the Corpus Christi chapter (the San Antonio chapter shunned the meeting), the Knights of America from San Antonio, and the League of Latin American Citizens, which had formed in Harlingen two years before.

Obreros Hall on Sunday afternoon, Feb. 17, 1929 was packed, with more 200 people present. Delegates elected Ben Garza as the meeting chairman and they agreed on the need for separate Hispanic civil rights organizations to merge into one effective organization, the League of United Latin American Citizens (LULAC). They agreed to hold a convention in Corpus Christi in May. That meeting was held at Allende Hall on Antelope.

At another convention at Allende Hall in May, Ben Garza was elected the organization's first president and Luis Wilmot, who was also from Corpus Christi, was elected treasurer; M. C. Gonzalez was elected vice president and Andres De Luna of Corpus Christi was named as secretary.

Ben Garza, LULAC's unifying leader and first president, was a self-made man. He grew up in Rockport. His father died when he was 15; he quit school to go to work to help his mother support the family. He moved to Corpus Christi, took a job as a waiter, worked at

13. *Members of Mexican-American organizations gather at Carrizo and Lipan in 1920. Groups represented included Woodmen of the World, the Corpus Christi Mexican Band (also known as the B. G. Rodriguez Band), and the Sociodad Concordia.*

a shipyard during World War I, and began to save his money and buy property. He and three business partners bought the Metropolitan Café on Chaparral in 1919. He became the leader of the Corpus Christi chapter of Council No. 4 of the Order of Sons of America.

Garza began to work to unite other Hispanic organizations in South Texas to increase power, reach and influence. In time, through the efforts of LULAC and Hispanic activists willing to take a stand, primary schools in Corpus Christi were opened to children of Latin descent, Hispanics were accorded the right to serve on juries, and other gains were made. As the new president of LULAC, Garza went to Washington to testify against legislation that was aimed specifically to restrict immigration of Latin-Americans as "undesirables."

Garza closed the Metropolitan Café in 1931 and entered a sanitarium for treatment of tuberculosis. He died at the age of 44 in 1937. Flags at the City Hall and Courthouse were lowered to half-mast and the White House sent representatives to his funeral.

Ben Garza's widow Adelaida said her husband's single-minded goal in founding LULAC was not only to fight segregation and discrimination, but to improve the educational opportunity for all Hispanics. "He wanted to better the Mexican-American in all aspects of life, and the way to do this was through education."

Obreros Hall was torn down in 1974 when the new county courthouse was built on the site.

Past Leopard, in the 700 block, was a blacksmith shop run by Marcus Russell, at 716. It's believed that this was the old Thomas Beynon Livery Stable. Beynon was a cavalry captain during the Civil War and later he was a trail boss for King Ranch. He was one of three appraisers for the estate after Richard King's death. Beynon's livery stable was on

Carrizo past Leopard on the east side of the street. J. L. Allhands wrote in "The Gringo Builders" that Beynon's Livery had an unusual feature, a windmill that pumped fresh water to each stall. Beynon was elected sheriff and also ran a stage line to the Rio Grande before the coming of the railroad.

Beynon's livery was still in business after the turn of the century. He died in 1913. The Beynon Livery building (and later Russell blacksmith shop) was torn down to make way for a Piggly Wiggly parking lot, across from the Villa Apartments. Next door to the north was the Dixie Ice Plant, run by Charles Dorsey.

Several homes stood on both sides of the street in the 800 block, between Antelope and Buffalo, including that of Nannie Griffin, who was county treasurer in the 1930s.

In the next block, past Buffalo, was the home of Dr. P. G. Lovenskiold, at 907 Carrizo. Dr. Lovenskiold, the town's first dentist, built the home in 1907. Lovenskiold was the son of Charles Lovenskiold, from Denmark, who came to Corpus Christi in 1852. He was trained as a lawyer and prepared the first city charter. He established the Corpus Christi Academy in 1854.

Lovenskiold served as a colonel of cavalry during the Civil War. He died in 1875. His oldest son, Oscar, was mayor for 12 years. And his youngest son, Dr. P. G. Lovenskiold, was mayor from 1921 to 1931. Dr. Lovenskiold would walk each workday from his home down the bluff to his office in the Gugenheim-Cohn Building on Schatzel Street. During the upheaval in the mid-1950s in that part of town due to the construction of access roads to the Harbor Bridge and Crosstown Expressway, the old Lovenskiold home was moved from 907 Carrizo to 813, one block south.

Because the doctor resisted the idea of moving the house, the family took pains to reconstruct the house at its new site to match the old location as closely as possible. Even the blue and white tile inlays in the sidewalk that spelled out "Dr. Lovenskiold" were replaced at the new site. He died in 1963 at the age of 95 and the house was demolished in 1971 after it was damaged by Celia.

ARTESIAN: This street runs north-south one block west of Carrizo, from Blucher to Winnebago. In the 400 block, between Comanche and Lipan, was the home of William and Lena McCurdy, at 401, past Comanche. McCurdy owned a jewelry store on Schatzel, across from the Gugenheim-Cohn Building. Past McCurdy's was the home of Conrad Uehlinger, who owned a confectionery on Leopard. At 409 was the home of Gregorio and Bertha Tamez. Across Lipan was the Blue Star Grocery, run by Vicente Rossi and his wife Trinidad, followed by the home of Mary Bluntzer, widow of Peter Bluntzer.

In the 700 block of Artesian, past Leopard on the east side of the street, was the Ideal Rooms boarding house, run by Lydia Parks, followed by the Old Virginia Café. This later became the Green Tree Bar, run by Fred Smith. It was converted into the home and office of dentist Constantine Menendez. Another dentist, H. B. Hall, was at 722 and an ice cream shop, Harris Quality Ice Cream, run by Joseph Harris, was at 712.

On the west side of the 700 block was the home of Ben (Benito) Grande, built in 1904. Ben Grande ran the famous Grande Saloon, founded by his father Francisco in the 1880s. The Grande Saloon was the dominant business on Leopard and perhaps the city's most popular saloon. After Francisco died in June 1902, Ben took over the operation and the saloon became known as the Ben Grande.

14. Rafael Garcia and his bride, Annie Dutailly, on their wedding day on June 4, 1910. They were married at St. Patrick's Cathedral by Father Claude Jaillet. Rafael Garcia was a salesman at Lichtenstein's. Annie Dutailly's father, Auguste Dutailly, was a lamplighter for the city. Their first home was at 823 Artesian.

In 1925 Ben Grande sold his two-story home at 709 Artesian to Ida Grossman Cohen, whose family established the Grossman Department Store on Leopard. The Grande home was operated as an apartment building before it was donated to the city in 1982 and moved to Heritage Park for preservation. The original site was cleared for a parking lot.

Beyond the Grande-Grossman house, at 723 Artesian, was a grocery store run by Mrs. Rose Moses. In the 800 block, at 823 Artesian, was the home of Rafael Garcia and his wife, Annie (Dutailly) Garcia. They later moved to 1010 Lipan.

On the west side of the 900 block of Artesian, past Buffalo at 901, was a 10-room house built in 1898 for William B. and Edna Hopkins. W. B. Hopkins was the judge of 28th district court.

15. *The home of A. M. French (and later Rafael Galvan) was moved from Waco Street to Heritage Park in 1983. It was built in 1908 at the corner of Waco and Comanche.*

WACO: This was a busy commercial street, intermingled with some homes, for most of its length, from Blucher to Winnebago. Past Winnebago was Topo, a short two-block street that ran from Winnebago to Old Bayview Cemetery. The name of Topo was changed to Waco in 1941.

In the 300 block of Waco, the first block north of Blucher, was Mother's Cookie Company. It was at 311, on the west side of the street, and it was run by Harry and Nora Spicer. That was in the 1930s. They changed the name to Spicer Bakery. Across the street at 324 was the Bay Grocery operated by John Mircovich. John and his brother Mateo were well-known throughout the area as successful fishermen who came from Yugoslavia.

John Mircovich was born in 1857 and came to the United States in 1871. He moved to Corpus Christi in 1881. He and Mateo built a fishing schooner in 1884 and called it "Two Brothers." They opened a fish market in Ingleside, also called "Two Brothers," and another in Corpus Christi. In 1889 John built the Bay Saloon and Restaurant at 224 Water Street. He was known for cooking seafood. Fishermen bought his macaroni soup, fish and oyster chowder and Italian beans to take home. After Nueces County voted for Prohibition in 1916, he converted the Bay Saloon into the Bay Grocery.

After the 1919 storm destroyed his home, grocery and restaurant on Water Street, John Mircovich moved to the 300 block of Waco Street. Soon after his arrival in Corpus Christi, Mircovich married Adela Flores and they had four children. She died at age 24 in 1897. Mircovich married Francisca Gonzalez in 1903 and they had five sons. John Mircovich died at his home on Waco on Sunday morning, June 12, 1949.

In the 400 block of Waco, on the west side of the street, was the A. M. French home, built in 1908 at 403 Waco. French, a trained engineer and surveyor, moved to Corpus Christi from New Hampshire in 1875. He went to work as a surveyor on building a railroad in Mexico. When the company lost its concession, he and other men employed on the line walked hundreds of miles from the interior of Mexico to Matamoros and then Brownsville. That was in late January 1876.

At Brownsville, French was told it would be easier if he walked up Padre Island to Corpus Christi; he could get food and water at ranches along the way. French and a man named James Hayes started walking home.

French wrote in his diary that when they started up the island on Friday, Feb. 4, a norther blew in and it turned bitterly cold. They built a fire on the beach that night to try to keep warm. On Saturday they found water and camped at an old abandoned corral. They met a fellow traveler who had no blanket and they took him in.

On Tuesday they ate a dead fish and on Wednesday they killed a half-dead water turkey, which they ate. They killed a possum, which French described as good eating. Nearly dead from thirst and hunger, they finally reached an occupied residence on Thursday. A woman at the house cooked a meal for them.

After breakfast on Saturday they waded across the Laguna Madre and then sat on a log to dry out. They reached a packing house at Flour Bluff and from there made it the last easy stage to Corpus Christi. After spending eight days walking up the length of the island, almost perishing from cold and hunger on the way, French decided that Padre Island was a great place to stay away from.

French continued to survey land for railroads and was the chief surveyor and engineer when the San Antonio & Aransas Pass Railroad was built. He surveyed land for Stanley Kostoryz in 1904 when he was selling farm parcels in his Bohemian Colony.

French was one of the directors of the First State Bank and maintained an office in the round tower of the bank. He married Frances Garrett, from Rochester, Minn., and built a new home on the bluff. They had been living in one of the Daimwood cottages at Broadway and Leopard, where the Nixon Building was later constructed.

A granddaughter said French "stood on the wharf and picked out the lumber for the house, board by board" that was built on Waco Street. French died on April 22, 1936. Mrs. French died on Jan. 6, 1956. The French home on the corner of Waco and Comanche was sold to Rafael Galvan in 1941. What became known as the French-Galvan house was moved to Heritage Park and restored in 1983.

The 500 block of Waco, between Lipan and Mestina, consisted mainly of small homes and apartments, which were subdivided from older houses. At the end of the block, on the east corner with Mestina, was a service station run by Erasmo Muguerza in the 1930s. That site was vacant by the 1940s.

The 600 block between Mestena and Leopard presented a thriving commercial scene in the 1930s. On the east corner past Mestina was Angela Chapa's Mexican Café in the early 1930s. It advertised "High class Mexican dishes." By the 1940s it was a beer saloon called the Alma Latina Club. It was followed by the Ideal Market, Dick Cross's jewelry store, and the furniture store of M. W. McGinnis. By the late 1930s, the jewelry store had become a café run by Marvin Clark and the McGinnis furniture store was a beer bar run by Ricardo "Dick" Godoy, later called the Waco Club.

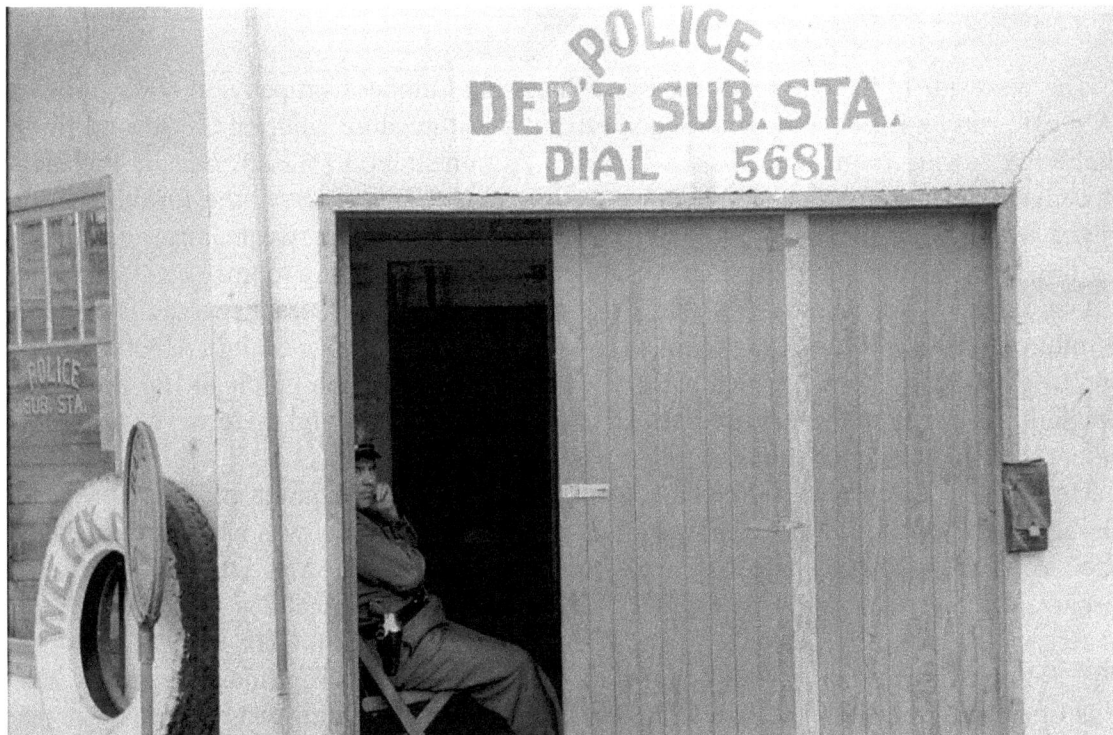

16 and 17. Lerma Poultry & Eggs, at 713 Waco, (top) was operated by Juan Lerma. The site in the late 1930s and early 1940s was occupied by Longoria Taxi and as a substation of the city police department (bottom).

18. *Felipe Castaneda, who owned Castaneda Funeral Service, sits in the driver's seat of a hearse as it passes the corner of Waco and Antelope. Castaneda's funeral parlor was at 811 Waco. The procession was passing Aquilino Rosales' general store at 724 Waco. He later moved to Antelope.*

The west side of the 600 block included Pickering Lumber Company, at 601, followed by a café run by Eliseo Villasenor, Joe Ferrer's furniture store, and, on the second floor, the WPA sewing room. The Works Progress Administration (WPA), part of President Roosevelt's New Deal, opened the sewing room at 613 Waco, above the furniture store, where women were paid up to $43 a month to make overalls, underwear, shirts and dresses for the needy. Mrs. Gladys Bonham was the director of the sewing room.

One of the WPA dressmakers was Rosa Esparza, wife of Pedro Esparza. The Ferrer furniture store and WPA sewing room were followed by the Anahuac Club, Alberta's Café, and Miguel Godoy's Café, which was soon closed and the White Elephant Bar opened in the building. Many of these businesses were gone by the 1960s and there were vacant lots where the buildings once stood.

On the east side of the 700 block were Michael Balle's restaurant, at 706, then Sport Barber Shop, at 708. Reyes G. Briones' tailor shop was at 710; it was later Ismael Luna's shoe shop after Briones went to work for Lichtenstein's. It was followed by Julian Esparza's grocery store at 720 and Juan Galvan's Black Cat Café at 724.

Across Waco on the west side of the 700 block was the Delta Club Billiard Parlor, at 709, followed by Lerma Poultry & Eggs at 713, owned by Juan Lerma. Longoria's Taxi was operating from this site by 1937. Part of the Lerma building was used as a police substation in the early 1940s. After this came the White House Café, with the Waco Hotel above it, the Palace Cleaners, Memo Medina's barbershop, and Tomas Maldonado's Grocery. The Green Tree Bar was moved from 710 Artesian to 723 Waco by 1942. It had gone out of business by the late 1940s and the Rumba Club, a bar operated by Tato Hernandez, occupied that location.

At 719 Waco was La India Bakery, established in 1937 by Mr. and Mrs. R. C. Garcia (Raymondo and Manuela) on Sam Rankin Street. They moved to Waco and at first called it Rivera's Bakery before settling on La India because, Mrs. Garcia said, her husband liked the name. The bakery became famous throughout the area for its French bread and pastries.

In the 800 block, between Antelope and Buffalo, was Rosales General Store on the corner lot. It was in a two-story building and the family lived upstairs.

Across the street, at 811, was the funeral home and residence of Felipe Castaneda, who moved to Corpus Christi from New Orleans and married Isabel Reyna. Castaneda later established the Corpus Christi Auto Livery. He died in 1926.

On that block, in the 1930s, there was Bill's Potato Chips, owned by William J. Horton.

Past Buffalo, on the east side of the street, was W. R. Haven's laundry and across the street was the Reyna family home, built in 1905 by Francisco Josefina Reyna. In the 1930s, a family bakery was operated at the rear of the home.

The old home and bakery were damaged by Celia and razed in 1970. Past the Reynas was the First Congregational Church at 921 Waco. The church was a descendant of the original Freedman's Congregational Church established on North Broadway after the Civil War. In the 1930s, the pastor of the church was Rev. William Bender, who was succeeded by Rev. S. J. Mayfield.

TOPO: This short street led from Winnebago to West Broadway, taking a right angle to the northeast. It was considered an extension of Waco and the City Council changed to that name in 1941. Two other short streets nearby were also changed in 1941: Media became an extension of North Tancahua and Jones became an extension of North Carancahua.

St. Matthew's Baptist Church was at 924 Topo in 1937, but its new address in 1942 was 1101 Waco. St. Matthew's was established in 1874, when several Baptists withdrew from the Congregational Church, composed of different denominations and organized in 1866.

In the early 1930s, St. Matthews, with Fred Davis as pastor, was located at 1200 Chipito Street. It moved shortly afterwards to 924 Topo, with Rev. B. E. Joshua as pastor. When the street name was changed, St. Matthews' new address was 1101 Waco. It also got a new name about the same time, becoming St. Mathews Missionary Baptist.

In that short addition to Waco there was D. Aguirre Munoz's home and grocery store. He later moved to the 1700 block of Antelope. Others in that block included Dr. W. C. Anderson's office, Esther Crecy's Beauty Shop, Jackson-Flowers Funeral Home, and a number of homes and apartments.

WINNEBAGO: The name of Winnebago originated with the town's founder, Henry Kinney. The Indian tribe it was named for came from the Midwest, around Lake Michigan. Kinney came to Texas from Illinois, so he was familiar with the Winnebagos. He named other uptown streets after Indian tribes with closer connections to South Texas — Carancahua, Tancahua, Lipan, Comanche and Waco.

The connection was a little too close in 1844 when Kinney's Rancho, as the settlement was first called, was attacked by Comanche warriors on horse-stealing raids. Kinney hired armed gunmen to help protect the town. Kinney himself relied on Lipan warriors to escort him on his trips to Austin to attend the Texas Congress. The uptown streets named for Indians were all very familiar to the early settlers, except for the misplaced Winnebago.

19. Nueces County Judge Walter F. Timon. He was instrumental in building the first causeway across Nueces Bay and pushed for the construction of a seawall to protect Corpus Christi. Timon Boulevard on North Beach was named for him.

Winnebago in the 1930s was mixed with homes and businesses. The more palatial mansions on the street were built in the first two blocks from Broadway. In the 700 block, between Carancahua and Tancahua, was the Walter Timon home at 711. Timon, before he was elected county judge, bought the house in 1902 from the Tito Rivera family. He sold it in 1945 to the First Methodist Church, which moved it to the 1000 block of Chaparral. It was torn down in 1962.

Timon was born in 1872 on the Timon ranch north of San Patricio. His father John owned cattle ranches in San Patricio, Live Oak and Bee counties. His mother Ellen's father was one of the Horse Marines in the Texas Revolution. John Timon built a home on Mesquite Street in Corpus Christi. One day in 1891, his wife and daughter returned home to find his body in the wrecked house. Who or what caused his death remained a mystery. As a young man, Walter was a star baseball player on the Bluff City Nine. He was once a sparring partner of Blacksmith Bob Fitzsimmons, who trained on North Beach.

Timon was elected county judge of Nueces County in 1906 and soon became a power in politics, a man who could hold his own against Jim Wells and Archie Parr, the big political bosses of the time. He was a politician of great skill. Timon and other county officials were tried in federal court in 1915 on charges that they bribed voters to win an election. Timon was found not guilty. After six terms as county judge, Timon was appointed district judge in 1920.

20. The Thomas B. Dunn home stood at the corner of Winnebago and North Carancahua. This 12-room Southern-style house, built in 1906, was torn down to make way for the Harbor Bridge approaches.

Judge Timon was wounded in a shootout on Chaparral Street in 1924. He was shot by his nephew, Harry Leahy. This was the result of a family squabble. Walter's older sister married Philip Leahy and the Leahy family believed that Walter had used his influence with their mother to cheat them of their fair share of the inheritance. Harry Leahy was later executed for killing a Mathis doctor. Walter Timon never ran for political office after his last term as county judge but his influence was lasting. The 1914 courthouse and the first causeway across the bay were built under his supervision and it was the Timon tax remission plan that was instrumental in building the seawall. He died on Aug. 2, 1952.

On the corner across the street was the Thomas B. Dunn home at 710 Winnebago. (The address was later changed to 1001 Carancahua.) The 12-room Southern-style house was built in 1906 on a site that had been in the Dunn family since the early years of the city. The Dunn home commanded a beautiful view of the bay from the home's white Southern-style verandas.

Dunn was chief of the city's volunteer fire department. His wife, Nellie Musselman Dunn, once said that when the house was filled with flowers it was a sign that the firemen's parade was coming up. Their home served as headquarters for women who decorated the floats with flowers. Early in the morning after the 1919 storm, volunteers brought survivors to the Dunn home, which became an emergency shelter and aid station. "It was awful to see them come in," said Nellie (Musselman) Dunn. They were all covered with oil and blood." The old Dunn home, an uptown landmark, was acquired in 1956 to make way for the south expressway to the new bridge. It was torn down soon afterwards.

21. Solomon M. Coles school was built in 1924 to replace a frame building that had been used as a broom factory. The school was expanded and remodeled over the years. It was a focal point of the black community in Corpus Christi and throughout the region.

In the 1930s in the 800 block of Winnebago, between Tancahua and Carrizo, on the north side of the street, was the Peter Coleman residence at 804. By the 1940s it was the home of K&M Cleaners, run by R. D. Kuykendall. The Gold Front Bar was at 806 and Walter's Pool Hall at 808. There were half a dozen homes on both sides of the street. Homes and apartments dominated the 900 block.

In the next block, between Artesian and Waco, was the Solomon Coles School. Solomon Melvin Coles, a former slave, was appointed principal of the black school near the end of the 1870s. Coles was known as a strict disciplinarian. One student recalled that "you had to be in your seat by 9 a.m. or you would get a whaling."

The colored school, next to the Central School on Carancahua, was moved to a four-room frame building on Winnebago. The new school for the city's black students was in a converted broom factory, with two outhouses and water supplied from a backyard rainwater cistern. The school opened in September 1893 with Coles as principal. He left the following year for San Antonio. A new brick structure was built in 1924 and additions were made in 1927 and 1929. The school was made a full high school in 1933.

In the 1930s and 1940s, the Solomon Coles school became a magnet not only for the town's black neighborhood, but throughout the region. Because there was no other high school open to blacks between Victoria and Brownsville, in that era of segregation, black students came from all over to attend Coles. Will Scott, who attended Coles and went on to get a doctorate in education, once said, "There was one group of kids who came over in an old battered car from Robstown every morning. There were kids from Kingsville who had some relatives they lived with in Corpus Christi so they could attend high school at Coles." In 1967, with the coming of integration, Coles was converted into a junior high and in 1973 it became an elementary school.

22. *The Michael Thomas Gaffney home was moved from 80 Leopard (where Corpus Christi Bank & Trust was built) to Buffalo where it was remodeled and enlarged. It became known as the Gaffney-Young home.*

Across from Solomon Coles, on the south side of the street, was Joseph Castaneda's grocery and market. The Castaneda family still occupied that address in the 1960s. Past North Staples, in the 1200 block approaching Sam Rankin, was Antonio Longoria's Grocery.

BUFFALO: In the 600 block of Buffalo, between North Broadway and Carancahua, was the home of Anna Brooks, at 616, next door to the Shaffer Apartments, at 624, which consisted of four buildings. The main building was built by Anna Brooks' father, Professor Alex A. Brooks, who moved to Corpus Christi from Goliad, where he had a boarding school, in the late 1880s.

Professor Brooks was a well-educated man with many years of experience in teaching. He was principal of the public schools in Corpus Christi for a short time before he built the large structure at Buffalo and Carancahua where he started Kensmar Seminary, a boarding and day school for young women. The town's most prominent young ladies attended Professor Brooks' seminary. Among the students in 1890 were Lulu and Blanche Rivera, Eva McCampbell, Selma Lichtenstein, Lottie Savage, Katie Ricklefsen, Nellie Chapman, May Ward, and Anna Mussett.

The school had been long closed when William Shaffer bought the building and converted it into apartments. He also purchased the old Episcopal rectory on Taylor Street and moved it up to Buffalo Street and turned it into apartment units. The whole complex was known as the Shaffer Apartments.

Shaffer was elected mayor in 1933 and served one term. The main building, Professorr Brooks' old Kensmar Seminary, was torn down in 1954 to make a parking lot for Sunray Oil Co. The other Shaffer Apartment structures were torn down in 1957.

23. *The Edward C. Timon home was sold to Maxwell P. Dunne in 1926 and converted to a funeral home.*

In the 800 block of Buffalo, between Tancahua and Carrizo, there were two places that stand out, from an historical perspective. The first was Robert Ritter's Grocery at 828, on the corner of Carrizo, on the north side of the street. Ritter brought his family from Heidelberg to Corpus Christi in 1883. He opened a racket store on Mesquite in the 1880s and built the Ritter Hotel and Bath House on a pier off Water Street in 1891. It was later destroyed by a hurricane. The Ritter store on Buffalo was in a small frame building. A sign said, "Ritter's Every Day Bargain Store." Ritter died in 1943 at the age of 93.

Opposite Ritter's store on the corner with Carrizo was the home of George R. Clark Sr., at 823. It was built in 1910 and the family moved in later that year. The family stayed in the home during the 1919 storm. Homes on the bluff, high above the storm tide, were hardly damaged during the storm. At the Clark home the wind of the storm blew in some water around the doors. That was all. Clark was at first a cashier and later the president of State National Bank. He became chairman of the board when it merged with Corpus Christi National Bank. He died in 1958. A daughter, Mrs. A. Hunt Cole (Maggie Clark) lived in the home until it was razed in 1964.

In the 900 block, between Carrizo and Artesian, was the old Gaffney home, on the south side of the street at 915. It was built by Michael Thomas Gaffney in 1877, at 801 Leopard. One of the four Gaffney children, Katherine, married Philip Young, a local attorney, and when he died of influenza in 1918 she moved back into the Gaffney home on Leopard. A building boom in the 1920s, after Maston Nixon built the Nixon Building, led to the transformation of Leopard Street. The Gaffney property was sold to make way for Robert Driscoll's Corpus Christi Bank & Trust. The Gaffney home was moved to 915 Buffalo,

238

24. *Mary Fisher in 1920. She operated a "house of pleasure" on Buffalo. She later moved to Palo Alto Street where she was murdered in 1946.*

where Kate Young lived. The frame house was remodeled, enlarged, and a stucco façade added. In later years, it was converted into apartments. Next to the Gaffney place was another old home at 923, first constructed by George Greer in the decade after the Civil War. Mrs. Philip Young bought the house, which became the residence of her daughter Mary after she married Sam Westergren. The house became known as the Greer-Young-Westergren house. It was moved from Buffalo Street to 234 Rossiter in 1952.

In the 1000 block, in the 1930s, stood two homes on the north side of the street. At 1020 was the home of Police Chief Lee Petzel. Next door was the home of Roger McGloin, the Police Commissioner. Petzel became chief of police in the 1930s. He was tried for murder, with Sheriff Frank Robinson, in the shooting death of Fred Roberts in 1922. Petzel in later years would reminisce about the days when he was the only officer working under Chief Mike Niland. He was mounted on a horse, wore a pith helmet and uniform with golden buttons. Petzel's brother J. W., known as Bill, served as chief of detectives and police chief in the Roy Miller administration. Lee Petzel died in 1948.

In the 1100 block was the well-known bakery of Alfonso and Hermila Reyna. Corpus Christi Transfer later moved in past the Reyna bakery.

Mary Fisher owned a property at 1313 Buffalo, though she lived on Palo Alto. She ran a "house of pleasure" and the young women who lived with her were described as boarders who were too good-looking to work regular hours. They would be called "sex-workers" in the non-judgmental term of today. Theodore Fuller in his memoirs said there were three brothels besides Mary Fisher's and all were supplied with young women circulating from Matamoros to New Orleans. Mary Fisher moved to Palo Alto Street where she was murdered on May 7, 1946. Hugh Smith, the man convicted of the crime, was sentenced to life in prison.

25. *The Shaffer Apartment building, at 624 Buffalo, was originally Professor Alex A. Brooks' Kensmar Seminary, a school for young women built in the late 1880s.*

26. *Tomas Cantu and family operated Cantu's Food Store on Sam Rankin, past Antelope Street.*

27. The Order of Sons of America with Ben Garza in the front (next to the sailor with a flag) stand on the steps of the First Methodist Church in 1929. The Sons of America was a forerunner of the League of Latin American Citizens which was formed in May at a convention at Allende Hall. Ben Garza was elected the first president and these Sons of America became founding members of LULAC.

ANTELOPE: Past the intersection of Carancahua, on Antelope Street, was the stately Edward C. Timon home, a real showplace. The Edward C. Timon home was on the north side of the street at 720, across from St. Patrick's Church. Timon's widow, Josephine Bluntzer Timon, sold the house in 1926 to Maxwell P. Dunne, who converted it into a funeral home.

This was Dunne's third location. The first was in the 500 block of Starr in 1908, next to where the federal courthouse was built. He moved to the 100 block of Mesquite in 1916. After the 1919 storm, Dunne was responsible for identifying and preparing death records for many of the storm victims. He moved up to the bluff in 1926. Dunne died in 1948. The old Timon home was razed in 1962 after the funeral home moved out to Morgan Avenue.

In the next block of Antelope was the bishop's home. It stood on the corner opposite of Dunne's funeral home, past the Tancahua intersection. The bishop's house was built before World War I for Bishop Paul Joseph Nussbaum, who was appointed to succeed Bishop Peter Verdaguer. The original house on the site was built in 1901 for Rev. Claude Jaillet.

When Nussbaum was appointed bishop of the diocese, the two-story Jaillet residence was moved across the street to the Incarnate Word grounds and a residence for Bishop Nussbaum was built on the site. It was a two-story 22-room house built at a cost of $10,000. Bishop Nussbaum was succeeded in 1921 by Bishop E. D. Ledvina. The home was being razed in 1971 when it burned.

Past the Carrizo intersection, on the corner at 902, was the Toups home, built in 1850 and considered one of the oldest homes in the city. Toups family members still lived in the house in the 1930s and 1940s. Susie Scott Toups was living in the old home when she died in 1958. She was the daughter of Henry Scott, a cattle rancher and vigilante captain. She married Joseph W. Toups in 1898. They owned a cattle ranch in Refugio County. The White House Food Store moved in next door in the 1940s.

In the 1000 block, between Artesian and Waco, on the north side of the street, stood the El Paladin printing office. The El Paladin, one of three Spanish-language newspapers on the Hill, was founded by Eulalio Marin and began publishing in 1928. He championed school desegregation, equal rights, and was a founding member of LULAC.

Leo Duran, the city's first Hispanic lawyer, said in 1988 that Marin didn't accept contributions for what he did, even though he was a poor man. "He didn't want credit or money; he just wanted to do good." It was said that he was a familiar figure on the Hill, always wearing a bowler hat and carrying a briefcase.

In the 1400 block of Antelope, past Sam Rankin, was Allende Hall, which stands tall in the history of LULAC. Ben Garza, owner of the Metropolitan Café, became the president of Council No. 4 of the Order of Sons of America. In 1929 it was merged with similar organizations in South Texas to form the beginning of LULAC.

The first convention was held May 18 and 19, 1929 at Allende Hall, where Ben Garza was elected president. (The first meeting was held at Obreros Hall on Feb. 17, 1929 to organize disparate Mexican-American groups.)

Fernando Pena, one of the men at that convention, said long afterwards, "These two days' experience will serve me all through my life. It is very seldom that you have the opportunity to hear men like this convention brought together and discuss issues as earnestly as they did Saturday and Sunday in Allende Hall." Another prominent and influential man at the convention, the genesis of much to come, was the El Paladin publisher Eulalio Marin.

MESTINA: This street runs west from Tancahua out to Black Street (later changed to North Staples. In the first 800 block was the Saenz Grocery, operated for years by Geronimo Saenz and after he died by his widow Sara. Mauricio Morales operated the old Saenz store in the 1940s.

In the next block, between Carrizo and Artesian, was the Cheston L. Heath School, at 907 Mestina, on the corner on the south side of the street facing north. (The school's address fluctuated over the years; it was sometimes listed at 500 North Carrizo and at other times as 907 Mestina.)

The site on block 26 of the Bluff Addition was purchased by the school board in 1901 for $400 from Corpus Christi National Bank, which in turn bought it from W. S. Rankin.

The wood-frame school building was constructed for $1,685 by Reid & Sutherland (Dan Reid and H. R. Sutherland Sr.). The keys to the three-room building were turned over to the school board on Sept. 8, 1902, and the board bought new stoves, and the coal to burn in them, for the coming school year.

One of the first students recalled that there was a water cooler under the outside stairway "and the janitor had to fill it up about every 30 minutes." It was first known as the Mexican Central School, and was intended to teach elementary age Spanish-language students to speak English before they could be assigned to the Central School on Carancahua.

28. Students on the playground at Cheston L. Heath School on Jan. 21, 1933. The two-story structure behind was the old school building originally constructed on Carancahua in the 1890s and moved to the Cheston L. Heath school grounds. It was demolished in 1937.

The name was changed to the Cheston L. Heath School in 1919 after Heath died in 1918. He was a longtime school-board member who was known for his generosity in buying schoolbooks for kids who couldn't afford them. His father, Cheston C. Heath, was a former ship captain and merchant who served a term as mayor of Corpus Christi. The family business was the Heath & Son Emporium, which sold groceries, crockery, and iron stoves.

The Cheston Heath school grew and a new brick building was built in 1927 while the older structure was still in use.

Rose Dunne Shaw was one of the outstanding teachers and later principal of the school. She established what was called "a bean line" at the school during the Depression years of the 1930s. She convinced the Rotary Club and merchants Alex Weil and Edwin Flato to donate foodstuffs, pots and pans, and an iron stove. She established an improvised kitchen at the end of the hall on the first floor and fed her students every day.

Before the brick building was constructed, and even afterwards, the Cheston L. Heath School consisted of a conglomeration of frame buildings as attendance at the school soared in the 1930s and 1940s. One building on the premises was the old frame building on Carancahua built in the early 1890s. It was torn down in 1937.

29 and 30. *Cheston L. Heath's main brick building, shown in 1939, (above), was constructed in 1927. The school building was demolished in 1974 to make way for the new Nueces County Courthouse.*

31. *Principal Rose Dunne Shaw (center) with teachers at Cheston Heath School in the 1940s.*

At its peak in 1934, attendance at Cheston Heath climbed to 1,600 pupils, with only 27 teachers to instruct them. Attendance began to drop after World War II as new schools were opened. The school was closed in 1960 and its student population moved to the George Evans School. When Northside Junior High (the old "Brick Palace") was closed and the site sold for a parking lot, the students at that school were moved to the Cheston L. Heath School, which was renamed Northside Junior High. A year later, the junior high students were moved to the old Solomon Coles School. The Cheston L. Heath building sat empty until the newly organized KEDT public TV and radio station occupied the building in 1972 for a year. The old school building, constructed in 1927, was torn down in 1974 to clear the site for construction of the new Nueces County Courthouse.

The El Parian Apartments were at 1016 and the Nueces Lumber Company was in the 1100 block. L.D. Garrison's lumber company was in the 1200 block, past Staples.

32. The home of Anton Samman, a Lebanese immigrant who owned a store on Leopard, was built at 1215 Mestina in 1911. City Hall parking lot is on that site today.

One home in the 1200 block (where the new City Hall was built) was that of Anton M. Samman, at 1215. It was built in 1911 by Samman, a Lebanese immigrant who operated a dry goods store in the 1200 block of Leopard, just past the Staples Street intersection. He later opened the Samman Grocery and Market on Leopard Street. In the 1400 block, past Sam Rankin, was the Mexican Presbyterian Church. The street consisted mostly of homes and apartments until the 2100 block where the Mirando Lumber Company was located.

LIPAN: There were homes on both sides of Lipan in the first four blocks, from North Broadway to North Staples. The home at 719 Lipan belonged to the widow of Dale Brickley. Brickley was an aviation enthusiast at Cliff Maus Field and was hired to dust crops in the Taft area, where he was killed on July 16, 1936. His widow Hilda, with four kids, rented the Charles Kelly home, a large three-story house at 719 Lipan, and opened a boarding house. After she married one of the boarders, Temple Ray, they moved to 15th street where Hilda Ray continued to operate a boarding house.

In the next block, at 818 and 820 Lipan, was the home and bar of Frank Huereca. The Huerecas lived at 818 and Frank operated his bar at 820. After he died, Eulalia sold the bar to Mrs. Natalia Betancourt, who converted it into a grocery store. In the 1960s, the Huereca home was occupied by a family member, Mrs. Severiana Huereca, though what had been Frank's Bar and the Betancourt Grocery stood vacant.

Past Staples was a Southwestern Bell warehouse. In the early 1930s the Roland Grande Grocery Store was at 1424 Lipan, at the Josephine intersection. The building, a combination store and home, was later sold to Fernando Villareal. The grocery store was short-lived and the address by the late 1940s was listed as the residence of Mrs. Juanita Galvan, widow of Eduardo Galvan Jr., a janitor at City Hall.

33. The original building for George Evans Elementary was constructed in 1912 and the school opened in 1913. The building was replaced by a new structure in 1967.

COMANCHE: There were several homes on Comanche, past Carancahua, in the 700 block. Past Tancahua, heading west, Blucher Park was the left, or south side of the street, and on the north were several homes, in the 1930s.

Before there was a Blucher Park there was an arroyo known as Chatham's Ravine, named after the Chatham family that lived nearby. Felix von Blucher bought the property from Henry Kinney shortly after the Mexican War.

The Blucher homestead was built west of the ravine. The land containing the park was donated to the city by the Blucher family in 1942 in memory of Charles Frederick Harvey Blucher, Nueces County surveyor from 1882 to 1934. That parkland is bounded on the south by the 800 block of Kinney Avenue, on the west by the 100 block of Carrizo, on the north by 800 block of Comanche, and on the east by the 300 block of Tancahua.

34. The Paul Court development stretched for five blocks along Comanche, from Sam Rankin Street to the west. The George Evans Elementary was sometimes referred to as the Paul Court School.

There were homes on the north side of Comanche in the 800, 900, 1000 and 1100 blocks, from Tancahua past Waco to Staples. On the north side of the street, past Staples, was the Sacred Heart Church, at 1222. Across the street, at 1223, was the J. M. Barrera Grocery.

Past Alameda (which had been known as Last Street) there was the Walter Lucas Grocery, ran by Walter and his wife Ruth, at 1324. It was across the street from George Evans Elementary, at 1315 Comanche.

George Evans Elementary was one of three new ward schools built in 1912. The other two were David Hirsch and Edward Furman. They were built using the same floor plan to save money. Theodore Fuller wrote in his memoirs, "When the Century and I Were Young," that the three new ward schools "were the last word in modern school architecture."

The school was named for George F. Evans. He was mayor in 1884-1885 and later served as vice president of the school board. Evans, from Boston, came to Corpus Christi and entered the "Mexican trade," buying wool and hides and selling other goods to traders from the interior of Mexico. He married Cornelia Moore, the daughter of Col. John M. Moore.

Early teachers at George Evans, soon after it opened, included Laura Savage, Mrs. Mae Decker, Mary Woods, and others. Evans was sometimes called the Paul Court school, in reference to the new subdivision developed near the school. A new building was erected in 1967 and the original structure was demolished.

In the 1400 block was the Moriada Funeral Home and in the 1600 block was the Mexican Methodist Church. The church was organized in 1874. The name was changed in 1948 to the Kelsey Memorial Methodist Church, after Anna Kelsey donated $75,000 to build a new

35. *The Eureka Laundry was located at 1111 Blucher, next to the Blucher's Lone Star ice plant. The laundry was established by James Walter Pittman in 1906. It was first on Chaparral at Starr then moved in 1920 to Blucher.*

brick building at Comanche and Mexico. Kelsey was the adopted daughter of early Corpus Christi settlers John Peter Kelsey and his wife Amanda. Kelsey ran a store and bought wool and hides. Amanda, a young woman from Ohio, taught school in his store. They moved to Rio Grande City. Farther west on Comanche was the Texas Star Flour Mills, at 1901, and Rose Hill Cemetery, at 2900. Comanche past Sam Rankin, in the 1400 to 1800 blocks, was part of the Paul Court addition.

BLUCHER: This street, which runs from the bluff to Staples, was originally called Chatham Street, named for Chatham's Ravine which in turn was named for the Chatham family, early settlers in the area. The name was changed to Blucher, at the request of the residents, by the City Council in 1913.

Blucher Street from Broadway to Carancahua included several homes, including that of Frank Tompkins, at 622, and Bertha Lacey, at 619. She was a dancing instructor. Bertha Lacey crossed paths with Fred Gipson, who wrote the book "Old Yeller." When he was a columnist for the Caller-Times, in the late 1930s, he was sent to write about a dance rehearsal at Bertha Lacey's studio, which was on William Street at Mesquite. He treated the assignment about the same way he would have if he was writing about a rodeo. Next day. Bob McCracken, the editor, said he was besieged by the angriest woman he had ever met, Bertha Lacey. McCracken said she didn't leave until she lost her voice from screaming about Gipson, "that awful cowboy."

Past Carancahua in the 700 block were homes on the south side of the street and several apartment buildings on the north, including the Castle Apartments and the Simank Apartments. There were more homes and apartments from Tancahua to Artesian. In the 1100 block, on the north side of the street were Clements Wilson's various business operations. Wilson and his wife Hazel operated three businesses across the street from the Lone Star Ice plant and the Eureka Laundry. They owned and managed Wilson's Produce, Wilson's Pool Hall, and Wilson's Café in the 1930s and early 1840s at 1118, 1122, and 1124 Blucher, between Artesian and North Staples.

Across the street was the Eureka Laundry. The laundry was established by J. W. (James Walter) Pittman in 1906. It was first on Water Street and moved to Blucher Street in 1920. J. W. Pittman died in 1938.

Past the Eureka Laundry was Marcus Russell's blacksmith shop. In previous years he was located on Carrizo where Thomas Beynon's Livery once stood. Russell's shop was followed by the Lone Star Ice Company, a Blucher family enterprise. In 1942, Arthur Blucher was president of the firm, Julius Blucher was vice president, and Jasper Blucher was secretary-treasurer.

Like much of the Blucher history, it is entwined with the history of the city. Jasper Blucher, the son of George and Alice Crawford Blucher, once recalled that Richard King built the first ice plant in Corpus Christi in 1878 and when King died it was sold to John Greer and in time passed to the Blucher family. Jasper said his father got a job at the ice plant. He would fire up the boilers and drive the ice wagon. After the 1919 storm, the ice plant was moved to Blucher Street.

Chapter 10. Ocean Drive

South from Emerald Cove past Cole Park, to the Louisiana intersection, and beyond to Three-Mile Point, the Aberdeen area, the Poenisch farm past Airline, and on to the Oso Pier, Cayo del Oso, Ward Island, and the Naval Air Station.

Elihu H. Ropes first envisioned an Ocean Drive. Ropes, from New Jersey, arrived in Corpus Christi in 1889 and described himself as a capitalist of unlimited means. He was certainly a man of unlimited ambition.

Ropes had a number of ambitious projects for Corpus Christi. He built a resort hotel at Three-Mile Point named the Alta Vista and began "The Cliffs" development south of town. He planned a street from the city to his development called Ocean Drive. A winding dirt road followed the bluff from the town south to Farmer Clark's farm where Ocean and Airline intersect today.

Decades before Elihu Ropes came to town, the area south of town along the bayfront around Three-Mile Point was part of the tract named for Col. William S. Harney. Harney's name is known to history as the man who was in charge of hanging deserters who were part of the San Patricio Battalion. They were mostly Irish deserters who changed sides and fought in the Mexican Army.

Harney's role came at the end of the Mexican War when 30 of the San Patricio men were ordered to be executed. The condemned men stood on heavy wagons beneath scaffolds on the outskirts of Mexico City on Sept. 12, 1847. Harney told them they would be hanged the moment the American flag went up at Chapultepec, the Hill of the Grasshoppers, where a battle was being fought.

The condemned men waited, with ropes around their necks, in the hot sun, one hour, two hours, then, through the smoke of battle, they could see a flash of red, white and blue, as the flag was raised in victory at Chapultepec. The guards cheered, the wagon drivers cheered, even the doomed men cheered. Through the cheering came Harney's harsh voice ordering the execution to proceed. The heavy wagons rolled from under 30 of the San Patricio deserters, leaving their bodies dangling from the scaffolds in the hot sun.

After the war, in the 1850s, Gen. Harney was in command of the Army's Department of Texas and army headquarters was located in Corpus Christi. During this time Harney bought much of the land south of town along what would become Ocean Drive. Old maps identify that area as the Harney Tract. Elihu Ropes purchased the Harney Tract for his development called "The Aransas Cliffs" then he went bankrupt. His resort hotel at Three-Mile Point, the Alta Vista, remained closed and shuttered and his other ambitious plans for Corpus Christi were abandoned.

The next chapter in Ocean Drive's history began after the outbreak of World War I in Europe in 1914. Corpus Christi and South Texas were focused on the revolutionary violence in Mexico that was spilling over the border. In March 1916, Gen. John Pershing was sent to the border with 10,000 troops and by August 1916 there were more than

1. *Soldiers at Camp Scurry in 1916. The camp was located in the area where Spohn Hospital and Del Mar neighborhood are today.*

100,000 state militia troops stationed on the border. Corpus Christi Mayor Roy Miller lobbied Gen. Frederick Funston, commander of the Army's Southern Department, to move some state militia units to Corpus Christi. Miller promised that Corpus Christi would provide a model camp.

After the 1916 hurricane flooded army camps in the valley, Gen. Funston ordered the Second and Third Texas Infantry Regiments, which made up the Texas Brigade, to move from the Brownsville section to Corpus Christi.

The camp at Corpus Christi was built in a pasture south of town, an area between Ocean Drive and Santa Fe, Buford and Louisiana, where Spohn Hospital and the Del Mar neighborhood are located today. City workers cleared brush, laid water lines, and dug drainage ditches around the camp. Electric lines were strung, wooden mess halls built, and the streetcar line extended to the camp.

The Third Infantry Regiment came by train from Harlingen on Thursday, Sept. 7, 1916. The Second Infantry Regiment arrived from Pharr the next day. Gen. John Hulen established his headquarters near Ocean Drive and named the camp after Gen. Thomas Scurry, a Texas veteran of the Spanish-American War.

The soldiers were put to work spreading shell on UpRiver Road as far as Calallen. For a long time, UpRiver Road was known as Shell Road.

A four-day field exercise began early on Wednesday, Nov. 8, 1916. Soldiers marched with full packs to Calallen and made camp across from the railroad depot. Before midnight the camp was drenched with heavy rain as a fierce norther blew in. Tents were blown down and orders given that it was every man for himself. They were a bedraggled sight as they marched through town on their way back to the camp.

2. The football team of the Second Texas Infantry in striped jerseys took on the New York Infantry in a game on New Year's Day 1917. Second Texas scored 102 points and the New York Infantry scored 0.

At Camp Scurry in 1916 the Second Texas Regiment fielded a football team made up of former college players, some from the University of Texas, Texas A&M and Baylor. They built a field at Santa Fe and Booty where the team trounced the country's best military teams. The Second Texas beat them by such lopsided scores that they were called "the best team that ever played the game."

From November 1916 into early 1917 the Second Texas ran up 432 points while allowing the opposition 6. The team never came close to losing. Perhaps that's why it was called "the best team that ever played." Knute Rockne, the legendary Notre Dame coach, was making some point at a football clinic when he said, "Not even the Second Texas could do that."

In February 1917, troops at Camp Scurry heard rumors that all Texas guardsmen were to be for demobilized. The rumors were true. They were going home and Scurry would be closed. Only a few of the 3,500 men would be left to dismantle the camp.

That changed on April 6, 1917 when the United States entered the war in Europe. Camp Scurry was designated as a training base. The Fifth Engineers from El Paso arrived on June 26 and began training for trench warfare. They were ordered to France in June 1917.

After the Fifth Engineers departed, Camp Scurry became the training base of the Fourth Field Artillery, which arrived on Sept. 7, 1918 from Houston. The camp was off limits during the height of the influenza epidemic that fall.

After the Armistice was signed on Nov. 11, 1918, which ended World War I, someone wrote, "a great quietness descended upon the Earth." Soldiers from Camp Scurry celebrated the end of the war with a parade downtown. On Jan. 4, 1919, the Fourth Field Artillery marched out of town for Camp Stanley near Leon Springs. There was no longer a need for Camp Scurry and it was permanently closed.

3. *Spohn Sanitarium was on the outskirts of the city, at Third and Ayers off Ocean Drive, when it opened in 1925. The name was changed to Spohn Hospital in 1930.*

Another chapter in the history of Ocean Drive began with the location of the second Spohn Hospital, built back of Ocean Drive at Third and Ayers. The original Spohn Sanitarium was built on North Beach in 1905. It was constructed on the site where the Miramar Hotel had burned. Spohn Sanitarium was all but destroyed in the hurricane of 1919 and a search began for a hospital site. While the search was underway, the John G. Kenedy home on North Broadway (Martha Rabb's old Magnolia Mansion) was used as a temporary hospital.

Alice King Kleberg convinced her mother, Henrietta King, the matriarch of King Ranch, to donate five acres of land along the bay for a new hospital. The prevailing opinion seemed to be that the place was too remote, too far outside the city, to be a suitable location. But the decision was made and the five-acre tract was turned over to the Sisters of Charity of the Incarnate Word.

A new Spohn Hospital was built at the corner of Third and Ayers, west of Ocean Drive and the bayfront. The three-story 50-bed Spohn Sanitarium opened on Aug. 25, 1925.

Leona Gradahl recalled the new hospital. Her family moved to Corpus Christi from the Panhandle in 1924. "When I arrived, Spohn was one little building, three stories and oblong in shape. The hospital was located at the end of the world because everything outside of Ayers Street was all cotton fields."

The first to be admitted to the new hospital was a patient of Dr. Harry G. Heaney. His father, Dr. Alfred Heaney, had admitted the first patient to the Spohn Sanitarium on North Beach when it opened in 1905. The hospital was originally intended to be a facility for the

4. *The Frank Crook home at 1717 Ocean Drive was built in 1927. The Crook home and the Donigan home at Three-Mile Point began the transformation of Ocean Drive as the city's most fashionable address.*

care of long-term illnesses but in 1930 it was changed to an institution aimed at the care of the critically ill.

The name was changed from Spohn Sanitarium to Spohn Hospital. A new 50-room annex was added to the original building in 1937. A new wing was completed in 1952, which was a five-story story addition with room for 120 more beds, giving the hospital a total of 250 beds.

The hospital continued to expand from its original site at Third and Ayers until it fronted on Ocean Drive.

The hospital had few residential neighbors. Most of the city's palatial homes were built on the high bluff, on North and South Broadway, with an unobstructed view of the bay. The first of the many fine homes that started Ocean Drive as a place of consequence was Frank Crook's home, built in 1927, followed by V. M. Donigan's white-stucco mansion at Three-Mile Point, built in 1931.

Crook was president of the Port Compress Company. He said in 1978 that when he bought the property from Austin Wright in 1931, "There was a small caliche road out here and if you wanted to go out to Three-Mile Point (where Donigan's home was built later) you had to go down to Water Street and take a boat. That's how bad the road was." When

5 and 6. Ocean Drive in the 1930s (above) and in the 1960s (below.) The top photo shows the street near the Municipal Wharf; this part of Ocean Drive, north of Buford, was changed to Water Street in 1960. The bottom photo shows Ocean Drive in front of the Crook house with Cole Park on the right.

7. *WPA workers in 1935 were employed to terrace the slope of Cole Park to prevent erosion.*

Crook bought the property, he said that Austin Wright assured him that nothing would ever be built in front of him. There was no Cole Park at the time. "Then we agreed to let the city have the property on the bay side in front of us to fill in and improve."

An iron fence around the Crook home was made in 1751. Crook said it was 175 years old when he bought it in 1926. "It was built by the Imden Iron Works in New Orleans and it was around an old New Orleans house that had burned." Crook said after Celia damaged the fence in 1970 he sold part of the ironwork to Lady Bird Johnson who used it for LBJ's grave site at the ranch at Johnson City.

A 1939 Caller-Times article described the Crook home: "White on the exterior, surrounded by palms, a landscaped yard that has no peer in the city, and an iron fence, the (Crook) home has an air of distinction."

In 1933 E. Barnes Cole gave the city land on the bay side of Ocean Drive, across from the Crook home, for a city park. Cole came to Corpus Christi during the Ropes boom in 1890. He owned a drug store and small hotel in Elk Falls, Kansas and one day he read a Kansas City newspaper that included a glowing account of the potential in Corpus Christi. Cole had never heard of Corpus Christi, but he moved here and became the sole agent for Elihu Ropes' real-estate sales.

8. *Aerial view of the expansion of Cole Park in 1967, showing the park from Emerald Cove at Buford to Louisiana Avenue. Fill material dredged from the bay added about 20 acres to the size of the park.*

9. May Watson's adobe-brick home was built in 1938 on the corner of Louisiana and Ocean Drive.

Cole once explained that the origin of Cole Park began with a mistake. City workers were plowing in the Austin J. Wright Park which adjoined Cole's property on the bayfront. The workers plowed up Cole's six acres by mistake. When city officials told Cole, he said, "I'll tell you what I'll do. I'll deed that six-acre tract to the city if the city will guarantee to use it permanently only for a public park." The bayfront land that Cole donated to the city in 1933 became Cole Park.

Two years later the Works Progress Administration (WPA) paid workers to terrace the slope and build a concrete base to stop the soil from eroding into the bay. Some 70 men worked in the park for six months in 1935.

Past the end of Cole Park (before it was expanded) on the south corner of the Louisiana Drive intersection, Harry and May Watson built a pueblo-style home they called "Watsonia."

The adobe brick house was built in 1938. It was the second notable house that May Watson occupied. For two decades, her home was La Quinta, a mansion on the north shore that was the headquarters of the Taft Ranch, one of the great ranches of South Texas.

May Watson was the daughter of Thomas Henry and Mary Nold Mathis. Her grandfather Henry Nold built a college at Ingleside before the Civil War. Her father was one of the founders of the Coleman-Mathis-Fulton Pasture Company. When the partnership ended in 1879, T. H. Mathis was granted the 24,000-acre Henry Bend Ranch. The town of Mathis was built on part of his ranch.

In 1907 May Mathis married Joseph F. Green, manager of the Coleman-Fulton Pasture Company, a 167,000-acre ranch. One of the original founders, Tom Coleman, sold his stock in the company in 1894 to David Sinton, a wealthy banker (for whom the town of Sinton was named) and Sinton's son-in-law, Charles Taft, both of Cincinnati. When Taft became the major stockholder, the ranch began to be called Taft Ranch.

When May married Green, the house that would be their home and serve as ranch headquarters was under construction on a site overlooking Corpus Christi Bay. The house was called La Quinta. President William Howard Taft stayed at La Quinta when he came to Texas in November 1909 to visit his half-brother's ranch. Joseph F. Green died on Nov. 20, 1926 and was buried in the Taft Cemetery. May married Harry H. Watson, a retired rancher from Colorado, and they built a new home in Corpus Christi at Louisiana and Ocean Drive.

The Watsons' home was built of adobe bricks that were made on the grounds and the clay used for the bricks was dug out of the bluff in front of the property. The bricks, five times the size of ordinary bricks, were fired in kilns fueled by mesquite and ebony.

The architect was William Doty Van Siclen, who designed notable buildings in San Jose, Calif., Seattle and Edmonton, Canada before he moved to Brownsville. He was 73 when he designed the Watson home.

The 15-room house was constructed of 55,000 bricks, each weighing 20 pounds. Tile from Mexico was laid on stairs, walks, tables and patio benches. The entrance hall was floored with colored flagstones and other floors were made of randomly sized boards secured with wooden pegs. One of the prized furnishings was a brass bed that President Taft slept in at La Quinta.

Almost 10 years after the house was finished, May's husband Harry died on Dec. 22, 1947. She died on June 21, 1966. The year after her death the adobe house was sold to Dr. H. Ross Garza.

Past the Watson place, at 2717, was the W. K. Shepperd home, a large two-story building of white stone constructed in 1939. Shepperd and his wife Hertha lived at 222 South Broadway, across from the G. R. Scott home, before the Ocean Drive home was built. Shepperd's wholesale grocery company was located on Laredo.

On the corner of Leming, at 2757 Ocean Drive, was a house built for oilman Douglas Corgey that was notable for a tunnel that extended from the garage basement under Ocean Drive to Cole Park.

The tunnel is now blocked off with masonry stone. The tunnel was built in 1940. It is 250 feet long, four feet under Ocean Drive, and measures six by eight feet inside. The concrete slab tunnel was lighted. Corgey owned the property on the bay side of Ocean across from his residence, where he had a swimming pool and boat dock. At that time, Cole Park did not extend past Louisiana.

Corgey moved to his ranch at Pleasanton in 1949 and sold the house to attorney Ben Vaughn Jr. Vaughn later sold it to former Mayor Farrell D. Smith. The tunnel was sealed off in 1967 when the city acquired additional land for Cole Park.

A yellow-brick home on the corner of Ocean Drive and Oleander, at 2831, was built in 1937 in an arroyo with the garage under the building. The house was constructed for attorney Sidney P. Chandler and his wife Billie Louise, who lived on Peabody on the bluff. They called their new Ocean Drive home "Arroyo Bonito."

Down the street at 3233 was the brick home of Joseph Knight and his wife Addie. They called their home Media Luna. It was built in the late 1930s. On down was the Alta Vista Apartment building at 3259 Ocean Drive.

On the east side of the street, at 3268, was the Creole style pink stucco home of Maston and Hallie Nixon, built in 1937. The Nixons moved into it from their house on Merrill Drive in Saxet Heights.

10. The home of Maston and Hallie Nixon was built at 3260 Ocean Drive, just north of Three-Mile Point, in 1937.

Maston Nixon, who had been a cotton farmer, built the city's first tall building on the bluff in 1925, the Nixon Building, and later founded a natural gas producing company, Southern Minerals Corporation, which he called "Somico."

Nixon, born in 1896 in Luling, was sent to boarding school in San Antonio, the West Texas Military Academy. His first job was to harness a mule to the ice wagon, for which he was paid $5 a week. He served as an artillery captain in France in World War I and later displayed the "Battery F" guidon on the wall of his office. After he was discharged in 1919, he moved to a cotton farm at Petronila, which he owned with his stepfather, and he started to raise cotton seeds near Robstown. He married Hallie Fincham and they moved to Corpus Christi.

It was Nixon's idea in 1924 to take farmers and civic boosters on a train trip to central and north Texas to promote "black land farming" in the Coastal Bend. Two years later, Nixon and H. L. Kokernut of San Antonio bought property at the corner of North Broadway and Leopard Street to construct a new office building, the largest in the city. The 12-story Nixon Building opened on April 2, 1927. The Nixon Building led the way for other tall structures on the bluff, including the White Plaza and Driscoll hotels. In 1946, the Nixon Building was sold to oilman Sam E. Wilson.

The Caller-Times described the Nixon home on Ocean Drive soon after it was built. "A stucco exterior finished in pink distinguishes it from other houses along the drive. It is two

11 and 12. A sketch of the Alta Vista Hotel (top) appeared in Frank Leslie's Illustrated Weekly on Oct.20, 1890. The hotel's grand opening was held on Aug. 14, 1891 (bottom photo) and closed shortly afterwards. It reopened briefly in the summer of 1905.

13. *Elihu Ropes' Alta Vista Hotel, a luxury resort patterned after one in Santa Monica, Calif., was closed soon after it was built. The old derelict burned in a spectacular fire in 1927.*

stories high, has eight rooms, and floor dimensions of 40-by-60 feet."

South of the Nixon home the high bluff bulges out into the bay at Three-Mile Point where Elihu Ropes' Alta Vista Hotel once stood. Ropes, who came to Corpus Christi in 1888, dredged a channel across Mustang Island and planned to build a railroad to Brownsville. He bought 20 blocks of land for a development called "The Cliffs" and built a steam-dummy streetcar line to his Alta Vista Hotel at Three-Mile Point.

A grand opening for the hotel was held on Aug. 14, 1891, even though it was unfinished. The dining room and ballroom were on the third floor. The guests dined and danced with a great view of the bay. One of the unusual features of the hotel was a curved staircase extending over the lobby. It was constructed of polished mahogany from logs salvaged on Padre Island by J. E. Curry, one of Preacher Curry's sons at the Curry Settlement.

The Ropes boom crashed during a national recession in 1893. Ropes could not pay his taxes or bills. Before Ropes left town, he was knocked on the head with a cane wielded by Matt Dunn, an old Texas Ranger who had invested his life savings on Ropes' inspired schemes. Ropes left for New Jersey. He died of a stroke, at age 53, on Staten Island in 1897.

In 1905, the long-empty Alta Vista Hotel was reopened by J. J. Copley. As part of that undertaking, the city, county and Copley paid one-third each of the cost of building a new shell-topped road to the hotel. They used Ropes' name for his planned street and called it Ocean Drive.

The Alta Vista Hotel was closed again. In 1911, it was leased for use as a boys' school by the Peacock Naval College. The Naval College soon closed and the Alta Vista stood

263

14. V. M. Donigan's home at Three-Mile Point, where the old Alta Vista Hotel once stood, was built in 1931 and designed based on Donigan's memory of his childhood home in Turkey. The home was built to feature a central three-story tower and flanking wings with red tile roofs.

vacant. Theodore Fuller in his memoirs said he and his older brother looked inside the hotel in 1921. "The dust of decades, quarter of an inch deep, formed a habitat for an infinity of fleas," Fuller wrote. "Heaven knows what they lived on."

Eight years later, on June 8, 1927, the Alta Vista burned in a spectacular fire. Smoke hung over the city as people drove out to see the fire. City firemen were not able to fight the blaze since there were no water connections that far outside the city.

The site where the Alta Vista burned was purchased in 1930 by V. M. Donigan, who owned the State Hotel in Corpus Christi. Donigan in 1931 built a residence at 3302 Ocean Drive that he called Alta Vista Place but most people called Donigan's Castle.

Donigan's father, Khatchadour Donigian, was a wealthy Armenian silkworm grower who immigrated from Turkey in 1892. The Donigian family bought a ranch southwest of Houston and changed the family name to Donigan.

When Khatchadour died in 1900, Vartan Manasseh Donigan — which he shortened to V. M. — spent his inheritance building the State Hotel on Mesquite Street in Corpus Christi. The hotel was operated by the Donigan family, including V. M. Donigan, his wife Anna Horope, and five children, Parnot, Mesog, Zareth, Lucille and Nectarine.

V. M. Donigan's family lived at the hotel until "Donigan's castle" was built in 1931. It was an eye-catching white-stucco structure with a touch of the Mediterranean in its design. The Donigan home featured a three-story tower with flanking stucco wings and red tile

15. *V. M. Donigan's red-tiled palace at Three-Mile Point was sold in 1979 to Mike McKinnon. The house still stands.*

roofs. It was said to be a replica of the family home at Geyve, Turkey, where Vartan had happy memories of growing up.

Vartan Manasseh Donigan died in 1943, when he was 77, at his home on Ocean Drive. His wife Anna died three years later. Mesog, who never married, died in 1979, when he was 80. His older brother Parnot died in 1992.

The house on Ocean Drive was sold in 1979 to Mike McKinnon. The exotic red-tiled mansion on Ocean Drive is still standing.

Ocean Drive featured a dangerous S curve that wound around the old Donigan home site. It became a hot political issue in the 1950s after several major accidents. Farrell D. Smith, elected mayor in 1955, ordered the curve straightened.

To accomplish that the city would have to buy part of the Donigan property, which led to a major political scrap. Smith was accused of trying to block the project, on one hand, and on another he was accused of standing to benefit personally from it since he owned property nearby.

The city went to court to buy the land needed to straighten the curve. A condemnation court awarded the Donigan property owners — Lucy Welch and Mesog Donigan — $21,000. Road equipment was moved to the site to begin work, but the project became an issue in the election campaign in 1959, which led to Farrell Smith's defeat by Ellroy King.

16. An aerial shot of Ocean Drive taken in 1937 shows the Donigan home, also known as Donigan's castle, on the bay side of the drive. After several bad accidents, the S curve around the Donigan estate became a major safety concern and political issue in the 1950s and 1960s.

The King administration returned the land to the Donigans and abandoned the project. But it was still an issue.

After several fatal accidents in the 1960s, including one in 1963 when three teenage boys were killed, property owners along Ocean Drive urged the city to install flashing lights and railings. The roadway was widened into a four-way drive in 1969, which did not eliminate but did smooth out the worst part of the serpent-like twists of the S Curve.

Across from the Donigan place, on the west side of the street, was the Grossman home at 3275 Ocean Drive, built by Edward and Sadie Grossman.

Edward Grossman was president of the Grossman Brothers firm which at one time owned seven dry goods and clothing stores in Corpus Christi. The Grossman family emigrated from Russia in the early part of the 20th Century (Chapter 7, pages 181-182).

The first home of Edward and Sadie Grossman was on Texas Drive in Oak Park before they moved to 2524 Ocean Drive. Houses along this part of Ocean Drive were demolished when Louisiana was expanded into Louisiana Parkway. They moved into their new home, set back from the street, at 3275 Ocean Drive, across from the Donigan home.

South of the red-tiled Donigan home, on the same side of the street, was the home of Bruce L. Collins, at 3352 Ocean Drive.

Collins, a member of a pioneer South Texas ranching family, moved from Alice to Corpus Christi in 1906. He later managed his family's interest in two earlier downtown theaters, the Amusu and the Aldine, and expanded the chain, with United Artists, to include 15 local theaters.

Collins became the prime developer and motivator of North Beach in the 1920s, after the 1919 storm leveled the earlier homes and structures on North Beach. He was a co-owner of the North Beach Bath House and the North Beach Amusement Park.

The Ocean Drive home of Bruce and Lucille Collins was finished in 1941 and described by the Caller-Times as a Monterrey hacienda style house with white-washed bricks, brown shingles and green shutters. The house was sold after the death of Bruce Collins Sr. and torn down in 2014.

The Shoreland and Terrace Apartments followed in the 3400 block and in the next block, on the west side of Ocean Drive, was the home of Roy Murray, who owned Roy Murray Motors. The Murray house, at 3505, was sold to jewelry store owner George Taylor.

Beyond the 3500 block going south, Ocean Drive did not include street numbers in the 1930s but mile markers. Street numbers were added in the 1940s then the numbers were changed in the 1950s when Doddridge was converted into a four-lane artery. The Farrell J. Smith place in this area was originally listed at the 4-mile mark then at 4005 Ocean Drive in the 1940s and finally as 3745 by 1955.

The home of Howard E. Butt, the food store magnate, was at 3701. Extensive files on the history of the Butt family include no references to the family home on Ocean Drive, presumably because the family members zealously protected their privacy.

Past the Butt home was the residence of another grocery store pioneer, Farrell J. Smith. After it was built in 1937, an article in the Caller-Times described the Smith home as "a rock house, a rambling structure, truly a giant of a house, two stories and capped with a roof of tile."

Farrell J. Smith's son, an attorney, Farrell D. Smith, was elected mayor in 1955. He also built a home on Ocean Drive, at 3343, at Alta Plaza.

17. An aerial shot shows the Farrell J. Smith home, upper right, under construction in 1937 on the corner of Ocean Drive and Doddridge. The home was sold to Sam and Ada Wilson 10 years later.

Ten years after the Smith home was built, in the mid-1940s, it was sold to oilman Sam E. Wilson Jr. and his wife Ada. At the same time, the house the Wilsons owned at 138 Southern in the Del Mar addition was sold to Smith.

Sam Wilson was an oil lease broker in El Dorado, Ark., when he met and married Ada Laverne Rogers in 1921. The couple moved to Corpus Christi in 1936 where Sam became successful in developing oil fields in South Texas. In 1936 he had 17 producing wells in the old Corpus Christi Field when water broke into the oil and he lost $550,000. He moved to Houston where he drilled 11 dry holes. He returned to Corpus Christi and with one rig bought on credit he began drilling in the Campbellton Field near Aransas Pass. An article in the Caller-Times said he branched out into Nueces County where he scored with 44 producing wells before hitting a dry hole.

18. Oilman Sam E. Wilson Jr. and his wife Ada at the Golden Strand Hotel in Miami in 1950. Wherever the Wilsons traveled, Ada would always hire a publicist to send their photos and description of their visit to the Caller-Times.

In 1943 Sam Wilson sold some of his oil production for $2.3 million and made similar sales in the next three years. He bought most of Mustang Island, excluding Port Aransas, with plans to develop a Miami-style resort.

He invested in real estate and bought the Nixon Building on the bluff, which he renamed the Wilson Building, built the Wilson Tower, and constructed a building on Chaparral that was leased to J. C. Penney's Department Store. He bought race horses and one of his horses, Royal Mustang, finished second in the Kentucky Derby in 1951. Sam Wilson Jr. died of a heart attack on Feb. 17, 1957 at age 58.

Wilson's wife Ada founded the Ada Wilson Hospital of Physical Medicine and Rehabilitation, which began in a small house on Chaparral before it was moved to a cluster of houses on Third Street. She later helped build a new facility next to Driscoll Children's Hospital. The Ada Wilson clinic was recognized as a pioneer in the rehabilitation of crippled children.

After Sam Wilson died in 1957, Ada built a round tower next to her home on Ocean Drive to give it a castle-like appearance. It was designed by architect Richard Colley on Ada's explicit instructions and used to store her antiques. She called the house the Wilson Manor. Ada was known as a flamboyant character whose capacity for self-praise was a matter of local legend.

19. *Ada Wilson's home, which she called Wilson Manor, on Ocean Drive at Doddridge in 1977. After her husband's death in 1957 she hired architect Richard Colley to design a castle-like turret tower which was built on the north side of the home.*

Ada Wilson decided to sell Mustang Island, which she called "my island," to the state for use as a state park, but the state didn't want it. She took her case to court and eventually it reached the U.S. Supreme Court, where she won.

The late Edward Harte, publisher of the Caller-Times, wrote that, "From a monetary point of view, Ada would have been better off to drop the whole thing and sell the island to private interests, but we can all be glad that she didn't."

Ada Wilson died on Feb. 17, 1977. The Wilson home was later sold to lawyer Dan Alfaro and recently was purchased by the Rachal Foundation, which plans to demolish the home and its pretentious tower and clear the site.

A Bird's-Eye View map by A. H. Meuly in 1909 shows the Chautauqua Grounds between Three-Mile Point and Aberdeen. The Chautauqua Grounds were a favorite gathering place for Sunday picnics and Chautauqua speakers. The name derives from an adult education movement that started in Chautauqua, N.Y., and spread across the country.

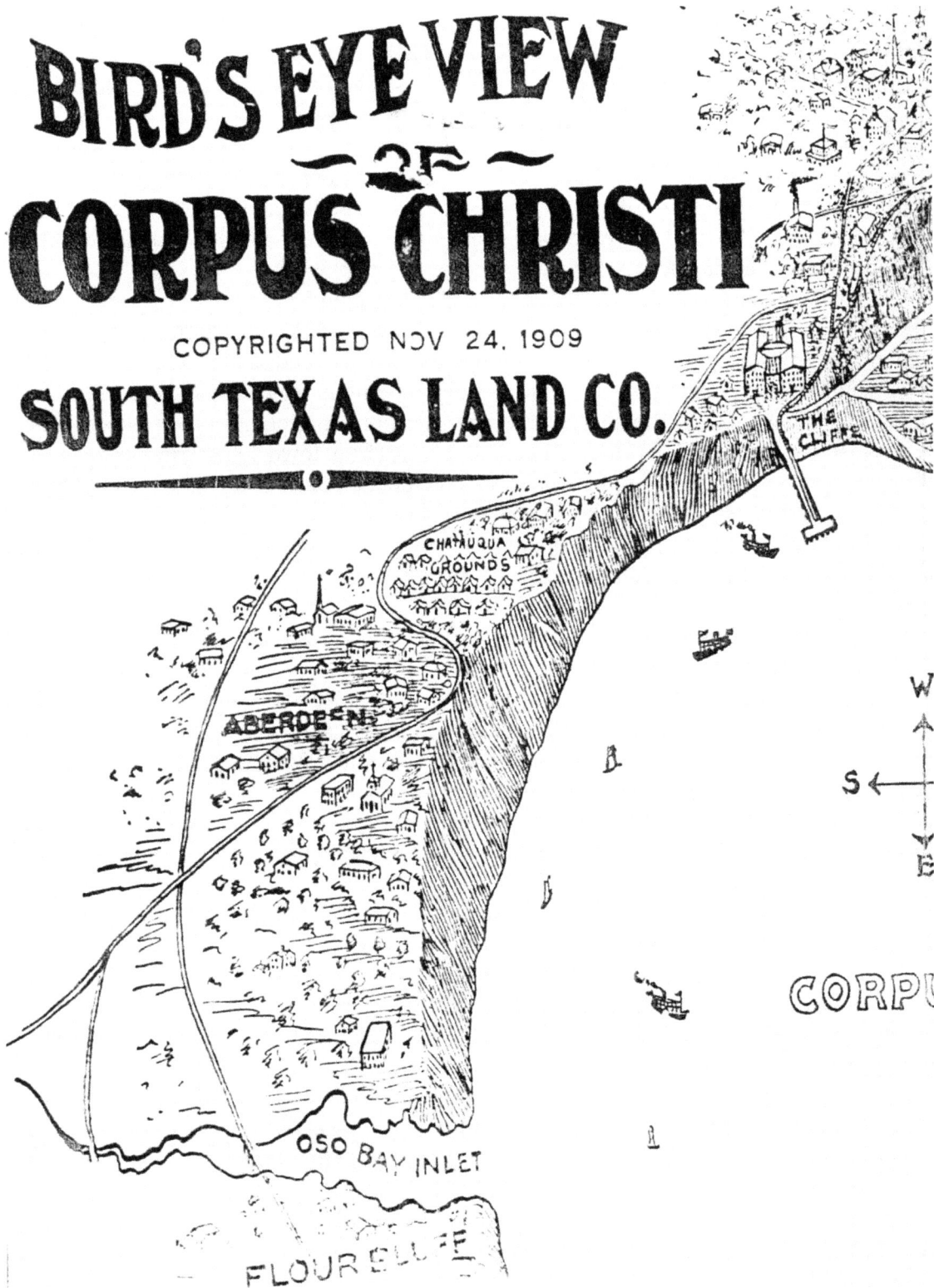

20. *Detail from A. H. Meuly's 1909 "Bird's Eye View" map of Corpus Christi shows the Alta Vista Hotel and the Aransas Cliffs, the Chautauqua Grounds and the Aberdeen community.*

A Chautauqua gathering featured speakers and experts and often entertainers and musicians. The Chautauqua Grounds on Ocean Drive were used as a public park, where picnics were held and families gathered. One news item of a Chautauqua gathering was printed in the Caller on May 25, 1894:

"A picnic party composed of Misses Annie Rogers, Maud Wareham, Beatrice and Minnie Graham, Lillie DuPuy, Rilla Weeks, Lucy Armstrong and Mssrs. Henry Mitchell, Chris Yung, Tom Pohlson, Gilbert Rogers, Luther Armstrong and Ed Sturges, chaperoned by Mr. and Mrs. Wareham, drives to the Chautauqua a few miles down the bay from Corpus Christi to spend the day outing on the bay shore.

"Well-filled lunch baskets were taken along with ice-cold lemonade to wash the eatables down. After dinner Mr. Pohlson entertained the crowd with a serio-comic stump speech, which was followed by some good old songs exquisitely rendered by the young ladies. After sundown the picnickers returned to town by moonlight, having spent a pleasant day."

Past the Chautauqua Grounds was the small farming community of Aberdeen, which was two miles beyond Three-Mile Point and five miles from town, located in the area where the Seaside Cemetery is today. Aberdeen was big enough to have a post office in the late 1890s and in the first decade of the 20th Century.

A news item from Feb. 28, 1896 announced that a phonograph concert would be given at Aberdeen and all who rode the streetcar from Corpus Christi to Aberdeen would be admitted free.

Maud Wareham (later Mrs. William Gerhardt) recalled in an interview in 1939 when she was a teacher in 1893. "I began teaching out at Aberdeen and taught four months. I had 10 pupils in one small room. Among my pupils were the Watsons, Grahams and Fondrens. Zed Graham was one of the pupils. His father, P. A. Graham, was the conductor on the trolley car to Alta Vista. He had a long prod for the mule, which was rather willful and delighted in taking lengthy periods for contemplation."

The small one-room school on Flour Bluff Road, where Maud Wareham taught, burned in September 1905. The Aberdeen school was later consolidated with the Sunshine school to become the Sundeen district.

A street that runs from Santa Fe to Ocean Drive is called Aberdeen, a faint reminder of the farming community that existed more than a century ago,

There were several homes and apartment buildings in the Aberdeen area in the 1940s. At 4204 was the Glenview Cottages, on the east side of Ocean, followed by J. G. Sullivan's apartments, at 4226. Past Sullivan's was the home of Robert L. Garrett, a farmer, and his wife Eleanor.

Across the street, on the west side of Ocean Drive, was the home of Morris L. Lichtenstein Sr. and his wife Margaret. Lichtenstein, grandson of the founder the city's famous department store, bought the controlling interest in the store in 1932 and ran it with his brother Albert.

At the Robert Drive intersection, on the bay side of Ocean, was the Sea Side Grocery Store owned by Price Chandler, followed by two other apartment buildings, Bayshore Courts and Eidson Courts, before the intersection with Airline Road.

W. A. Clark's home was on the bay side of Ocean Drive at Airline. He was known throughout the town as "Farmer" Clark. He and his wife Rachel brought their family in a covered wagon from Bell County, near Temple, in 1895. They bought property south of

21. *Looking north, a buggy traveled south on Ocean Drive past the intersection with Airline Road in 1910. On the right was the home of W. A. "Farmer" Clark. North of Clark's farm was the Aberdeen community around where the Seaside Cemetery is today.*

Aberdeen and began a dairy farm. "Farmer" Clark was said to have brought the first registered Jersey cattle to Nueces County. (One of the Clarks' 11 children, Curtis Clark Sr., became a pioneer seed and grain dealer whose business, Eastern Seed Company, was in the 300 block of South Staples; page 199.)

Past Airline, on the west side of Ocean Drive, was the home and farm of Ernest M. Poenisch. The Poenisch family moved from Sherman to Corpus Christi in 1889 and purchased farming tracts around the city, which later became prime real estate as the city grew southward. The father, Friedrich Poenisch, bought land that today is between Port Ayers shopping center and Del Mar College. His sons started their own farms. Herman bought land and farmed where the Country Club golf course is today. Robert established a farm from Airline to the Oso. Ernest's farm was off Ocean Drive, extending to Airline.

Harriet Tillman, Poenisch family historian, said that after Ernest married Mary Pearse he bought 80 acres and built a large home facing the bay, where Ocean Drive and Poenisch Drive intersect today. She said his home was built with porches around the lower and upper floors, with a white picket fence around the front yard and a mulberry tree in the back yard.

Tillman said that in 1903 Ernest was bitten by a rattlesnake. Mary put his leg in a bucket of kerosene and by the time they reached town, six miles away, the kerosene had turned green, but his leg was saved. She said that Mary Poenisch kept carefully wrapped bottles of beer in a barrel of cool water and on wash-days, when she had finished her labors, she

22. *Mary (Pearse) and Ernest M. Poenisch. Their farm and home were located off Ocean Drive near where Poenisch Park is today.*

would drink one of her beers. No one else, Tillman said, was ever allowed to drink her beer.

A Corpus Christi newspaper, the Crony, on April 5, 1902 carried an account of a fish fry at Ernest Poenisch's place. "Besides raising cabbage to the tune of at least $100 an acre, Nueces County farmers find opportunity to have some gay old times. A recent occasion in the Encinal tract, six miles south of Corpus Christi, is an instance. Out there they have big fishing frolics very frequently. The other day the Poenisch brothers invited a lot of neighbors and friends to join them in a seine-baptizing.

"When they have a fish fry, the finned creatures are captured from the bay in a seine. The old seine had worn out and a new one, 300 feet long, had been made. April 1 was the day designated for the first use and crowds repaired to a pretty spot near the Aberdeen school house to help baptize the seine. Before the first haul was made, Mrs. O. S. Watson broke a bottle of buttermilk on the seine's head-line. Then the seine was hurried to the water and drawn out into a great circle which was tugged toward the beach where hundreds of imprisoned trout, redfish, sheepshead and croakers were soon being prepared to sizzle on glowing embers. Many other eatables were at hand and everyone had plenty of fish. It was a great day, the sort of day which comes to men who dwell on such a coast as this."

Mary Poenisch died in 1948 and Ernest died four years later. Their son, Ernie Jr., continued to farm until 1963 when he moved to his Escondido Ranch in Karnes County. Poenisch Park was named for the family.

23. *A short-lived restaurant was located in a lighthouse-style building on Ocean Drive about 1930-1931. The name, owner, and exact location are unknown; it was outside the city limits and not included in the City Directory.*

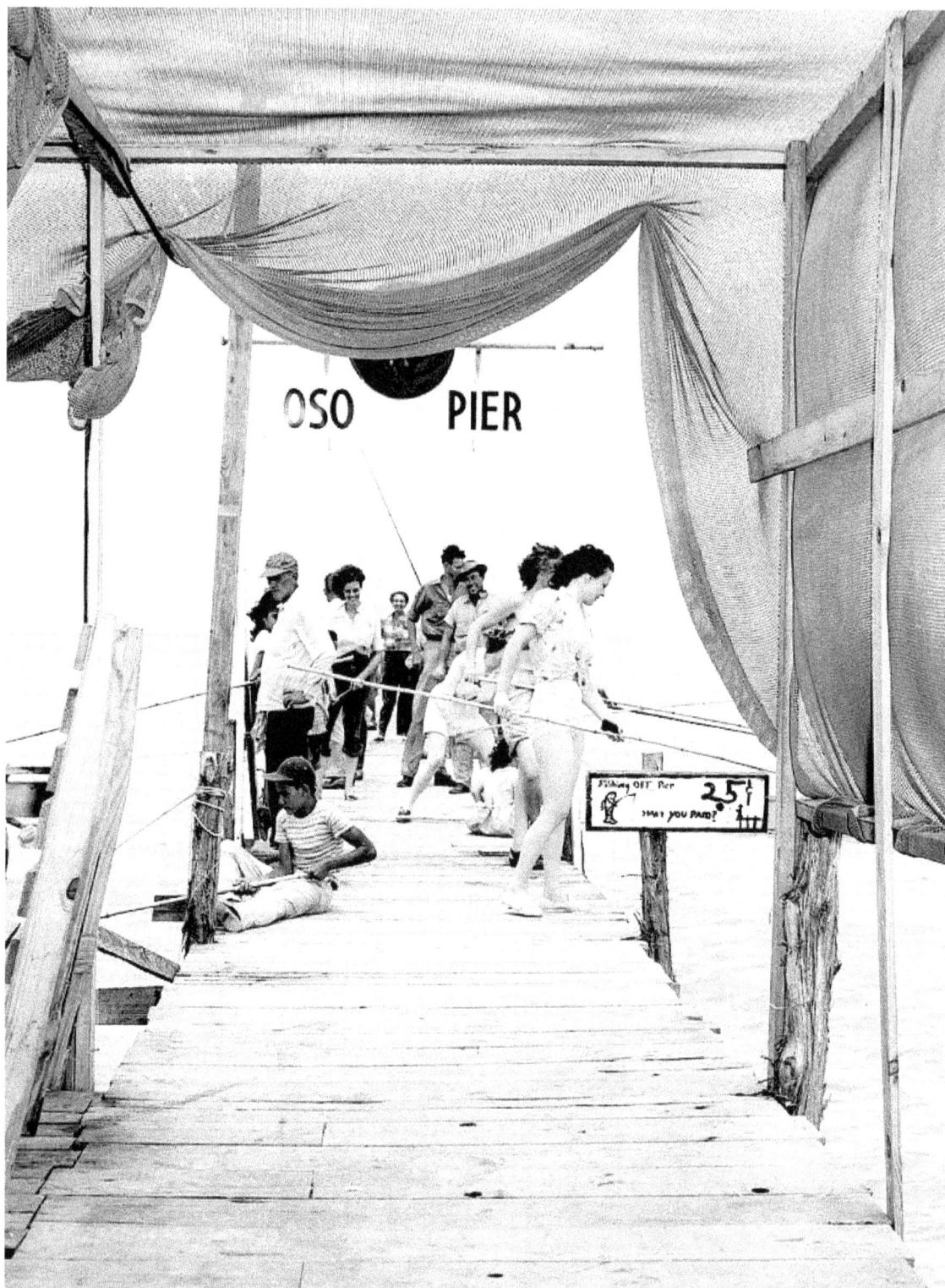

24. *The Oso Pier, at 6124 Ocean Drive, shown in 1950, was built in 1948 by Jack Maddux. He once said of his pier and bait stand business, "If you don't like fishing and talking about fishing, this could get to be like work."*

25. Aerial view shows the Naval Air Station under construction in December 1940. Near the top, on the left, is Ward Island, with Ocean Drive along the shoreline.

26. Sentries at the North Gate of the new Naval Air Station check visitors at the base in March 1941. Beyond the gate, Ocean Drive retains its name on the base.

Past the Poenisch farm, in the 5300 block, Ocean Drive approached the Oso Tourist Courts, run by Frank Chilson, the Edgewater Grocery and Market, the Oso Package Store, and the Oso Pier and Bait Stand, run by Jack Maddux.

Beyond was Ward Island, the University of Corpus Christi (now Texas A&M University-Corpus Christi) and the Naval Air Station.

Stephen Fox, an architectural historian, described Ocean Drive as the kind of grand avenue that passed from the scene in most American cities. Fox wrote that most grand avenues began to decline with the rise of the automobile after the turn of the 20th Century, but Ocean Drive got a late start. Among Texas cities, he wrote, "Corpus Christi has the advantage, shared only with El Paso, of being visible as a whole. From any point along Corpus Christi Bay you can turn and see the city spread out before you. A broad boulevard traces the contour of the shoreline from Emerald Cove, south of downtown, to Cayo del Oso, nearly six miles to the southeast. This is Ocean Drive."

Chapter 11. North Beach

Major north-south streets on North Beach included Rincon, North Water, and Timon Boulevard. Short east-west streets included Bessie, Bennett, Pearl, Market, Garner, Vine, Elm and Burleson. Some of the names were changed.

A rectangular wedge of land between Corpus Christi and Nueces bays was called Rincon then Brooklyn and finally North Beach. After Henry Kinney founded Corpus Christi in 1839 he hired men to slaughter wild horses for their hides, an enterprise conducted on the Rincon. Kinney's men one day were forced to hide in a thicket when Comanche warriors in a raiding party appeared. The men watched from their hiding place as the Comanches spread buffalo robes across the shallow bayou to keep their ponies from bogging in the mud.

On another day, a company of Rangers chased a Comanche war party to Rincon Point. It was sundown and the Rangers waited for morning so they could get reinforcements and attack the Indians at first light. When the sun came up, the Rangers discovered the Indians were gone. Not a feather from a warbonnet was left behind. The Rangers found tracks leading into the bay and realized that the Indians had escaped by riding over a submerged oyster reef.

This underwater land bridge became known as the reef road. It was three miles from Rincon Point on North Beach to Indian Point on the north side of Nueces Bay. It was crooked as a worm fence as it made zig-zag turns across the bay. It was marked with stakes to show the way. To one unused to the sight, it was described as surreal watching wagons and horses crossing on the water. Although the reef was marked, it was easy to stray into deep water where horses could bog or get cut by razor-sharp oyster shells.

On Aug. 1, 1845, the first companies of Zachary Taylor's army landed on the beach at sundown. The men from companies K and G of the 3rd Infantry were tired, hungry and wet. The waves were too high to land their supplies from the small fishing boats that ferried them from St. Joseph's Island. They ate hard ship's biscuits for supper and slept on the sands of North Beach, without tents or blankets. In coming days, they cleared the campsite and put up tents. Order began to emerge with tents squared in military fashion in neat rows that stretched along the shoreline from North Beach across the mud slough to the small village of Corpus Christi.

A letter to the New Orleans Daily Picayune from Corpus Christi, dated Aug. 30, 1845, said, "The position taken by Gen. Taylor is one of extreme beauty, and when the eye first rests upon his camp, clustered with a thousand spotless white tents along the shelly margin of the shore of Corpus Christi Bay, irresistible bursts of admiration follow. It is a position of security, as well as beauty."

In the months ahead Corpus Christi became a major military outpost with the concentration of half the U.S. Army in Taylor's command. It was a small trading post of some 100 people when Taylor's soldiers pitched their tents on North Beach. It became a

1. Daniel P. Whiting's sketch of the Zachary Taylor encampment at Corpus Christi in 1845.

boomtown of 4,000 soldiers and perhaps as many as 2,000 citizens, many of them camp followers, gamblers, prostitutes, and grog-shop purveyors.

Army engineers, looking for an easy way to transport supplies to a detachment at San Patricio, gouged out a cut in the reef that divided Nueces and Corpus Christi bays. This allowed small boats to pass over the reef, enter Nueces Bay, and sail up the Nueces River to San Patricio. For years afterwards, during high tides, horses were forced to swim across the spot where Taylor's engineers made a passage-way through the reef.

The months of October and November 1845 were wet and cold. It rained with a steady drizzle. On. Dec. 3 the temperature dropped to 23 degrees and the cold stunned fish and turtles in the bays. Cartloads of fish and sea turtles were gathered along the shore. Soldiers surrounded their camps on North Beach and along the shoreline past the bayou with chaparral brush to screen the bitterly cold wind.

The army began its move to the Rio Grande on the morning of March 8, 1846. First to leave was the 2nd Dragoons, camped on North Beach, followed by a company of artillery. Elements of the 3rd Infantry, which had been the first to arrive on Aug. 1, 1845, were the last to leave and as they marched out of the small village the army drummers beat out a traditional tune for departure, "The Girl I Left Behind Me."

On Jan. 11, 1847, the first work ordered by the new Nueces County Commissioners Court was to stake the reef road.

Years later, during the Civil War, on Aug. 16, 1862, Union ships landed 30 men with a howitzer on North Beach in an effort to seize a Confederate battery from behind. Confederates charged the landing party and forced them back to their ships.

2. House on North Beach rented by "Blacksmith" Bob Fitzsimmons in 1895.

After the war, one of the first acts of the reorganized county government was to order the stakes that marked the reef to be replaced. They were removed during the war.

William Ohler, a Corpus Christi merchant, bought a large portion of North Beach (or the Rincon, as it was then called) in 1870 and renamed it Brooklyn. He filed a plat with the county that showed plans for streets, parks, and public squares. New homes were built and Jacob Ziegler, who owned a hotel and restaurant on Mesquite Street, planted salt cedars and opened a beer garden at Rincon Point.

During the beef packing era in the 1870s, three packing houses, called packeries, operated on North Beach. One packer operation was owned by John B. Hall, a former Union soldier and immigrant from England. Hall dumped rotten meat in the mud slough that separated North Beach from Corpus Christi proper, which became known as Hall's Bayou. (Bob Hall Pier was named for his son, a county commissioner.)

In the hurricane of 1874, tides were so high that Hall's Bayou was a reported 12 feet deep and running like a torrent. After the storm was over, the damage on North Beach included the destruction of Norwick Gussett's wharf. Afterwards a rickety bridge was built across the bayou at what was called the Brooklyn Crossing.

In 1886, the San Antonio and Aransas Pass Railroad (SAAP) built a trestle across Nueces Bay near the reef road. In the 1880s, the name Brooklyn was dropped in favor of the old name, Rincon. In the 1890s, during an economic boom stimulated by the activities of Elihu Ropes, a resort hotel called the Miramar was built on the north side of Hall's Bayou.

The Miramar Hotel opened on June 1, 1891. It registered 4,000 guests in three months before it burned on Sept. 11, 1891. Some guests escaped by jumping from the second floor to mattresses on the ground. Lillie (Anderson) Rankin recalled that "it was a beautiful night when the Miramar burned. There was no wind at all and the flames leaped high. The two-story hotel was completely destroyed. No one was killed in the fire but many people in Corpus Christi who had invested in the enterprise took heavy losses.

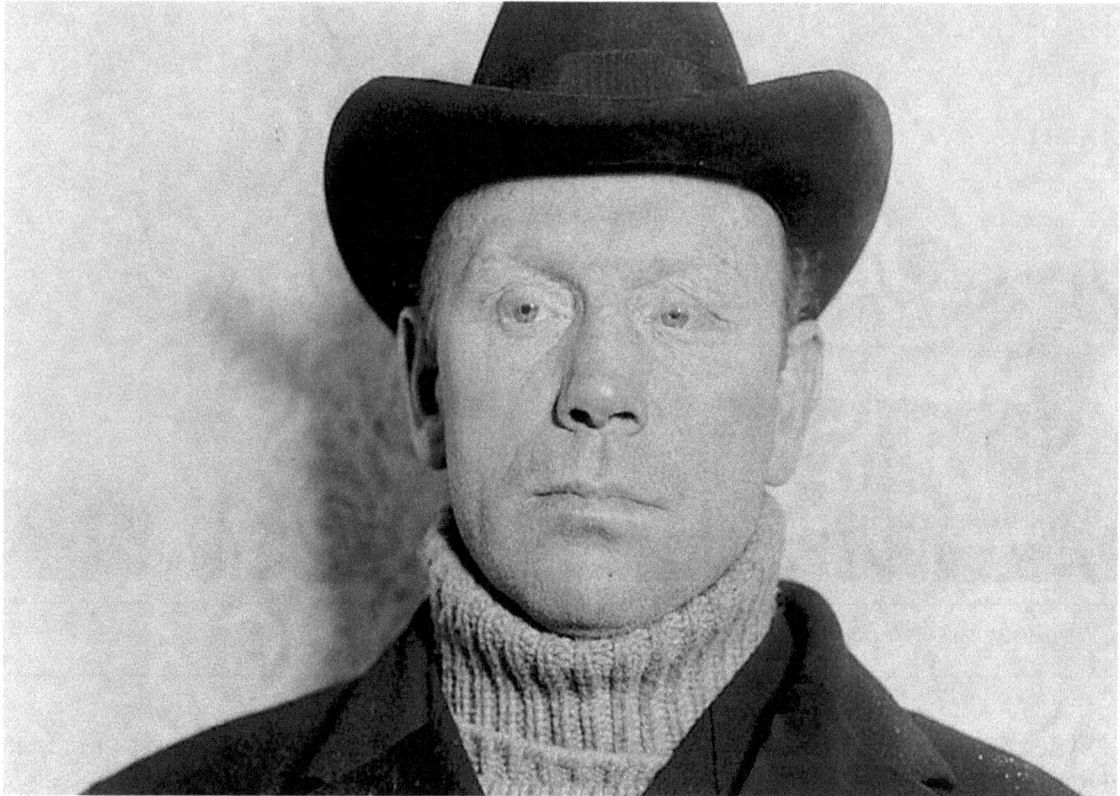

3. *"Blacksmith" Bob Fitzsimmons trained on North Beach for a planned championship match with "Gentleman" Jim Corbett in 1895.*

In 1891, D. Mahoney built a two-story brick house on North Beach, along the shore north of the Miramar Hotel. Four years later, in 1895, heavyweight champion "Blacksmith" Bob Fitzsimmons rented the Mahoney house and opened a camp on North Beach to train for a planned fight with "Gentleman" Jim Corbett.

Fitzsimmons' pet lion would run with him when he did wind sprints on the beach. An alarm spread one day that the lion was missing. People loaded their guns and mothers kept their children inside. The lion was eventually found napping peacefully under a porch.

During Fitzsimmons' stay, F. E. Ring built tourist cottages to capitalize on the heavyweight boxer's presence. The Ring Villa were the first tourist courts in Corpus Christi.

After Fitzsimmons departed, the Mahoney house was converted into the Shell Beach Sanitarium operated by Dr. W. E. Carruth. It was located at 2811 Rincon. It was destroyed in the hurricane of 1919.

During the Spanish-American War, Corpus Christi volunteers called the Kenedy Rifles were sent to Cuba while a volunteer unit from Longview, the Longview Rifles, were stationed on North Beach.

In 1905, Spohn Sanitarium was built where the old Miramar Hotel had burned. James F. Scott donated lumber for the east gallery of the hospital and Joseph Hirsch paid the labor costs to build it. Spohn was opened and turned over to the Sisters of the Incarnate Word to

4. *Spohn Sanitarium on North Beach was built on the site where the Miramar Hotel burned.*

5. *Tents of the annual Epworth encampment on North Beach.*

manage; the $15,000 hospital was built with contributions from the people of Corpus Christi. Before the hospital was built, doctors performed surgeries in the homes of patients, sometimes using their kitchen tables.

On Aug. 8, 1905, the Epworth Revival opened. Beginning that year and continuing for a decade, North Beach turned into a religious oasis each August of a Methodist revival called Epworth by the Sea, a summer encampment where families attended religious services and frolicked on the beach. SAAP Railroad built a depot across from the Epworth grounds.

6. The Country Club in 1914 was converted into the North Beach Bath House.

Roy Terrell, a Corpus Christi resident, remembered the Epworth encampment. A frame building called Epworth Inn was constructed and contained lodging places and a large auditorium. Smaller buildings went up and the overflow lived in tents stretched along the sandy shores of North Beach. Terrell said preaching "took place night and day but there was time for games and bathing. There was a big tent where they served meals. The first time I ever tasted ice tea was at one of the Epworth meetings."

Epworth by the Sea was held every year for a decade. Each summer, hundreds of Methodist families and missionaries from around the world gathered on North Beach. The beginning of Corpus Christi as a tourist destination can be traced to two events.

One was in 1895 when heavyweight champion Blacksmith Bob Fitzsimmons trained on North Beach for his prize fight with Gentleman Jim Corbett. Corpus Christi got a lot of national attention that year. The other was the annual Epworth by the Sea encampment, which introduced many Texans to North Beach and the summer pleasures of Corpus Christi Bay.

After the turn of the 20th Century, the reef road across Nueces Bay, discovered in the 1840s, still served as a unique underwater land bridge. People coming in wagons to shop in Corpus Christi tried to time their trip to return before dark. If they stayed too late, they would try to see the marker posts on the reef road by the phosphorous glow kicked up by the horses' hooves.

May (Mathis) Watson recalled traveling across the reef. "Trips were made by wagon to bring back supplies and if the tide was in it would be dangerous crossing the reef, with occupants of the wagon having to stand up in their seats while the team was forced to swim." This was over the old cut made in the reef by Zachary Taylor's engineers.

On Oct. 22, 1909, President William Howard Taft delivered the dedication speech at the opening of Corpus Christi's first Country Club. It was on North Beach. Taft struck the first ball on a new nine-hole golf course and, as the rotund president bent over to make his

7. *John Dickenson's Beach Hotel, built in 1912, was leased by the government for use as a rehab hospital for soldiers wounded in World War I. It survived the 1919 storm and was later converted into the Breakers Hotel.*

swing, a photographer couldn't resist taking a picture of the seat of government. For years the Country Club displayed the golf club, ball, and photo of the president's rear end.

The Country Club building was sold in 1914 and turned into a bathhouse and confectionery. It was a business venture of L. G. Collins, a cattle rancher from Alice, and H. M. Kelley, who owned the Alcove Confectionery on Mesquite, across from Market Hall. Kelley's wife said they lived on Leopard and "every afternoon I would take the children on the streetcar to the beach. My husband served wonderful sandwiches at the bathhouse and we would stay until he came home with us."

North Beach was the setting for the first airplane flights in the area. Eight years after the Wright brothers first flew at Kitty Hawk, N.C., the Wright Brothers company gave demonstration flights over North Beach on July 3-4, 1911. A crowd gathered on the salt flats north of the Epworth encampment. Admission was 50 cents for adults, 25 cents for youngsters. Aviator Oscar Brindley flew a Wright Brothers' plane that had been shipped in crates and assembled here.

In 1912, John Dickenson built the Beach Hotel on a pasture where the city's butchers kept their cattle for slaughtering. The hotel faced the bay, surrounded by oleanders and palms. A streetcar stopped at the front door and the grounds ran down to the water. Room rates at this luxury hotel began at $3.50, three times the price of a room at the State Hotel on Mesquite Street downtown. Six years later, in 1918, it was leased by the government for use as a convalescent hospital for soldiers wounded in France.

8. Army Hospital No. 15 (the former Beach Hotel) was surrounded by water in the wake of the 1919 hurricane. The hospital served as a refuge during the storm.

In 1915 Nueces County dedicated a new causeway across Nueces Bay which replaced the reef road. Not long after the new arched causeway opened, it was badly damaged in the 1916 hurricane. Three years later came a far deadlier storm.

On Sunday, Sept. 14, 1919, a powerful hurricane swept across North Beach. At the former Beach Hotel, which had been converted to U. S. General Hospital No. 15, more than 100 refugees were taken in during the storm.

One of those was five-year-old Lemmawayne Burnett. Her father took her, her sister and mother to the hospital for safety. "You could hear the storm and every so often a big wave would smash into the windows. I'm sure my parents were terrified, but we sat on the beds, and the soldiers told us stories to help us pass the terrible hours."

At Spohn Sanitarium, Ben G. Whitehead, a patient and a newspaper editor from McAllen, said it was the most horrible night that could be imagined. "Wing after wing of the hospital was swept away. Once we were all huddled in the rear portion of the building and the Sisters (of the Incarnate Word) were saying their prayers in concert. I did not know how to say them their way, and I was sorry, for it was a time for prayer."

On Monday after the storm only three battered structures remained standing on North Beach: Judge McDonald's home, Spohn Sanitarium, and the Beach Hotel/Government

9 and 10. The Judge Henry McDonald home (top) on the afternoon after the storm. Barely visible, two men in a rowboat approach the home to rescue the inhabitants. Below, the home was among only three buildings that survived the storm.

11. A National Guard soldier patrols on North Beach after the 1919 storm. In the distance is Spohn Sanitarium, which was damaged but survived the storm.

Army Hospital. Hundreds of people were killed in the storm and their oil-coated bodies recovered at White Point.

Some of the finest homes in the city were destroyed. North Beach was left as empty as an open field. "The only thing we found of our possessions," said one North Beach survivor, "was a cut-glass bowl that had been on the mantel. Daddy found this bowl, with three pennies still in it, in the sand. That's all that was left." The 1919 storm brought home the age-old warning of What Can Happen When You Live on the Coast.

North Beach began to rise from the ruins, beginning with the North Beach Bath House, built in 1920, a joint venture of Bruce Collins and his cousin John Mosser. Collins' father, L. G. Collins, a cattle rancher in Alice, was one of the investors who converted the County Club into the North Beach Bath House in 1914. Collins was 18 at the time.

Collins enlisted in the Navy after he left Corpus Christi High School and served with the Pacific fleet during World War I until he was discharged in 1919. He returned home and got a job as a salesman for Edwin Flato's Corpus Christi Hardware.

After the 1919 storm left North Beach in ruins, with the remains of three buildings still standing, Bruce Collins and John Mosser collected wood from wrecked buildings and rebuilt the North Beach Bath House. It was the first business to reopen on North Beach after the storm. While Collins traveled throughout the Rio Grande Valley as a salesman for Corpus Christi Hardware, Mosser ran the bath house and confectionery. Collins also built the North Beach Pleasure Park in 1922.

In 1927 Collins purchased an old wooden sailing ship abandoned in the port turning basin. He moved it to North Beach and sank it in the sand to keep it stable. The side of

12. Bruce Collins Sr. behind his desk in December 1957. He was born in Alice in 1896. His father was L. G. Collins, rancher and cattleman, and his mother was Catherine Adams Collins, the daughter of rancher Robert Adams. Bruce Collins started the transformation of North Beach beginning in 1919 after the hurricane. He and his partners built the North Beach House, the Saltwater Pool, the North Beach Pleasure Park, and operated "Dance On the Ship." He died in 1986.

the ship was painted in large letters, "Dance on The Ship." Dancing on the deck under the stars, with an evening breeze blowing off the bay, attracted large crowds, especially on Saturday nights.

The Saltwater Pool was built in 1926. The large oval pool was filled with piped-in saltwater, filtered to keep out jellyfish. It had indoor lighting and stadium seating, where parents could sit to watch their children swim. North Beach in those years was called "The Playground of the South."

In 1925 and 1926, as the bascule bridge was being built, dredges worked behind it in the salt flats digging a turning basin for the coming port. The port and bascule bridge opened on Sept. 14, 1926.

The new bridge attracted a crowd to watch it go up and down. The bridge was called the bascule, French for "seesaw" that described the counter-balanced lifting action.

13. *"Dance On The Ship" operated on North Beach from 1927 to 1933. Dances were held nightly but the most popular were on Saturday nights. The ship was damaged in a hurricane in 1933 and moved shortly afterwards.*

The old Beach Hotel — the Army convalescent hospital during the 1919 storm — was remodeled and renamed "The Breakers." Its Spanish village ballroom was designed to resemble a rose garden in moonlight.

The Crystal Beach Park Ballroom and pier were built south of the bathhouse in 1929. The following year, a dance marathon contest was staged in the Crystal Beach Park Ballroom.

The large ballroom building, on piers over the bay, had bleacher seats to accommodate the large audience of spectators, who paid 50 cents to watch what became a grueling endurance contest.

The marathon regulations were printed in the paper: "A one-hour period will be taken every morning at 7 o'clock for attending to laundry, bathing, shaving, and otherwise preparing for the day's grind. One 15-minute rest period in the morning and one in the evening would be devoted to meals."

The marathon event began on July 24 with 19 couples who danced (or rather shuffled their feet) 40 minutes of every hour to the music of Clarence Schenk and his "Rio Grandians" playing tunes like "I Love You Truly." By the third day, only three people had dropped out.

14. *Promoter Harold J. Ross in front of the Crystal Beach Park Ballroom in July 1930 before the start of a marathon dance contest. The contest lasted 31 days. The winning couple received $675.*

Before it began, an article in the Caller estimated the contest would last no more than two weeks but after two weeks the promoter Harold J. Ross said "We have some tough-muscled entries."

After 31 days, two couples, one from Corpus Christi and one from the Valley, were left: Mary Myers of Mercedes and Tommy Thomas of Weslaco; and Doris Hunt and August Spies of Corpus Christi.

The Valley couple got married while they danced. On the last day, Aug. 25, August Spies forgot to move his feet and started to doze off, despite the frantic efforts of Doris Hunt to keep him awake and active. That made the Valley couple the winners. They received $675, a sizable sum when few people were acquainted with folding money in that Great Depression year. The Corpus Christi couple received $375 for second place.

A top attraction on North Beach was the rollercoaster called Skyrocket on the Bayside Amusement Park near the "The Ship." On July 27, 1931, a 15-year-old girl, Tessie Mae Hunsucker, was killed when she was thrown from the coaster. The newspaper account said the accident happened when the girl stood up and lost her balance and fell through the supporting framework. She died from a fractured skull. Her family had moved to Corpus Christi from McGregor a short time before and were living at the Sunset Camp on Rincon.

Not long after the Hunsucker girl's death, a woman was killed when a car jumped the track. The Skyrocket was closed and the abandoned framework was left standing for years.

291

15 and 16. A top attraction on North Beach was the rollercoaster called Skyrocket. It was shut down after two fatal accidents. Below, a crowd gathers on the beach in front of "The Ship."

17 and 18. The Saltwater Pool pumped in filtered saltwater from the bay. It was in operation from 1926, when it was built, until the mid-1950s when it was torn down. Below, a weekend beach scene in 1937. North Beach, virtually destroyed by the 1919 storm, became the playground of South Texas from the 1920s until the 1950s.

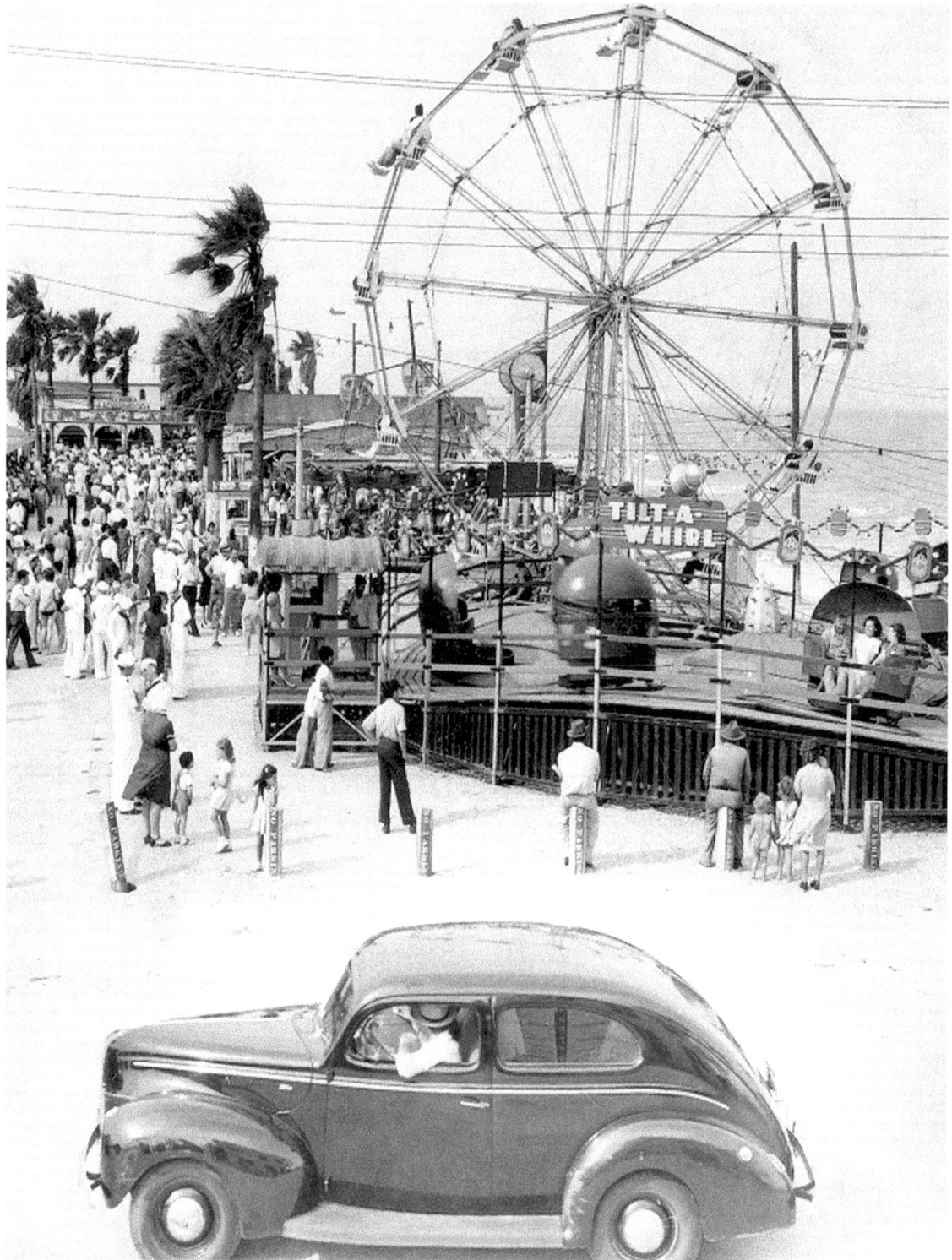

19. The North Beach Amusement Park featured a Ferris wheel, merry-go-round, bingo parlors, and typical carnival concessions. The park was an especially busy place in the early 1940s when thousands of military personnel were stationed at the Naval Air Station. The park and North Beach in general began to decline in the 1950s. It was torn down in 1957.

20. *The Bohemian Village Restaurant on North Beach on a day in 1938. It had formerly been a sandwich shop called Peacock Alley on Rincon Street.*

In the late 1920s and early 1930s net shrimpers would spend their evenings on the old Epworth Pier putting out crab baits and waiting for dark before lighting kerosene lanterns. After dark, they would throw cast nets and catch large white bay shrimp, which they sold to seafood buyers waiting in Model-T trucks.

When the USS Constitution, Old Ironsides, visited Corpus Christi in 1932, the wake of its destroyer escorts lifted the Dance Ship from its base and it broke free of its moorings. The vessel was finally returned to its berth at the pier. In September 1933 a hurricane destroyed tourist cabins, a diving platform, and the Bayside Park and Ballroom. Timbers from the pier and pavilion were scattered for blocks on the beach. The Nueces Bay Causeway, a temporary wooden structure built in 1921 to replace the concrete causeway destroyed in 1919, was heavily damaged and so was the Dance Ship, which was moved soon afterwards to the Houston area.

North Beach soon returned to business as usual. On a good weekend, the North Beach Amusement Park, the carnival midway, the Ferris wheel, merry-go-round and other rides would attract as many as 4,000 visitors, or 20,000 on a holiday.

In the 1930s Rincon Street ran along the shore. (It was later renamed Avenue A and then Shoreline Drive). Rincon ran along the bay to the amusement park, with tourist cottages along the way. On the water side were pleasure boats that offered fishing excursions and bay cruises. Among the businesses between the bascule and Bennett Street were Edgewater

21. *The North Beach Theater (later called The Beach Theater) opened in 1939. It was at 3122 North Water Street, near the North Beach Church of Christ.*

Beach Cottages, run by Arth and Maxine Landsman, and the Harbor View Courts, owned by Harry and Catherine Trombley.

Past the Bennett intersection was the Yacht Beach Court, at 2700 Rincon, owned by race-car driver Barney Oldfield, the first man to drive a car 60 miles an hour, in 1903. Past the Pearl Street intersection was Jack Tunnell's Fish and Oyster Market followed by the Palace Fish Market.

Across Market was the Sea Breeze Apartments, run by Foster and Mary Douglas, followed by the Rincon Camp, the Palace Bath House and the Long Island Fish Market. On the other side of the Garner intersection were the Bay View Apartments, Sunset Camp, and past Vine was Dave's Reliable Mattress Factory and a roller-skating rink. Beyond Elm Street was the North Beach Bath House, run by John Mosser.

On North Water Street were the Shell Beach Lodges and the Curry Cottages, run by Louie L. Curry, Mary Hubbard's Las Palmas Courts and the Aztec Curio Shop. Past Pearl was J. D. Brown's Barbecue and Brown's Courts, Jack McCormack's Grocery, and the Cloverleaf Camp, run by Charles and Hattie Belknap. Across Garner was the North Beach Drug Store followed by Biel's Grocery No. 4 and several other camps and tourist cottages. The North Beach Theater was at 3122 N. Water, past the Vine Street intersection.

Timon Boulevard began several blocks north of the bascule bridge, in the 3500 block, past the silver Humble Oil Refinery tanks. To reach the causeway a driver turned left from North Water Street about four blocks past the bascule bridge, crossed the railroad tracks and drove north on Timon Boulevard to the causeway. "There was little on the way to Nueces Bay," William Radeker recalled, "except for a few tourist courts, the Ma Harris Bar on Avenue F and the Breakers Hotel on Hamilton Road."

22. *Linn K. "Doc" Mason's Dragon Grill, on Timon Boulevard, was a North Beach night club known for its fine food, lively entertainment, and illegal gambling. It burned on Jan. 15, 1944 and Mason relocated his club to the Elks Building in downtown Corpus Christi.*

At 3501 Timon was the Castle Beach Hotel, owned by George and Ruth Blethen, followed by the Silver King Tourist Court. There were several service stations, refinery tanks, fish markets and cafes on Timon. The North Beach School was at 3901, across Garner, and Doc Mason's Dragon Grill was at 4325. For seven years the Dragon Grill on North Beach was Corpus Christi's top nightspot until the morning of Jan. 15, 1944 when it burned. Firemen trying to fight the fire were hampered by the explosion of cans of cooking oil stored in the kitchen. The place was a total loss. Mason moved his nightclub into the Elks Building in downtown Corpus Christi (Chapter 1, page 19).

At the end of Timon Boulevard was the Causeway Inn near the entrance to the Nueces Bay Causeway. This was the area where Royall Givens' fish canning building was located in the early part of the century. Mrs. Royall (Leona) Givens recalled that "wonderful fish fries used to be held at Mr. Givens' fish house on the shore of Nueces Bay near the reef. Fifty or sixty young people would gather for these occasions, spreading the supper on the long tables that were used for opening the oyster shells."

It was in this area, near Rincon Point, where Jacob Ziegler planted a grove of salt cedars. Long after his beer garden was closed, dances were held at the "mott" of salt cedars. E. H. Caldwell in his memoirs said that "The Cedars" was the name given to a dance held there. "North Beach was like a prairie, no trees at all, except that someone (Ziegler) planted some salt cedars and they grew well and spread."

23. *Fire Station No. 4 on North Beach was built at 213 Bessie, near the bascule bridge, in 1937. It was shut down in 1968.*

The North Beach Fire Station at 213 Bessie was built in 1937 as the city's fourth fire station. John Mosser's La Palma Drive-In was on Elm Street, at 215, on the corner with North Water. The original building of La Palma was the first structure built after the 1919 storm; lumber debris collected after the storm was used in the building. (Besides La Palma, Mosser owned two "Giantburger" drive-ins on Weber and Alameda.)

The history of the street names on North Beach has been obscured by name changes. Rincon Street, a long-established name, was changed by the City Council to Avenue A, then changed again to Shoreline Drive. North Water and its extension Hamilton Street were changed to Surfside, Bessie was renamed Canal, Market changed to Breakwater, and Vine was renamed Coastal. Other names of east-west streets on the north end of North Beach were also changed.

After Corpus Christi annexed North Beach in 1935, some honkytonks and juke joints became a source of trouble because of frequent brawls and illegal gambling. Mayor H. R. Giles in 1936 said he would push to close the worst joints but not all. "We don't want an air-tight city," Giles said. "There are certain pleasures the citizens and visitors demand." The police chief, Lee Petzel, did close down one North Beach bar called the Cat's Meow because of complaints over loud music and repeated fights.

The city also made a push to clean up a migrant camp of tents and tin shacks that sprouted up during the Depression. Most of them were at Rincon Point. In 1939, when Corpus Christi won the battle for a new naval base, the migrant camps on North Beach filled with workers looking for jobs building the installation.

The fat years for North Beach came in the 1940s when thousands of Navy cadets trained at the Naval Air Station. On Saturdays the amusement park would be crowded during the day and the popular night spots would be packed at night. On an average weekend on North Beach in its heyday in the 1940s, the beach, the North Beach Amusement Park, the carnival

24. The Breakers on June 17, 1937. It was built in 1912 as the Beach Hotel. It was leased by the government for use as a convalescent hospital for soldiers wounded in World War I. It survived the 1919 storm and was remodeled as the Breakers. It was demolished after it was damaged by Celia in 1970.

midway, the Ferris wheel, merry-go-round and other rides would attract as many as 4,000 visitors. On a holiday weekend the number could climb to 20,000 or more. The boom years in the 1940s were prosperous times when it seemed that the whole world converged upon North Beach.

After the war, by the end of the 1940s, the number of visitors began to fall and continued to fall in the 1950s. One cause was the opening of the Padre Island Causeway in 1950, which provided a new island playground for tourists and residents. Bruce Collins Sr., the "father of North Beach," blamed the decline on interminable waits at the bascule bridge. For every ship entering or leaving the port, the bridge would be raised and stay up sometimes for 20 minutes or more. The bascule bottleneck no doubt kept people from going to North Beach, but if they didn't love the bascule, they loved the Harbor Bridge even less.

Some blamed Harbor Bridge for the decline of North Beach and that became the authorized answer of "What Happened to North Beach?" But North Beach was in decline *before* Harbor Bridge was built. The amusement park and the boardwalk were torn down in September 1957, two full years before the bridge was opened to traffic. The roller rink was razed the following year. The Saltwater Pool had already been demolished.

Restaurants and curio shops and tourist courts were closed. The beach was no longer crowded with people basking in the sun. What had been a lively seaside purlieu turned into resort ghost town. One owner of a tourist court said there was nothing left to do except fish and drink.

25. *A boy wades in the aisle of the Beach Theater after a weak hurricane struck on the coast at Freeport, causing flooding in low-lying areas, on Oct. 4, 1949. The storm tide left standing water up to the 10th row of seats in the theater.*

26. John Mosser's La Palma Drive-in, shown on May 12, 1938, was at the corner of North Water and Elm, west of the North Beach Bath House.

27. Sheffield's Grill, shown on Feb. 8, 1940, was owned and operated by J. O. Sheffield. It was located at 2724 North Water past the Marine Bar and Marine Hotel (just visible on the right) and across the street from the Midway Service Station.

28. North Beach (or Corpus Christi Beach, as it was then called) on Oct. 9, 1966. The Harbor Bridge interchange shunted traffic away from what was once the main business district of North Beach.

The Harbor Bridge opened in October 1959. The shape of the bridge resembled Napoleon's Hat, which gave it a nickname by sailors, and it turned out to be something of a Waterloo for North Beach. It threw traffic over the business part of North Beach and, in the blink of an eye, onto to the causeway to Portland. While Harbor Bridge was a great improvement for Corpus Christi and most of its people, it made a bad situation worse for North Beach. The North Beach merchants could look at the traffic streaming off Harbor Bridge and remember, in the glory years of the 1940s, how it was when all the cars passed right by their front doors. And suddenly they were on the wrong side of the bridge.

Bruce Collins and other North Beach property owners urged the City Council to change the name to Corpus Christi Beach in the hopes that it might improve North Beach's prospects, serving to remind the people of Corpus Christi that North Beach was a vital part of the city. The council complied but it didn't stop the decline.

A combination of factors — the bascule bridge, the Padre Island Causeway, and the Harbor Bridge — was almost as damaging as the 1919 hurricane. One can rebuild after a storm but without the prospect of business there was no reason to rebuild or hang on in anticipation of better times. And probably there was another factor at work, changing tastes of changing times. What North Beach had to offer was no longer so exotic or unique enough to slow the passing traffic. The tourists quit coming and those who depended on them for their livelihood packed up and left.

29. A scene in the off-season on North Water Street in February 1939 during the golden years of North Beach when a weekend could attract 20,000 or more tourists and local residents.

After the bridge came Hurricane Carla, in 1961, which made landfall near Port Lavaca on Sept. 11, 1961. The storm knocked down power lines and flooded low-lying North Beach.

Six years later, Hurricane Beulah made landfall near Brownsville on Sept. 20, 1967. The storm demolished nearly 200 buildings on North Beach and the streets were turned into lakes draining into the bay. U. S. 181 was closed for days and when it opened motorists were warned to keep going, not to stop on North Beach, which was off limits to all but those with special permits from the police department. North Beach suffered more than $2 million in damage from Beulah.

Three years later, on Aug. 3, 1970, Celia made landfall north of Corpus Christi. A storm tide of five feet flooded North Beach and high winds damaged many buildings.

30. Sign on a North Beach building after Hurricane Allen struck on Aug. 10, 1980. North Beach during the storm was under five feet of water, above the window sills of many buildings. After the storm, 154 lots were cleared and 210 buildings were demolished or removed for salvage.

Celia claimed the Hotel Breakers, built in 1912 and the survivor of many storms, including the 1919 hurricane. The Breakers was so smashed up by Celia's destructive forces that it was torn down later that year.

In the almost half a century since 1970 North Beach has recorded major successes, notably the Texas State Aquarium and the Lexington, but the effort to return North Beach to its golden age as a major tourist mecca is still a work in progress and the attempt may be unimpressive for those who remember the old North Beach.

In its heyday, North Beach was the place to be and then it became the place to pass by, a place glimpsed from insulated windows of passing cars. The sun-warmed waters of the bay and honey-colored sands along the shore were still there, but the crowds that once strolled ceaselessly along the beach and boardwalk were gone.

People talk of the lost gaiety of the old North Beach and think it will be like that again, embracing what Samuel Coleridge defined as "the willing suspension of disbelief." What they hunger for is the past restored. One resident quoted in a 1983 story said, "I like North Beach like it is, but Lord I miss it like it was."

The small peninsula known over the years as Rincon, Brooklyn, North Beach, Corpus Christi Beach, then North Beach again, has a long and proud history. It has survived many storms and economic slumps and reversals of fortune.

31. *Looking north from the top of the bascule bridge in 1937 presented a view of cars waiting on North Water Street for the bridge to be lowered. At upper left, past the refinery tanks, was Timon Boulevard stretching to the Nueces Bay Causeway.*

Street Names

Agnes west of South Staples was formerly Ladd Avenue. Who or what Agnes was named for is not known. It may have been the mailboat "Agnes" that made the regular run from Indianola to Central Wharf in Corpus Christi in the 1870s and early 1880s before the railroads.

Airline Road, from Ocean Drive past Alameda west to city limits. The name of the road predates public air transit, which began after 1914. It is presumed to have derived from an earlier use of the word "air-line," which goes back to the 1850s and means a straight line between fixed points, like "bee-line."

Alameda south from Kinney Avenue to Booty was Chamberlain Street until the name was changed in 1941. Alameda north of Kinney Avenue was called Last Street before it was changed.

Alaniz was formerly Garwood Street. The name was changed in March 1970 to honor Paul Alaniz, killed in the Vietnam War.

Alta Vista Road, a shell drive from the city to the Aberdeen area past Three-Mile Point, was changed to Santa Fe Street.

Angel Avenue, for two blocks next to Incarnate Word Academy, was formerly Breezeway. It was changed in April 1974.

Aubrey Street was named for William Aubrey, Kinney's business partner when they set up a trading post on Corpus Christi Bay in 1839. They dissolved the partnership at the beginning of the Mexican War in 1846.

Ayers was likely named for businessman David Ayers. It has been attributed over the years to Thomas Carlton Ayers, who was a principal at Solomon Coles School, but the Ayers street name appears on maps that predate T. C. Ayers' tenure at Solomon Coles.

Baldwin was named for the first president of the Chamber of Commerce, Henry Baldwin.

Battlin' Buc Boulevard, next to Miller High School, was formerly Fisher Street, which had been Palmer. The name was changed to accommodate the school student body in January 1971.

Belden Street was named for Frederick Belden, a merchant who came to Corpus Christi before Taylor's army landed in 1845. His store was on Chaparral and his home on Mesquite Street. He married Mauricia Arocha in Matamoros and was considered a spokesman for, and keen supporter of, the Hispanic community of Corpus Christi.

Black Street was changed in 1929 to North Staples.

Bluntzer Street was formerly Steele Street, from Mary to Kinney, and 24th Street, from Mary to Buford. The two streets were renamed Bluntzer in 1941.

Bonner Drive, in the Gardendale area, was named for Jack W. Bonner, who moved to Corpus Christi from Oklahoma and founded the Jack Bonner Company, an office supply and commercial printing operation, originally in the 400 block of Peoples Street.

Born Street was named for E. A. Born, a businessman. He was secretary of the CCISD school board in 1910 when the new Corpus Christi High School was built on Carancahua.

Breakwater on North Beach was formerly Market Street.

Breezeway changed for two blocks next to Incarnate Word to Angel Avenue.

Brewster was named for Kinney's brother-in-law, Dwight Brewster, who married Emily Catherine Kinney.

Brownlee, north and south, was formerly 13th Street. It was changed to Brownlee to honor William John Brownlee, killed on Hickam Field at Pearl Harbor on Dec. 7, 1941. He was the city's first casualty of World War II.

Buddy Lawrence Drive was Lawrence Drive. The name was changed in April 1966 to reduce confusion between Lawrence Street in downtown Corpus Christi and Lawrence Drive, off Leopard and past Nueces Bay Boulevard. T. M. (Buddy) Lawrence was a county commissioner for 26 years. He was the grandson of Dr. D. H. Lawrence, for whom Lawrence Street in downtown Corpus Christi was named.

Buford Street was named for Buford Craig, a landowner around the Spohn Hospital area. Craig Street was also named for him.

Burlington was changed to 16th Street.

Cantwell Lane, named for M. J. Cantwell, was changed to Navigation Boulevard in April 1949.

Carrizo was probably named for a band of Indians, since it is in the same area as other streets named for Indian tribes, including Carancahua, Tancahua, Lipan, and Comanche, although some have attributed it to the Spanish word for cane, consistent with Mesquite and Chaparral.

Callicoate Road was named for George Callicoate, a farmer who moved to Corpus Christi from the Panhandle in 1920 and married the sister of Sheriff John Harney.

Carancahua was changed to Liberty in April 1912, part of the City Council's sweeping revision of street names, but it didn't last. It was changed back to Carancahua in September 1913.

Chamberlain Street, from Kinney Avenue to Booty, was changed to Alameda in 1941.

Chaparral, defined as a clump or mott of thorny shrubs, may have been named for a thicket at the south end of the street beyond Cooper's Alley or generically for the brush country of South Texas.

Chipito was named by Kinney for his friend, Chipito Sandoval, who was also known as a "scout" or "spy" who brought news from Mexico to Kinney and Zachary Taylor before the Mexican War.

Coastal Avenue on North Beach was formerly Vine Street.

Colorado Street, from Six Points to Dump Road, was changed to South Staples.

Cooper Street was changed back to its original name, Cooper's Alley, in 1977. The street was named for J. M. Cooper, a driller of artesian wells who came to Corpus Christi from Alabama in 1848 to drill for water on Kinney's ranch and in the arroyo near Kinney's home.

Coral Street, from Louisiana to South Staples, was changed to 15th Street in 1941.

Corn Products Road was named for a major plant located on UpRiver Road. The Bluebonnet plant of the Corn Products Refining Company began operations in 1949 and continued until it was closed and sold in 1979. It produced starches and dextrose sugar for animal feeds from grain sorghum and corn. The old Corn Products site is now part of Valero Refining.

Craig Street was named for Buford Craig (See Buford).

Davis Street, named for Gov. Edmund J. Davis, a former judge from Corpus Christi elected governor after the Civil War, was changed to 13th Street and finally Brownlee Boulevard.

DeMoines was changed to 17th Street.

Doddridge Street downtown, from South Broadway to Water, was later changed, along with Railroad Avenue, to Kinney Avenue.

Doddridge Street, from Ocean Drive to Staples, was named for Perry Doddridge, a former wool dealer, banker, and mayor. He was elected mayor in the first city election following the Civil War. When the street was extended west from Staples, the new extension was named Weber Road.

Dunn Street was renamed Naples Street.

Dwight Street was later changed to North 13th Street and that was changed to North Brownlee.

Ennis Joslin was named for the president of Central Power & Light.

Everhart Road was named for Czech farmer and landowner W. E. (Dad) Everhart. The name has been attributed to Park Everhart, his son.

Fifteenth (15th) Street, from Louisiana to South Staples, was formerly Coral Street.

Fisher Street was renamed Battlin' Buc Boulevard in 1971.

Floral Street, from Louisiana to South Staples, was reamed 13th Street in 1941.

Fourth Avenue was changed to Coleman Avenue.

Fourth Street was changed to Santa Fe.

Garwood Street was changed to Alaniz Street in honor of Paul Alaniz, killed in Vietnam in 1970.

Gavilan was changed to Tancahua in 1941.

Gollihar was named for Charles Gollihar, a rancher. The Gollihar family home was located on the site where the 1914 county courthouse was built. Among the extensive Gollihar family was Ed Gollihar, who was a pitcher on the Corpus Christi Kids baseball team around the turn of the 20th Century.

Greenwood was formerly Rabbit Run Road, which ran from South Port Avenue to out in the country, past the city's garbage incinerator. Greenwood was believed named for a subdivision development in the area, which preceded the change in names from Rabbit Run Road to Greenwood Drive. It was not named for Jim Greenwood, a Caller-Times reporter who covered City Hall at the time.

Gussett Street, named for prominent businessman Norwick Gussett, was changed to 10th Street.

Hamilton Road on North Beach was changed to North Water and then to Surfside.

Highway 9 from the city limits to Calallen was changed to Leopard in 1963. A group of businessmen in 1962 petitioned the City Council to change the name of Leopard to Main Street. The city turned down the petition. Mayor Ben McDonald said, "One hundred and ten years of history should support retention of Leopard's name." Ten days later, the council voted to change the name of the entire street from Corpus Christi to Calallen to Leopard.

Holly Road was named for rancher Hugh Holly.

Holly Street, near Mary Carroll High School, was changed to Sacky Drive and then, in 1962, to Tiger Lane.

Kinney Avenue was formerly Railroad Avenue. Portions of the street were also known as Neal Street, Britton Street and Doddridge Street.

Kostoryz was named for Stanley Kostoryz, who bought 7,000 acres of the Grim Ranch southwest of town in 1904 and resold the land to Czech farmers.

Ladd Avenue, west of South Staples, was later considered to be an extension of Agnes Street and changed to that name.

Laguna, from North Broadway to Water Street, was renamed John Sartain Street for a policeman killed by a sniper on Aug. 19, 1971. Henry Kinney named the original street for the arroyo nearby that emptied into the bay.

Lamar Street, between UpRiver Road and Leopard, was formerly called Palmer Street.

Last Street was the last street at the end of town to the west. Last, from Kinney Avenue north to the ship channel, changed to Alameda in 1929.

Lawrence Drive changed to Buddy Lawrence Drive to avoid confusion with Lawrence Street downtown.

Leming Street was formerly known as Texas. It was changed in 1941. The street has had three names over the years, Williams, Texas, and Leming.

Leopard was one of the original streets named for Kinney. He once said he named it for the place where he shot a "tiger or leopard" (likely a cougar) on the hill above the beach. Efforts in the 1960s to change the name of Leopard Street to Main Street were rejected.

Lexington Boulevard was changed to South Padre Island Drive in January 1966.

Lott Street was named for wool merchant and railroad promoter Uriah Lott. It was changed to 12th Street.

M Street was changed to 15th Street.

Mann Street was named for William Mann, the city's wealthiest merchant in the 1840s who was engaged in the Mexican trade. His combination store, hotel and warehouse on Water Street was called Mann's Red House, for the red shellcrete bricks used in its construction.

Marguerite was formerly Rogers Avenue.

Market Street on North Beach was changed to Breakwater.

Mary Street was formerly known as Bluett. It was changed in the general revisions of 1912.

Media Street was changed to North Tancahua in 1941.

Mesquite, as the case with Chaparral, may have been named for mesquite trees at its southern end or the origin may have been more in general for the hardy trees that invaded South Texas and spread over the savannahs and coastal prairies.

Mestena Street. The City Council changed the spelling in 1941 to Mesteyna in an effort to influence the correct Spanish pronunciation, but it soon reverted to the older name of

Mestena. (Besides Mestena, Kinney's original "creature" names include Leopard, Buffalo, Tiger, Lobo, Zorro, Oso, Cabra, Topo, and Gavilan.)

Morgan Avenue's name origin is unknown. It may have been named for shipping tycoon Charles Morgan, whose Morgan Line ships were important to the Corpus Christi economy. Rand Morgan was named for a farmer in the Saxet area where oil and gas were discovered.

Mussett was named for the pioneer family or for City Marshal Elias Tyre Mussett, who was killed in the line of duty in 1892.

Mustang Trail was formerly Sheridan Drive. The name was changed in May 1966.

Naples Street, from South Staples to Ocean Drive, was formerly known as Dunn Street. The name was changed in 1941.

Navigation Boulevard was formerly Cantwell Lane. The name was changed, despite Cantwell family protests, in April 1949.

North Staples was formerly known as Black Street. The name was changed in 1929.

North Water Street on North Beach was changed to Surfside.

Ocean Drive downtown, from Cooper's Alley to Buford, was renamed Water Street in July 1960. Families with homes on South Broadway whose property extended to the street below opposed the change.

Ocean Drive near the ship channel, from Dan Reid to Hughes, was formerly known as Rincon. The name was changed in 1941.

Palmer Street, between Leopard and UpRiver, changed to Lamar Street in 1941, then to Fisher, and finally to Battlin' Buc Boulevard.

Peoples Street downtown was named for John Peoples, Mexican War correspondent and editor of the Corpus Christi Star who left in 1848 to join the California gold rush. He drowned on the way.

Rabbit Run Road was changed to Greenwood in 1959. Some believed Greenwood was named for City Hall reporter Jim Greenwood and others believed it was named for Roy Greenwood who operated Roy's Barbecue Pit on Rabbit Run Road. However, it was likely named for the Greenwood subdivision which was built before the name was changed from Rabbit Run to Greenwood.

Railroad Avenue was changed to Kinney Avenue, after the town's founder, Henry Kinney. They used to construct railroad boxcars in a large shop on Railroad Avenue. John Anderson, from Sweden, said the operation included a blacksmith shop, a brass foundry, and they turned out a boxcar or gondola a day.

Rincon Street on North Beach was renamed Avenue A in 1941 and then Shoreline Drive.

Rincon Street on the south side of the ship channel was changed to Ocean Drive in 1941.

Rodd Field Road was named for the auxiliary air field which in turn was named for Herbert C. Rodd, an aviation pioneer killed in a crash in 1932.

Roy Street, from Morris Street to Kinney Avenue, was renamed 20th Street.

Sam Rankin was named for a property owner and real-estate agent whose home and office were in the 700 block of Mesquite. Sam Rankin Street, the first street west of Last Street, was named for Sam Rankin before he died in 1909. His widow, Lillie (Mussett)

Rankin, was a civic leader and instrumental in organizing the Old Bayview Cemetery Association.

Santa Fe Street was formerly Fourth Street and Alta Vista Road.

Savage Lane was named for a pioneer family. Best known was Russell Savage, attorney for the port of Corpus Christi and state representative. His father, Bob Savage, worked at Norwick Gussett's store on Chaparral.

Schatzel Street (the spelling was corrupted over time) was named for John Peter Schatzell, a wealthy merchant in Matamoros who was a friend of Henry Kinney. He moved to Corpus Christi in 1850 and built Mansion House on the bluff. He loaned Henry Kinney $45,000 to host the Lone Star Fair in 1852. He died in 1854.

Seabreeze, from Booty to Louisiana, was considered to be an extension of Carancahua and renamed that in 1941.

Second Avenue was changed to Park Avenue.

Sheridan Drive by King High School was changed to Mustang Trail in May 1966.

Shoreline Boulevard, from Hughes to Craig Avenue, was renamed Ocean Drive in 1941.

South Padre Island Drive was formerly Lexington Boulevard. The name was changed in January 1966.

South Staples, from Ayers to Dump Road, was formerly Colorado Street.

Staples Street was named for W. N. Staples who owned a lumberyard, grocery and dry goods store on Chaparral, was a co-owner of the beef packing house on Packery Channel, and was appointed mayor in 1866 and served until 1868. He later moved to Alice, where he died in 1893. Staples Avenue in Alice was also named for him.

Starr Street was named by Henry Kinney for James Harper Starr, a doctor and land agent who was secretary of the treasury of the Republic of Texas, 1839-1840. Starr County was also named for him.

Steele Street was renamed Bluntzer.

Tancahua was changed to Pleasant Street in 1912 and after a year of public resistance changed back to Tancahua.

Tarlton Street was named for Dudley Tarlton, an attorney. His daughter, also an attorney, ran for governor. Her name is "Sissy" Frances Tarlton Farenthold.

Taylor Street, from Broadway to the bay, was named for Gen. Zachary Taylor, who brought nearly half the U.S. Army to Corpus Christi in 1845 in preparation for an expected war with Mexico. The encampment stretched along the shore from North Beach to the vicinity of Artesian Park and the later-named Taylor Street.

Tenth (10th) Street, from Booty to South Staples, was formerly 12th Street. The name was changed in 1941.

Texas Street, between Alameda and Santa Fe (and later Ocean Drive) was renamed Leming.

Third Street, from Booty to Hancock, was renamed Carancahua in 1941.

Thirteenth (13th) Street, from Louisiana to South Staples, was formerly known as Floral Street. North Thirteenth, from Kinney to Leopard, was formerly Dwight Avenue. Thirteenth Street, north and south, was changed to Brownlee in honor of William John (Billy Jack) Brownlee, killed at Pearl Harbor on Dec. 7, 1941.

Tiger Lane by Carroll High School was formerly Holly Street, which was sometimes confused with Holly Road, and the name was changed to Sacky Drive, then, in 1962, to Tiger Lane.

Tiger Street was one of Henry Kinney's original streets. It ran five blocks from Mann to Brewster. It was later decided that Tiger Street was an extension of North Broadway and the name was changed in December 1938.

Timon Boulevard on North Beach was named for Walter Timon, Nueces County Judge from 1906 to 1920 who was instrumental in building the first causeway across Nueces Bay. Timon Boulevard led directly across North Beach to the causeway.

Topo Street, from Winnebago to Broadway, was changed to Waco Street in 1941.

Treptow Street was named by the Blucher family for an ancestral home in Germany. The first block of Carrizo past Railroad Avenue was called Treptow until 1913 when the City Council changed the name to conform to the rest of the street.

Twelfth Street was formerly Lott Street. Twelfth 12th, from Booty to Staples, was renamed Tenth Street in 1941.

Twentieth (20th) Street, from Morris to Kinney, was known as Roy Street.

Twenty-fourth (24th) Street, from Mary to Buford, was renamed Bluntzer.

Twigg Street was named for Gen. David E. Twiggs (the city misspelled the name). Twiggs, from Georgia, was commander of the Second Dragoons when Zachary Taylor's army was concentrated in Corpus Christi in 1845 and early 1846. Twiggs was in command of U.S. forces in Texas at the start of the Civil War and was roundly criticized for turning over federal munitions and forts in Texas to the Confederates.

UpRiver Road was for a time referred to as Shell Road, after it was spread with shell from town to where Corn Products Road was built later. At Mayor Roy Miller's request, soldiers at Camp Scurry in the fall of 1916 were diverted from training to spread oyster shell on UpRiver Road as far as Calallen. Afterwards, it was called Shell Road, even after it was paved in 1933, until its original name was restored. An earlier name was the San Patricio Road.

Vine on North Beach was changed to Coastal Avenue.

Waldron Road was named for Lt. Cmdr. J. C. Waldron, killed at the battle of Midway.
Weber Road was named for the family of farmers named Weber in the area.
Wilkie was changed to 14th Street.
William Street downtown is sometimes spelled Williams, though old plats clearly show the name as William. It was one of Kinney's original street names, though who was it named for has been lost.
Winnebago was named for an Indian tribe in Illinois and Lake Michigan area, where Henry Kinney had lived before he moved to Texas and founded Corpus Christi.

List of Photographs

1. Water Street

1. Central Wharf, Caller-Times Archives.
2. Municipal Pier, the "Doc" McGregor Collection, Museum of Science and History.
3. Water Street, Caller-Times Archives.
4. Purple Cow, "Doc" McGregor.
5. Conrad Meuly, Texas A&M University-Corpus Christi.
6. Shoop's Grill, Jim Moloney.
7. Goodyear Tire, "Doc" McGregor.
8. 400 block, "Doc" McGregor.
9. Pleasure Pier, Pier Café, "Doc" McGregor.
10. Pleasure Pier, "Doc" McGregor.
11. Pier Café, "Doc" McGregor.
12. Water Street, "Doc" McGregor.
13. Women attendants at Texas Star, "Doc" McGregor.
14. The Ladies Pavilion, Corpus Christi Central Library.
15. Ohler's building, 1850s, Central Library.
16. Anderson's home and windmill, Caller-Times.
17. Nueces Hotel, "Doc" McGregor.
18. Nueces Hotel dining room, Murphy Givens.
19. Nueces Hotel lobby, Murphy Givens.
20. Water Street, "Doc" McGregor.
21. Shoreline stabilization 1, "Doc" McGregor.
22. Shoreline stabilization 2, "Doc" McGregor.
23. Water Street, "Doc" McGregor.
24. A&W hamburger stand, "Doc" McGregor.
25. Mary Sutherland, from frontispiece "Story of Corpus Christi."
26. Seaside Hotel, Jim Moloney.
27. Seaside Pavilion, Karl Swafford, Jim Moloney.
28. Water Street, "Doc" McGregor.
29. Princess Louise, "Doc" McGregor.
30. Ritter's Hotel & Bath House, family photo, Harriett Tillman.
31. Lighthouse Restaurant, "Doc" McGregor.
32. Tourist Park, Jim Moloney.
33. Humble Service Station, "Doc" McGregor.
34. David Hirsch School, Central Library.
35. David Hirsch baseball team, Murphy Givens.
36. Waiting traffic, "Doc" McGregor.
37. Borglum seawall sketch, Central Library.
38. Seawall work, "Doc" McGregor.
39. Seawall work, "Doc" McGregor.
40. Seawall work, "Doc" McGregor.
41. T-heads, "Doc" McGregor.

42. Completed seawall, Russell Lee, Library of Congress.
43. First traffic on Shoreline, "Doc" McGregor.
44. First traffic to T-head, "Doc" McGregor.

2. Chaparral Street

1. Meuly home, Arthur Stewart, American Buildings Survey, Library of Congress.
2. Chaparral Street, "Doc" McGregor Collection, Museum of Science and History.
3. CPL building, "Doc" McGregor.
4. Chaparral Street, Corpus Christi Central Library.
5. DeWitt Reed Auto 1, "Doc" McGregor.
6. DeWitt Reed Auto 2, "Doc" McGregor.
7. St. James Hotel, "Doc" McGregor.
8. Vacant lot where St. James stood, "Doc" McGregor.
9. Girls on bikes by Doddridge Building, Murphy Givens.
10. Henry Kinney, Central Library.
11. Doddridge Building, "Doc" McGregor.
12. Old Grace-Headen building, "Doc" McGregor.
13. Lichtenstein's fourth building, "Doc" McGregor.
14. Centre Theater, "Doc" McGregor.
15. Nimitz Day parade, Caller-Times.
16. Corpus Christi National Bank, 1890, Central Library.
17. Keller's Saddlery, Caller-Times Archives.
18. Lichtenstein's third building, "Doc" McGregor.
19. Chaparral parade, "Doc" McGregor.
20. Chaparral street, "Doc" McGregor.
21. Street scene, "Doc" McGregor.
22. Thomas' Model Drug Store interior, Jim Moloney.
23. Laying streetcar rails, Jim Moloney.
24. 1920s street scene, Jim Moloney.
25. DeRyee's Drug Store, Louis de Planque Photo, Central Library.
26. City Bank Building, Karl Swafford Photo, Caller-Times.
27. Load of well-casing, Caller-Times.
28. Lichtenstein receipt, Jim Moloney.
29. Drawing of Lichtenstein's second store, Murphy Givens.
30. Woessner's store, Louis de Planque Photo, Central Library.
31. Nueces Hotel, Jim Moloney.
32. J. C. Penney's block, "Doc" McGregor.
33. Simon-Cohn Department Store, "Doc" McGregor.
34. Sale at J. C. Penney's 1, "Doc" McGregor.
35. Sale at J. C. Penney's 2, "Doc" McGregor.
36. Rooftop view, Central Library.
37. Mayflower Café, street scene, "Doc" McGregor.
38. Chaparral Street, "Doc" McGregor.
39. Ritz Theater, "Doc" McGregor.
40. Rio Theater, street scene, "Doc" McGregor.

41. Vaky Court, Givens' home, "Doc" McGregor.
42. Chaparral Street, "Doc" McGregor.
43. Wrather house, Caller-Times.
44. Rivera house, McGregor studio, "Doc" McGregor.
45. Rainbow Café, Henderson Hotel, "Doc" McGregor.
46. Giles Hotel, street scene, "Doc" McGregor.
47. Whitehouse Hotel, Jim Moloney.
48. Chaparral Street, "Doc" McGregor.
49. Elite Café, "Doc" McGregor.
50. Cohn house, Caller-Times.
51. Pig Stand, "Doc" McGregor.
52. Bascule bridge, Russell Lee, Library of Congress.

3. Mesquite Street

1. Steam Laundry, Caller-Times Archives.
2. Louis de Planque, Corpus Christi Central Library.
3. Mesquite Street, "Doc" McGregor Collection, Museum of Science and History.
4. Turnout for President Taft, Central Library.
5. Spohn Park, "Doc" McGregor.
6. Pitts Livery, Caller-Times.
7. Zip Battery, Caller-Times.
8. Daily Herald staff, Caller-Times.
9. Snow on Mesquite, Caller-Times.
10. Bidwell Hotel, Caller-Times.
11. Heath & Son Emporium, Central Library.
12. Ritter's racket store, family photo, Harriett Tillman.
13. Mesquite Street, Central Library.
14. Western Auto, Weil building, "Doc" McGregor.
15. Market Hall 1, Central Library.
16. Market Hall 2, Central Library.
17. Rankin Grocery, McCampbell building, Central Library.
18. Seeligson building, "Doc" McGregor.
19. First State Bank, "Doc" McGregor.
20. First State Bank corner, "Doc" McGregor.
21. Volunteer firemen, Louis de Planque, Central Library.
22. City Hall, "Doc" McGregor.
23. Blossman's Grocery, Central Library.
24. Furman building, "Doc" McGregor.
25. Hatch & Robertson building, Caller-Times.
26. Port opening parade, Caller-Times.
27. A&G Army Navy store, "Doc" McGregor.
28. State Hotel, 1910, Caller-Times.
29. State Hotel, looking north, "Doc" McGregor.
30. State Hotel, looking south, "Doc" McGregor.
31. Artesian Park 1, Caller-Times.

4. Dr. Spohn's auto, Caller-Times Archives.
5. Martha Rabb's Magnolia Mansion, Louis de Planque Photo, Central Library.
6. John G. Kenedy home 1, "Doc" McGregor.
7. John G. Kenedy home 2, "Doc" McGregor.
8. Henrietta King mansion, Caller-Times.
9. North Broadway street scene, Jim Moloney.
10. Henrietta King, Caller-Times.
11. Corpus Christi Cathedral, "Doc" McGregor.
12. J. A. Barnes' home site, "Doc" McGregor.
13. Nixon and Plaza, "Doc" McGregor.
14. Redmond home, First Presbyterian, Caller-Times.
15. Bluff Balustrade, Karl Swafford, Jim Moloney.
16. Driscoll under construction, "Doc" McGregor.
17. Clara Driscoll, Portrait, Caller-Times.
18. Homes on North Broadway, "Doc" McGregor.
19. Post Office, "Doc" McGregor.
20. Bluff before the balustrade, Caller-Times.
21. Tunnel opening day, Sammy Gold, Murphy Givens.
22. Tunnel, Caller-Times.
23. Peel Funeral Home, "Doc" McGregor.
24. Caller-Times building, "Doc" McGregor.
25. Craig home, Caller-Times.
26. Confederate Memorial Fountain 1, Caller-Times.
27. Confederate Memorial Fountain 2, Caller-Times.
28. Detail 1 from 1875 Street Map, Jim Moloney.
29. Detail 2 from 1875 Street Map, Jim Moloney.

6. South Broadway

1. G. R. Scott home, Jim Moloney.
2. Pat F. Dunn home, Murphy Givens.
3. Joseph Hirsch home, Caller-Times.
4. Herman Cohn home, Caller-Times.
5. W. W. Jones home, "Doc" McGregor Collection, Museum of Science and History.
6. Clark Pease home, Murphy Givens.
7. Carrie Lichtenstein home, "Doc" McGregor.
8. Giles-Farenthold home, "Doc" McGregor.
9. Homes on South Broadway, "Doc" McGregor.
10. Church of the Good Shepherd, "Doc" McGregor.
11. Caldwell home, from E. H. Caldwell memoirs.
12. E. H. Caldwell, Caller-Times.

7. Leopard Street

1. Nixon and Plaza 1, "Doc" McGregor Collection, Museum of Science and History.
2. Nixon and Plaza 2, "Doc" McGregor.

3. Nixon Café, "Doc" McGregor.
4. Perkins Department Store, "Doc" McGregor.
5. Street scene, "Doc" McGregor.
6. Corpus Christi Bank & Trust, "Doc" McGregor.
7. Little Mexican Inn, "Doc" McGregor.
8. Street scene, "Doc" McGregor.
9. Leopard, 900 block, "Doc" McGregor.
10. Ben Grande Saloon, Caller-Times.
11. Street scene, "Doc" McGregor.
12. Braslau's, "Doc" McGregor.
13. Grande Theater, "Doc" McGregor.
14. Melba cowgirls, "Doc" McGregor.
15. Melba Theater 1, Central Library.
16. Melba Theater 2, Central Library.
17. Street scene, "Doc" McGregor.
18. Sears, Cudd's, "Doc" McGregor.
19. Chat 'N Chew, "Doc" McGregor.
20. Bunks Café, "Doc" McGregor.
21. Horses and wagon on Leopard, "Doc" McGregor.
22. Nueces Coffee, "Doc" McGregor.
23. Oil-supply firms, "Doc" McGregor
24. Corpus Christi High School 1932, "Doc" McGregor.
25. Aerial of Corpus Christi High, "Doc" McGregor.
26. 1950 graduates show their legs, "Doc" McGregor.
27. Flag ceremony, Caller-Times.
28. Fred Roberts Hospital, "Doc" McGregor.

8. Staples and Six Points

1. KC Barbecue, "Doc" McGregor Collection, Museum of Science and History.
2. Lozano's, Caller-Times.
3. Kardell's Pharmacy, "Doc" McGregor.
4. High Hat Drive-In, "Doc" McGregor.
5. Furman Avenue, "Doc" McGregor.
6. Superior Ice Cream, "Doc" McGregor.
7. Oriental Laundry, Jim Moloney.
8. Six Points Grocery, "Doc" McGregor.
9. Six Points roadwork 1, "Doc" McGregor.
10. Six Points roadwork 2, "Doc" McGregor.
11. Alameda Pharmacy, "Doc" McGregor.
12. Wynn-Seale Inn, "Doc" McGregor.
13. Butter Krust, "Doc" McGregor.
14. Pick's Drive-In, "Doc" McGregor.
15. Fruit Stand, "Doc" McGregor.
16. J. J. Gonzalez, Caller-Times.

9. Uptown Streets

1. Central School, Caller-Times.
2. High School, Caller-Times.
3. Incarnate Word, Jim Moloney.
4. St. Patrick's Cathedral, Jim Moloney.
5. Bagnall home, Caller-Times.
6. Philip Scott home, Caller-Times.
7. Felix Blucher sketch, Caller-Times.
8. Maria, Felix wedding photo, "Maria von Blucher's Corpus Christi" from Blucher Collection, Texas A&M University-Corpus Christi.
9. Blucher homestead, "Maria von Blucher's Corpus Christi" from Blucher Collection, Texas A&M University-Corpus Christi.
10. Julia Blucher home, Caller-Times.
11. Charles Blucher home, Caller-Times.
12. Obreros Hall, Murphy Givens.
13. Groups at Obreros Hall, Galvan Collection, Texas A&M University-Corpus Christi.
14. Garcia wedding photo, Caller-Times.
15. French-Galvan home, Caller-Times.
16. Lerma Poultry, "Doc" McGregor Collection, Museum of Science and History.
17. Police sub-station, Library of Congress.
18. Funeral on Waco Street, Caller-Times.
19. Walter F. Timon, Corpus Christi Central Library.
20. Thomas Dunn home, Caller-Times.
21. Solomon Coles School, "Doc" McGregor.
22. Gaffney home, Caller-Times.
23. Maxwell Dunne Funeral Home, "Doc" McGregor.
24. Madam Mary Fisher, Murphy Givens.
25. Shaffer Apartment Building, Murphy Givens.
26. Cantu Food Store, "Doc" McGregor.
27. Sons of America, Central Library.
28. Cheston Heath playground, "Doc" McGregor.
29. Cheston Heath School 1, "Doc" McGregor.
30. Cheston Heath School 2, "Doc" McGregor.
31. Rose Dunne Shaw and teachers, "Doc" McGregor.
32. Samman home, Caller-Times.
33. George Evans Elementary, Caller-Times.
34. Paul Court subdivision, Jim Moloney.
35. Eureka Laundry, "Doc" McGregor.

10. Ocean Drive

1. Camp Scurry, by Karl Swafford, Jim Moloney.
2. Camp Scurry football team, Central Library.
3. Spohn Hospital, photo by Harvey Patterson, Murphy Givens.
4. Frank Crook home, Caller-Times.

11. North Beach

20. Bohemian Village, "Doc" McGregor.
21. Beach Theater, "Doc" McGregor.
22. Dragon Grill on North Beach, "Doc" McGregor.
23. North Beach fire station, "Doc" McGregor.
24. Breakers Hotel, "Doc" McGregor.
25. Beach Theater after storm, Caller-Times.
26. La Palma Drive-In, "Doc" McGregor.
27. Sheffield's Grill, "Doc" McGregor.
28. North Beach, Harbor Bridge, Caller-Times.
29. North Beach 1939, Russell Lee, Library of Congress.
30. Aftermath of Hurricane Allen, Caller-Times.
31. North Beach from bascule bridge, "Doc" McGregor.

Index

Benjamin's Furniture (Benjamin Roach), 198
Berry, Bob, 55
Berry, Henry W., 11, 13, 40
Berry, Irenah (Gravis), 40
Bertch, Charles, Pharmacy, 201
Bessett, Eber W., 180
Betancourt Grocery, 246
Betancourt, Natalia, 246
Betty Maid, 51, 66
Beyer, Leonard, 203
Beynon, Thomas, 226-227, 250
Bickford, David, Drug Stores, 175
Bidwell Hotel (former Constantine), 89, 90, 92, 131-132
Big Chief Camp, 30-31
Biggio, William, 41, 45-46,
Biel's Grocery, 120-121, 202-203, 296
Bingham, Robert H., Drug Store, 99-100, 101, 123
Bismarck Café, 60
Black Cat Café, 232
Black, Elise, 9
Blacknall, J. C., 40-41, 201
Blackshear, Thomas, 219
Blackstone Café, 9
Blaine, Johnny, 184
Blake's Drug Store, 197-198
Blanck Brothers Dry Goods, 181
Blethen, George and Ruth, 297
Blossman, James, 219
Blossman, R. G., Grocery Store, 99-100, 123-124
Blucher, Arthur, 250
Blucher, Charles, F. H., 223-224, 247
Blucher, Felix, 13, 220-223
Blucher, George, 7, 224, 250
Blucher, Jasper, 250
Blucher, Julia, 223-224
Blucher, Maria, 13, 164, 220-223
Blucher, Mrs. Charles F. H. (Mary Meuly), 224
Blucher Park, 217-218, 247
Blucher, Richard, 223-224
Blucher's Creek, 1, 31, 135, 218
Blucher's Ice Plant, 7, 132, 250
Blucher Street, 249-250
Blue Bonnet Café, 201
Blueprint Shop, 129
Blue Star Grocery, 227
Bluff Balustrade, 118, 135, 147, 152, 156
Bluff Drug Store (J. L. Welch), 180
Blumenthal & Jordt (later Jordt-Allen), 50
Bluntzer Hardware, 99-100
Bluntzer, Mrs. Peter, 227
Bluntzer, Nicholas, 89, 216
Bluntzer, Vincent, 95
Blythe Grocery Store, 204
Blythe, Samuel J., 204

Bob Hall Pier, 281
Bob's Café (Robert Day Jr.), 208
Bobys, Dr. Ernest, 171
Bohemian Village Restaurant, 295
Bonham Foods, 203
Bonham, Gladys, 232
Bonham, J. Forrest, 203
Bonham, Otha, 203
Bonham Service Station, 203
Bonner, Alma, 45
Bonner, Frank, 145
Bonner, Jack, Office Supplies, 124, 307
Borglum, Gutzon, 32-33, 315
Borjas Ranch, 169
Born, E. A., 171, 307
Boucher, Thomas, Pharmacy, 100, 123
Brandon, Frank and Mae, 92
Braslau, Abraham and Isaac, 201
Braslau, Frank, 181
Braslau, Morris, 181
Braslau, Sam, 180-182
Braslau's Dry Goods, 180-181
Braslau's Furniture, 180-181, 184
Braun, Leo, 201
Breakers Hotel, 70, 285, 290, 296, 299, 304
Brennan's Bakery, 184
Brennan, Ed, 71
"Brick Palace" (High School), 193-194, 202, 212-213, 245
Brickley, Dale, 246
Brindley, Oscar, 285
Briones, Reyes G., 232
Britton, Forbes, 137-139, 214
Broadway, Lower, 152-156
Broadway, North, 135-152
Broadway, South, 159-171
Brooks, Alex A., 237, 240
Brooks, Anna, 237
Brose, Frederick, 55
Browning Paint Store, 203
Brown, Jack, 70-71
Brown, J. D., 296
Brown Skin Café (Mary Graves), 219
Bryant, Charles, 45
Bryan, William Jennings, 23-24, 159
Bryden, James, 138
Buckley, Ed, 24
Buck's Garage, 11
Buffalo Street, 237-240
Bunk's Café (B. J. Spence), 188-190
Burke's Barbecue (Mrs. Anna Burke), 208
Burnett, Lemmawayne, quoted, 286
Bush, Julius, 201
Butter Krust Bakery, 206-207
Butt, Howard E., 267
Buttrey's Ladies Wear, 47, 51-50

OTHER BOOKS AVAILABLE FROM NUECES PRESS

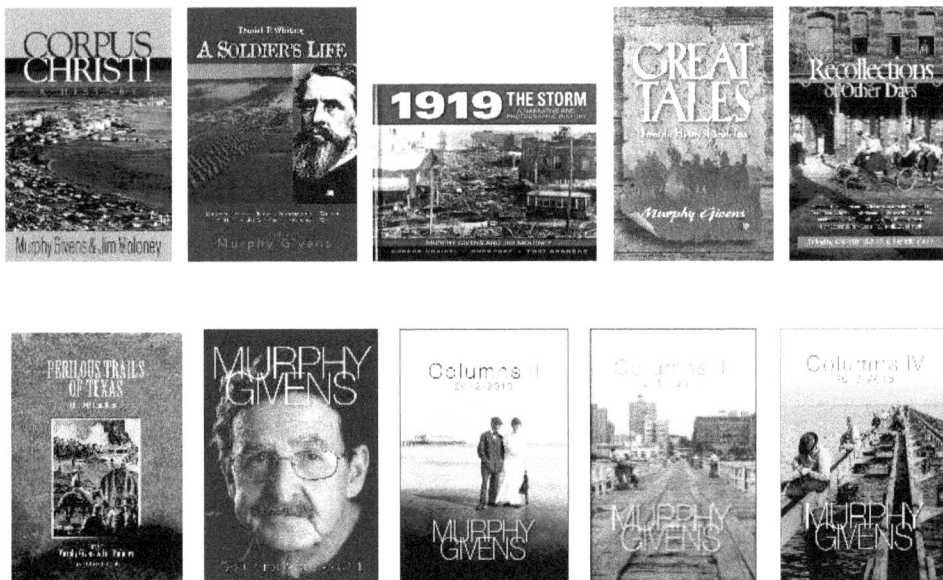

1919 – The Storm

Corpus Christi – A History

A Soldier's Life

Great Tales from the History of South Texas

Recollections of Other Days

Perilous Trails of Texas

Columns   2009 – 2011

Columns 2 2012 – 2013

Columns 3 2014 – 2015

Columns 4 2016 – 2018

Autographed copies are available from

www.nuecespress.com

www.ingramcontent.com/pod-product-compliance
Lightning Source LLC
Chambersburg PA
CBHW050408110426
42812CB00006BA/1831